COWBOY DOWN

A WWII MARINE FIGHTER PILOT'S STORY

GLENN " BUD" DANIEL

FIGHTER PILOTS & THEIR PLANES

YOU LOVE A LOT OF THINGS IF YOU LIVE
AROUND THEM. BUT THERE ISN'T ANY WOMAN
AND THERE ISN'T ANY HORSE, NOT ANY BEFORE
NOR AFTER, THAT IS LOVELY AS A GREAT AIRPLANE.
AND MEN WHO LOVE THEM ARE FAITHFUL TO THEM
EVEN THOUGH THEY LEAVE THEM FOR OTHERS.
MAN HAS ONE VIRGINITY TO LOSE IN FIGHTERS,
AND IF IT IS A LOVELY AIRPLANE HE LOSES IT TO,
THERE IS WHERE HIS HEART WILL FOREVER BE.

Ernest Hemingway

THIS BOOK IS DEDICATED TO THE MEMORY OF
MAJOR "COWBOY" ROBERT STOUT
UNITED STATES MARINE CORPS
1938 GRADUATE - UNIVERSITY OF WYOMING

MAJOR ROBERT STOUT, USMC, A HERO OF THE BATTLE OF
PELELIU, THE CACTUS AIR FORCE AT GUADACANAL AND
SQUADRON COMMANDER OF VMF-114.

HE LOVED HIS COUNTRY, THE MARINE CORPS, AND HIS FAMILY OF
MARINE FIGHTER PILOTS OF VMF-114, WHO WERE BLESSED WITH
HIS LEADERSHIP. HIS DEDICATION TO THE WELFARE OF EACH MAN
UNDER HIS COMMAND WAS EXCEPTIONAL.

I WAS HONORED TO BE HIS WINGMAN ON COMBAT FLIGHTS FROM
THE TIME HE SELECTED ME, UNTIL HIS DEATH ON A LOW-LEVEL
NAPALM RUN ON BATTERY HILL, KOROR ISLAND, MARCH 4[TH,] 1945.
HE WAS MY IDOL, FRIEND AND I TREASURE THE ASSOCIATION AND
TIME I HAD UNDER HIS COMMAND.

HE IS REMEMBERED AS FIGHTER PILOT ACE, COURAGEOUS
MARINE AVIATOR, AND WARRIOR!

TABLE OF CONTENTS

Acknowledgements

I want to thank the people who have helped me make this project possible. Yes, I wrote the original script, but without their cooperation, expertise and encouragement, this three year project might still be in production.

I will be forever grateful to my son, Colonel (Ret.) Tim Daniel, for the many hours spent in utilizing his expertise with the computer, editing and coordinating text and pictures into the manuscript. His graphic arts ability in separating the many pictures and presenting them in such an interesting style made the enjoyment of this project possible. He spent a great deal of his valuable time in making "the 'ole man look good!"

Then my best friend and caretaker, Connie my wife, without her "bulldog tenacity'' for perfection, the manuscript would have been full of many English mistakes and spelling. She was relentless in helping me write the proper words and phrases, in spite of my saying, "Damn it, that was not the way I intended to say that!" Yes, 44 years of married bliss and never a harsh word! "She was always there to help me, willing and able in spite of a heavy load. Thanks, partner!

Norma Gray, our neighbor, has self published family histories and military memoirs. Her encouragement and always-excellent advice, kept me going when I thought, "this is way too difficult."

The Pima Air and Space Museum has enriched not only Tucson, but also my life. The volunteer docents are many, giving enormous amount of hours to provide an education of military history and information about the over 300 planes on the grounds. We are a "band of brothers" representing many branches and ranks of the military. Every day that I spend with them I learn something new or hear another story that might embellish a wee bit on the facts, but adds to the fun of working under the wings of those awesome planes in Hangers 3 and 4.

I have been encouraged by so many and I would like to express heartfelt thanks to *George Matais, Tom Campbell, Harry Wells, Dick Casey, Al Raines, Dick Brown, Floyd Dickerson, John Edris, Tom Collins, Bill Kinney, Chet Harvey, Frank King, Tom Howard, Bill McGuire, Chuck Mitchell, Bill Stickel, Tom Bohan ...and the rest of the Museum team.*

Karin Militello, our Volunteer Coordinator, made certain that each Wednesday the cart was available for my use, responded to every request to make my presentations under the Corsair easier, and always had her camera at the ready to record the latest interesting activity of her band of volunteers.

Preface Where the Rails End and the Trails Begin

My journey in life began on 5 May 1923 in Belleville, Kansas, not far from the center of the United States of America. My parents were both born in the USA, my mother in Kansas and my father in Texas. My dad was a lifetime railroader, having learned telegraphy (dit-da Morse code) in his family kitchen on a knife and spoon. Mother, a loving housewife was noted for her beautiful voice, most notable in the church choir.

The Rock Island Railroad was infamous for transferring their employees. Moving to another city was normal every few years. I was the only boy and had two sisters, Jeanne and Arlene. For me, moving was a case of being able to handle or out run the athletic leader in every new class. Each of the following towns had some thing that I vividly remember. The moves occurred from six years of age on, starting in El Reno, Oklahoma. There was a valley between two rail tracks a couple of blocks from our house where the "hobos" lived. My friends and I sometimes wandered around there watching these men cook their food. They were out of butter, so I volunteered to run home and get them some. You can imagine my mother when she found this out! For some reason my parents gave me two beautiful white rabbits. We built a pen in the garage and it was my job to feed them each morning. One early morning I went the garage to feed them, and they were gone. Suddenly, I noticed our 1928 Willys Night touring sedan was no longer in the garage. My father had come home at midnight from work so obviously it had been stolen. What a strange feeling I had when both my rabbits and the car had disappeared. The State Police later retrieved the car about 70 miles east of El Reno; but no rabbits, I was furious.

We moved to Shawnee, Oklahoma when I was nine, at the beginning of the Depression. The town was in the throes of an oil boom gone sour, and we lived in a $50,000 home we rented for about $25.00/month. It was here that my father came home from work one morning stating that the Rock Island had just laid off 25,000 employees. We were moving north to Mankato, Kansas where my grandmother lived. I was heart broken because I had to give away my Scottish terrier. I never owned another dog.

Mankato was located in the center of the terrible drought and dust storms of the early '30's. We lived in a two-bedroom apartment, and the temperature for 30 days was never below 100 degrees. For two years, my dad sold knife sharpeners at fairs and rodeos! My mother worked in a grocery store 12/hours a day making $40.00 per month plus some groceries. I had a paper route, sold magazines and worked the weekend popcorn stand at Hale's Drugstore. My older sister had a job and my 3 year old younger sister was "unemployed."

Fortunately, Roosevelt started the Soil Conservation Service (SCS), and after two long years, Dad was employed in a Federal job and we were moving to Salina, Kansas. My baseball career started here. We lived a block from an area that had two school buildings, separated by a two block recreation area. It was here that I started playing baseball almost every day. Noontime between class and until dark we practiced there. My baseball ability enabled me to excel in basketball and football as well, until my father nixed football due to his fear of ruining my baseball future. He had been a good player in town teams until his late middle age. The junior high school in Salina had Lincoln's Gettysburg Address inscrolled above the entrance to be read daily upon entering school. I loved living in Salina. My classroom studies were interesting and I was above average scholastically. I remember school was suddenly fun and the athletic programs were wonderful. The Soil Conservation employees really enjoyed life. We had many good times at picnics, parties and family gatherings.

In 1938, my sophomore year in high school, Dad was transferred to Lincoln, Nebraska. I had just had a great summer playing American Legion Baseball, and was picked for the All-Star team at the Kansas state tournament. I was not too happy with the decision to move to Lincoln. Much to my surprise the move turned out to be great for me.

We lived a comfortable life, and I enjoyed Lincoln High School. I went to work after school, baseball or basketball practice at the Terminal Building drugstore soda fountain, taking a 10:30 PM evening bus home nightly. I made the varsity basketball team and was the catcher on the baseball team. Both teams went to the finals of the high school State Championships, and I was selected to the baseball All State High School team. Playing summer ball on an American Legion team, I was also selected to the Tournament All Star Team at the four state play offs. *Everyone in our family was having a wonderful time living in Lincoln. I knew it was too good to last.*

I can remember getting home late one evening, turning on the bedroom radio in time to hear that Hitler had invaded Poland and the war had begun in Europe. I had no idea how this would change our lives. Soon after, my father came home and handed me a brochure that proclaimed the "Wonders of Living in Wonderful Wyoming." We were about to move to Lander, Wyoming whose motto was "*Where the Rails End and the Trails Begin.*" I thought, "Where in the hell is Lander?" It was a fly casting fisherman's paradise, and Dad was excited.

Instead…the family moved to Casper, Wyoming! I enrolled in Natrona County High School where they had a Junior Reserve Officer Training Corps (JROTC). I wore an Army uniform four school days a week. Casper was a great place to live. The Soil Conservation Service was a wonderful group and this was one of the outstanding eras of my Mom and Dad's life. I can remember we had steak and fried potatoes cooked in a big black skillet over a wood fire many times up on Casper Mountain. Dad bought a beautiful yellow and black Studebaker, and believe it or not, let me drive it on a date as long as I got home in time for his pre dawn fishing trip.

As a senior, soon I would be making one of the most important decisions of my life. What path would my choice of college and academic major take me and would my athletic ability enable me to excel on the ball field as well?

Chapter 1   The USMC...A Dream...A Story... A Reality Check

It was a stormy winter day in October 1940, Tom Doty, my father and I had just spent a snowy morning driving in his new Oldsmobile from Casper, Wyoming through the winding mountain road to Laramie. My father was working for the Soil Conservation program that had been instituted by President Roosevelt during the throes of the big depression of the thirties. I was a student at Natrona County High School about to graduate the next year. I had been an above average student and successful athlete. My father's friend, Tom, a University of Wyoming Alumni, was dead set on my going to the University next fall upon my graduation. We had tickets for the Homecoming football game the next day.

We woke the next morning, and headed out the door for breakfast. Looking up at the Snowy Range the weather was questionable. We were ready to watch the Homecoming Parade and prepare to root for the Cowboys against their biggest football foe, Colorado State A&M.

The reason all of the above is important in my life time story, is that a happening that day would turn out in my future to become one of my life's most important events.

We proceeded to our seats in the old Cowboy Field and watched the important battle begin! It was the normal, annual rowdy beer soaked crowd, wildly rooting for their team! At half time, some of the most athletic fans decided to exhibit their powers in a touch football contest in the south end zone. Later in the afternoon I had the opportunity to speak casually to a young man, USMC 2nd Lt Bob Stout, who was wearing the coveted *GOLD WINGS, OF A NAVAL AVIATOR AND THE FAMOUS SAM BROWN BELT*! I was immediately and deeply impressed with him. It was then and there I decided if I ever enter the military, it would be to pursue those wings and to be on the same team as Bob Stout.

The clouds of war were beginning to cover Europe but they seemed years away from the United States. The dye was cast. I would be going to the University of Wyoming in September of 1941! I completed my senior year at Natrona County High School, Casper, Wyoming. The school had a mandatory Army ROTC program and that meant wearing a uniform Monday-Thursday. I can remember my history teacher warning that the Japanese Army was rattling their swords in Asia.

I participated in a successful basketball season starting every game and making the District All-Tournament Team played in Gillette, Wyoming. The C Club annual Boxing Tournament was a fascinating completion to my high school athletic activities, as I lost a final match in an upset to a swimmer…a definite smack to my pride! I recovered by playing semi-pro baseball during the summer, winning the state championship in Worland, Wyoming. I spent my summer workdays at the Casper Grocery Store, saving my pay for the coming University of Wyoming expenses!

I still have the memory on my graduation night of returning home shortly after midnight, after a party and my mother coming into my bedroom crying with the words, "Buddy, you will never be living at home again in the near future!" She was a prognosticator of my future!

Chapter 2   Future Marine – From College Student to Navy Preflight

September 1941

It was a bright sunny morning when my father, mother and I loaded our beautiful black and yellow 1940 Studebaker sedan and headed out on the drive through the winding roads from Casper, Wyoming to the 7,200 ft. high plains of Laramie to enroll in the University of Wyoming. My bags in the trunk contained a special bag so that I could send my laundry home each week to be washed and mailed back to me, hopefully with a package of special cookies, and other goodies.

I had completed the necessary pre-registration papers and had a reservation for a shared room at the Men's Residence Hall on campus. I paid my first month's rent, a whopping $3.00 per week. My mother's first words, as I started to proceed up to the third floor, were "Buddy, I need to see your room!" My answer was "Mother, this is a Men's Residence Hall!" She informed me that she was not leaving until she saw my room! You know how that decision ended! Little did I realize that while room 302 of the Men's Residence Hall would be my room for my freshman year, it would also be my room when I returned in 1946 from WWII and until I graduated in 1948.

I adjusted to college life and had a short-lived job to earn my meals at a brand new sorority house, Kappa Kappa Gamma. I had successfully completed four weeks of serving the girls their evening meals when on a dark and stormy evening, one of the windows on the second floor was rattling. The housemother requested that I get a hammer and nails and go repair the shutter! I promptly climbed the ladder and was preparing to nail the shutter when, suddenly, the light in the room came on. There were no curtains, and I had a complete view of one of the campus beauty queens returning from the shower minus any towel or body cover. I almost fell off the ladder. I completed my job and returned to the dinner hall. We served the dinner meal, and suddenly I was unable to serve this gorgeous coed without shaking. Being a well-mannered young man, I presented my resignation and promptly found a job at the University Student Union Fountain Room.

Little did I know that a big part of my life would be wrapped around my job at the Student Union Fountain working for manager Edna Tichac. My pay was about 12 cents per hour. It was a fantastic job as with the name of BUD, and my outgoing personality, I immediately was acquainted with almost every one of the few thousand students at the University. I had worked at the soda fountain of the Tenth Street Drug store during my Lincoln, Nebraska high school days and in the evening the young manager invested several hours to teach me to throw a scoop of ice cream behind my back and catch it in a cone, much to the entertainment of any customer. Needless to say, I won the appreciation of many Wyoming students during quiet evenings, with no manager in attendance, performing this act as I served them their ice cream cone. I also pocketed a few bets from the football coaches too!

I enrolled in the Pre Med student program as I had made up my mind that a career in medicine would be my future goal. I was tremendously impressed with my advisor, Dr. Clark, whom I learned to love as my friend and advisor in the future years of my life!

I was asked to join the men's fraternity, Phi Delta Theta, and was immediately challenged with their "frosh-hazing program!" I was introduced to my Phi Delta paddle, which I have in my possession to this day. My rear-end bruises have healed! As a freshman plebe in PDT, I was "volunteered" into two jobs for the fraternity. The first, much against my better instincts, as a male cheerleader for the University football games and, due to my baseball position as a catcher, it was determined that I would be a natural to become the Phi Delta Theta hockey squad goalie in the Intra-Mural Hockey program. This, however, was a job that would be short lived. In those days, hockey goalies were well padded but the game was played without a mask. First game, the whistle blew, one of the best players said to me, "ONE MORE SHOT IN THE WARM – UP." The lighting on the rink was sub-par, and I only saw it in time to turn my head as the puck traveled to me! The result was my nose was moved to the left of my face, and I was a bloody mess! END OF BUD'S HOCKEY CAREER! Two weeks later my parents visited Laramie and thought I had been in an automobile accident!

December arrived, and war clouds were blowing. Sunday, December 7th dawned bright and sunny, and I had an early morning shift at the Student Fountain. The small radio on the fountain ledge suddenly blared "THE JAPANESE HAVE BOMBED PEARL HARBOR—THE UNITED STATES HAS BEEN ATTACKED!" Amazed young men and crying co-eds immediately began to congregate in the fountain room. All were wondering what this would mean for their future. I was as shocked as the rest and realized that my life's course would soon be changed. I was 18 years old and flooded with thoughts of an uncertain future. I had to prepare!

I called my parents and told them not to worry. I had some initial thoughts that I needed to develop; I told them that I would take some time and not be panicked into a quick decision. Some of my immediate thoughts were that if I went into the service that I would want to go into aviation. First and foremost was the fact that I needed to finish my second semester of my freshman year before going into any program.

The U.S. Army was starting to evaluate their programs. My good friend Bob Cook and I decided to go to Cheyenne and see if we would qualify for their aviation program and we learned that the U.S. Navy was soon coming to campus to seek men for their programs. We decided to try the Army and discuss their requirements. We both passed all of their tests and seriously evaluated our choices. I had seen a movie a few years before with the title U.S. Navy "FIGHT SURGEON" that had fascinated me. I decided I wanted to wait for the Navy people to come to Laramie. I talked my buddy Cook into waiting. I also remembered the Marine fighter pilot I had previously met.

April-May 1942 – Civilian Pilot Training, Brees Field, Laramie, Wyoming

We took all the tests when the Navy arrived, and both of us passed with good results. They completed the mental and physical testing and tentatively accepted my desire to want to finish the second semester before going on active duty. They were sponsoring a program at the university called Civilian Pilot Training "CPT." This was very interesting as it was a way to qualify for my civilian pilot license. I would have approximately 50 hours flying the all metal, high wing 150 HP Luscombe. I had a very interesting young instructor, Jack McConnell. He was a daring, but good pilot. I soloed after nine hours of instruction and went on to receive my private license.

I learned that the Navy was not going to be able to send us into the program until June and this was perfect as I would be able to complete my second semester at the university. It also allowed me to take and pass a German class after promising the professor that when the war was over I would not take his language course again. School was over in early May and while awaiting orders to active duty I went to Cheyenne and worked for the Cook Plumbing Company. I learned how to lay pipe for them at Warren Air Force Base.

Chapter 3   U.S. Navy Preflight School

June 1942

In May, I enlisted in the U.S. Navy's V-5 Aviation program. I had earned my private pilot's license and waited for orders in June sending me to St. Mary's University in California to start the Aviation Cadet Pre-Flight School. In late June, the orders finally arrived, and I lined up my departure plans.

Anchors Away! I boarded the Union Pacific's *City of San Francisco* in Laramie and headed out for San Francisco. I will always remember the tall building with a clock on the top overlooking the bay! My first trip to the west coast! I boarded a bus to the other side of San Francisco Bay to go to St. Mary's University. We found ourselves going through the stages of the first day of active duty in the U.S. Navy – needles and shots, clothing issue, hair cuts and receiving all sorts of gear. There was a moment of shocking realization that I was finally an aviation cadet in the United States Navy!

I was assigned to the 3rd Battalion and housed in what had been a student dormitory. It was very nice California style building with two cadets per room. My room partner was Terry Dalton, a track athlete from Washington. We became close friends immediately. Our daily routine began at 6:00AM with a bugle blowing revile and a fast paced shower, shave, dressed, and ... ready for the daily inspection before formation for breakfast! The whole system was to follow the identical routine of the cadets at the U.S. Naval Academy at Annapolis. We soon thought Ensigns were the rank of Admirals! After breakfast we marched to classes covering various subjects to include Identification, friend or foe, where an image flashed on a screen for a 50th of a second, which resulted in us becoming speed readers and Sector search (carrier ops). These were one hour in duration and varied from 7 AM to 10 AM. We then dressed into our athletic gear and worked at various sports and close order individual combat methods. After lunch, we were back into athletic gear and physical training exercises counted out by a USMC Drill Instructor. We then went to various athletic individual sports at 3:00 PM. We had three choices, not necessarily your favorite. I drew boxing. Yeah! I participated in Junior Gold Glove bouts at a YMCA as a kid! We were scheduled for ten three minute bouts as a team sport. My first draw was the NCAA Champion in my weight class from Fresno State. I finally managed a lucky draw and survived! My instructor, Ensign Mosconi, was demanding. Our final challenge was a two-mile run around a lake with a one-pound weight in each hand, holding it above our heads! We then headed for a much needed shower. We had "gang showers." Lined up, first man ran, turned on showerheads, last man turned them off! Five minutes! No delay, immediate completion! This was the "BOOT CAMP" of the United States Navy!

After 30 days of being quarantined to the base, we were issued the much desired dress blue uniforms! Snazzy, sharp, well dressed cadets with a single star on the sleeves, and the great white hats. We cadets were now ready to dazzle the world on our few hours of leisure time, otherwise known as "Liberty."

Happy Saturday! Making certain our dress blues were freshly pressed, we boarded a bus for the ferryboat stop, and for a nickel crossed the channel to San Francisco. We are now at Fisherman's Wharf to board the cable car to the Mark Hopkins Hotel where we took the elevator to the "Top of The Mark" for a couple of drinks and then reversed course back to the base at St. Mary's University.

Elapsed time approximately six hours! This short "liberty" was vital to our weekly schedule.

The most awesome event of our stay at Pre-flight Training was the Saturday in October when the entire Corps of Cadets, dressed in blue uniforms, paraded into the University of California football stadium. We formed an impressive block on the 50-yard line where we remained at attention for the playing of our National Anthem. This was prior to the Cal/USC football game! What a thrill this was!

Because of our schedule each day, the pace of the training left little time to think! It was very physical; full speed ahead at all times. Yes sir, no sir, fall in-fall out of formation. It seemed the months passed very quickly. Soon I was in the prime physical condition of my life with a 30 inch waist a 15 inch plus neck and the confidence that I could handle any emergency.

Weather in the area was very cool in the early morning hours. Our training sessions in the outdoor swimming pool were the only uncomfortable times of our stay at St. Mary's. I had trouble coordinating the breaststroke and kick procedure. This was to train you to survive in the event of an emergency, if you had to swim in flaming water. However, I was finally able to pass the test for the above emergency but I almost froze to death learning survival! 6 AM---brr!

I was scheduled to go home on a two week Christmas leave before going to my next assignment. I was able to schedule a flight to Pocatello, Idaho for a wonderful time with my parents and younger sister. She was very busy; scheduling dates with her friends to make certain her brother was entertained! All too soon it was time to board the train to the Naval Air Station at Pasco, Washington for Primary Flight Training. My parents again were rock solid in saying goodbye to their only son who was heading into a future that was hard for them to understand. They made me feel very good, and it was full speed ahead!

Years later, as I read my squadron buddy Bill Cantrell's book, FRIENDS, DEAR FRIENDS, AND HEROES, I was amazed to learn he was in the same battalion at St. Mary's as me. The 3rd Battalion was so large I never met him at that time. We flew together in VMF114 until his injury and evacuation from Peleliu.

Chapter 4   Primary Flight Training

December 1942

All aboard for a train ride to U.S. Naval Air Station, Pasco, Washington! The Daniel family had done a great job in celebrating an early Christmas as US Navy orders ruled. As I boarded the train in Pocatello, Idaho it definitely was not FIRST CLASS! Because of wartime needs, every passenger car in the Union Pacific Railroad's inventory seemed like it had been built in the 1800's! Some even had an old time lantern fixture on the walls of the cars.

We arrived in the Pasco area that was adjacent to the newly constructed Hanover Atomic TOP SECRET project, about which very little knowledge was available. It was out in the "boondocks" with nothing much in sight as large sand dunes hid the scenic view. Naval Air Station, Pasco, was a base built in a hurry. The barracks were two story buildings, each housing forty cadets. We had twenty-two level steel beds, double storage cabinets and footlockers which are large wood cases for the storage of shoes, shaving kits, extra clothing, and personal gear. Special racks were available for hanging our snazzy blue uniforms and jackets. We had little use of the good looking uniforms as this Navy Air Base was lacking in "liberty" opportunities. Every item of gear had a designated special spot that was checked each morning during the white glove inspection prior to breakfast. The officers tried to make this much like Marine Boot Camp.

After we had seen the rows of biplanes lined up on the taxiways, we were very excited to get flight training started. We were issued heavy winter flight gear, pants, jackets and boots. In spite of excellent heavy fur lined equipment our flights during the cold winter months proved to be quite uncomfortable.

Each day we went to the "Ready Room" to meet our assigned Flight Instructors and to have our daily outline of activities explained. Half of each day was classroom instruction and the other half was devoted to flying. There were two types of planes we would fly, the two wing open cockpit Boeing N2S and the similar Navy N-3N that was actually built by the U.S. Navy. Both planes were nicknamed "Yellow Peril!" Compared to the planes we would soon learn to fly, these were indeed elementary! However, they were wonderfully efficient machines for student Naval Aviators to acquire the fundamentally necessary life saving habits and skills that young pilots required to succeed in meeting the challenges of Navy and Marine Corps wartime flight. The program was life insurance for later challenges! Amen!

Comical events would happen each day. In the open cockpit instructors communicated with cadets in the aft cockpit by "Goss port metal tubing and rear view mirrors!" One never knew what "gem" our instructors would pass through the tube next! My instructor, Ensign Isely, had acquired his wings through the PBY Flying Boat training program, a plane whose airspeed was 115 knots no matter what position the plane was in! Naturally my fighter pilot ambitions were aghast with this situation. He once asked me "Daniel, what do you want to do when you get your gold wings?" My answer, hand signals portraying a fighter pilot! He then said, "Yeah, all you little midgets want that!"

Naturally, my attitude was ignited! A day or two later we were in the aerobatic C stage, and he informed me "I'm gonna show you something you've never done!" My initial reaction was, "Yeah, show me!" He then put the aircraft into an INVERTED SPIN, which was amazingly new to me! Near panic set in as I was almost being ejected from the plane! Through the mirror I saw he was enjoying my reaction. On landing, I told him I owed him an apology. "Why?" he asked. "What was that maneuver we just did?" Answer, "INVERTED SPIN of course!"

My first Christmas away from home and the 1943 New Year's Day came and went without much celebration. We were busy absorbing Naval Aviation instruction in a completely new type of plane. Through January the first stage was moved rapidly. We were acclimating to the cold temperatures in the open cockpits. I was logging flights of one and one half hours every other day along with classroom indoctrination to several different subjects. From

Morse code, "da-dit-dit-da" to celestial navigation and the instant identification of enemy planes and ships. After eight hours in the air and a check ride by a Navy Lieutenant on 24 January, I had my solo flight requirement completed. There was a celebration of completing Stage A training. Stage B was now real flying – stalls, spins, cross wind landings and S turns to a small field landing. After another check ride with a different check pilot, I received a verdict of B+ and it was on to Stage C – aerobatics. Now this is what a fledging fighter pilot loves!

Now my fledgling career as a fighter pilot was truly on the line. After an additional several hours of practicing aerobatic maneuvers, I was not perfect, and I flunked a check ride. My whole world was about to crumble! It was time for the Marine Corps to come to save me! We had two USMC flight instructors and with extra time in the air they figured out my problems. My legs were two short for me to obtain full extension of the roll maneuvers. They recommended an additional two pillows that aided my foot position under the instrument panel, and I was able to sail by the next check successfully! My cadet career was salvaged!! These two Marine pilots cemented my future decision to become a Marine fighter pilot.

During the month of March we trained for two of the most interesting and exciting flights that were part of the syllabus and were introduced to night flights. The runway lights consisted of small smoke pots lining part of each side of the runway. The planes in the air at the same time were divided into groups and each group distributed to designated altitudes. At certain intervals the rotating signal light atop the tower would signal for the groups to alter altitudes. Your instructor accompanied you on your first short introduction flight. He constantly complimented you on your progress and landing, and before you taxied back to your starting spot patted you on the head and departed for you to continue on your own. It turned out that, on the entire flight, he had also been on the controls. This certainly did not reinforce your confidence! Nevertheless the next two night landings were a "piece of cake" in spite of, or because of, his unusual style of instruction.

It was on one of these flights that my constant cadet companion, Ralph Lagoni, struck a hill on his landing approach and did a good job of changing his plane's condition and appearance! We did not attempt to kid him on his performance! Ralph was prone to a "short fuse" at times.

C stage and all of the above had taken up the days of March. My logbook now showed almost ninety hours in the "Yellow Peril" aircraft. My self-esteem and confidence had soared. On "April Fools Day" I had my D stage check ride with Lt. Bearden and passed it with "flying colors!" Pardon the pun! I could feel that the end of primary flight was near as the final stage, E stage, was five days away! April 6, 1943, my final check ride with R.M. Baslach, gave me grade of E+. I was now well into Naval Aviation and ready for what the Naval Air Station, Corpus Christi, Texas had in store for me. My logbook showed 75 flights and my confidence and pride had soared!

I now had "the" big decision to make. Upon satisfactory completion of the US Navy Flight School Program, I would have to choose between becoming an Ensign in the US Navy, OR a 2nd Lieutenant in the United States Marine Corps. I made my choice and fulfilled my long time desire to wear my Gold Wings on a Marine Uniform.

Chapter 5   Naval Aviation Training

April 1943

The tenth of April was the start of a fantastic trip by rail that toured the Western half of the United States. At the completion of more than ten days on a 42-passenger two-deck sleeping car, we finally completed our tour! Forty-two Naval Aviation Cadets assembled for departure with Cadet Ralph Lagoni assigned as Commanding Officer and Cadet Glenn Daniel to the position of Executive Officer of our traveling cadet detachment. It was pointed out to everyone that any problems or trouble during the trip would bring serious consequences to the command. This guaranteed that "playful events" would happen during the trip! Amen.

During WWII, the US railroad system was loaded to the hilt and each section or division point could change your movement. We first traveled from Pasco, Washington to Portland, Oregon, then aboard the Coast Line for a wild ride to Southern California. The passenger car we boarded in Pasco was never changed. We parked on a siding, moved onto a fast Coastal Line and then were dropped off at the next convenient siding to await an available train. We spent time in Stockton, California and then, several hours later, we arrived in Bakersfield. Each stop provided the cadets an opportunity for a short liberty, and this led to some interesting "situations!" At Bakersfield, the cadets took the opportunity to not let Ralph, the CO, on board the train until the very last minute! A constant problem for the two of us who were in command was to make certain that the full complement of cadets were indeed aboard after each short stop.

East from Southern California across the Colorado River to Arizona and then across the desert to Las Vegas, New Mexico, then to El Paso, Texas and Abilene, finally southeast to Corpus Christi and our destination, the big Naval Air Station.

The tour was enlivened during our time aboard as the cadet stewards for the car were ordered to make certain one of the rest room facilities had a 24 hour supply of iced beverages on board. Each Division stop in route gave the cadets time to refill the inventory. The last day gave the "motley" crew of cadets the time to make certain they were presentable upon arrival at their new command and the last stop on the road to our *"GOLD WINGS!"*

WWII was raging in Europe. The U.S. Navy was fighting to stop the Japanese war machine that had now rolled over most of the islands and countries in the Pacific and Far East. Australia was in the gun sights of the Japan War Lords. Naval Air Station Corpus Christi had ballooned into a huge aviation operation with the mission to provide pilots to fly every type of aerial warfare. As a result, they were rapidly developing all types of training on the Main Station as well as at many other airfields outside of the city. Our group of cadet pilots had not yet been moved to train into specific types of mission aircraft such as fighters, dive-bombers, multi-engine bombers and large PB-Y flying boats.

Main Station was a beehive of officers, cadets, enlisted personnel and military protocol ruled. Cadets immediately faced physical examinations of all types and, of course, conditioning training was not neglected. The biggest initial event was the issuing of all types of personal equipment for our footlockers and super snazzy uniforms, dress blues, whites and flight gear. It was now time for a big move up from the "YELLOW PERILS!" Cadets were beginning to feel a part of the war as daily reports from the Naval Fleet reported what the carrier pilots were facing in combat with the Japanese!

STEARMAN N2S " Yellow Peril"

May 1943

Lagoni and I were sent to Beeville, Texas Field for Basic Flight training after putting our names in-between #1 and # 4 on the sign up sheet. It was a brand new field, one of the many smaller bases near Corpus. There we were introduced to the North American SNV BT-13, code named the "Vultee Vibrator." The code name referred to the vibration that existed in various flight positions. In

SNV BT-13 Vultee Vibrator

addition, it had only three bolts holding the tail on the plane! We ignored that information. It had 2-way radio flaps that lowered for landing and a variable pitch propeller, which were additional items we had to learn. The flights were generally one and ½ hours in length. A most memorable time was when I forgot to fasten my seat and shoulder belts on take off. My instructor, noting this, promptly climbed to altitude and rolled the plane on its back putting me up against the top of the cockpit cover! I wildly grabbed my belts and locked them tight. His comment was "I'll bet you never will forget that again!" Lesson learned!

Our schedule was flying in the morning, then classes, marching, physical training and time in our favorite toy, the Link Trainer. The Link Trainer was equipped with a radio and "needle/ball" altimeters used for instrument flight training. You had the necessary items to teach you to find a landing facility in bad weather by utilizing radio and low frequency Morse code broadcasts. Two hours in that box and you were almost a mental case. I logged 28 hours in the "black box"! It was a great but tough training aid. It was, however, important life insurance for the actual "under the hood" and unusual position flying that we had to learn for the advanced SNJ-model plane in our future. We received some flights in cross-country navigation going from city to city over Texas. April and early May flew by and on May 5th, my 20th birthday, I flew my one hour check flight with Captain Schwarz and was ready to proceed to Advanced Fighter Training. What a great birthday!

Beeville was so new the base housing did not have screens and still had upper/lower bunks with about 20 cadets to a large room. We carried our Liberty Cards in our pockets, which was unheard of in the Navy. This led to great liberty in San Antonio, Texas. The cadets from the Army Air Base there thought we were *HIGH RANKING* Naval flyers from the single stars we had on our jacket sleeves. Lots of laughs and salutes on the streets of San Antonio.

June- July 1943   Naval Air Station Advance Fighter Training, Kingsville, Texas

Navy Waves washing SNJ Advanced Fighter Trainer

On to NAS Kingsville, Texas, and on a banner day I checked out in SNJ #27399 with Instructor Ensign Felice. What a thrill to now be in a plane with a top speed of 208 miles per hour, a Pratt & Whitney 1340 HP engine, retractable landing gear, a 1200 ft. a minute climbing speed, and .30 machine guns in low wing. Was this next to heaven?

On June 5th the Texas coast's weather was hot and muggy, "the big H, humidity" was now here. We were headlong into the dual instruction flying. From 6 June to 18 June I spent 18 hours total flying instrument flights under a hood doing all kinds of "needle/ball/air speed recovery from unusual positions, learning approach procedures to radio beams that were identified by Morse Code (da dit—dit da) and altitude level procedures and directions by the magnetic gyro. On June 18, I passed my instrument and radio check ride! Boy, what a multitude of aerial knowledge I had accumulated in that length of time. On 28 June "A" type check rides in the N3N "Yellow Peril" with Ensign Swan and on the 29th and 30th of June three hours solo in the SNJ. I now had a total of 150 hours of Naval Flight training in my Logbook!

July's flight schedule called for gradually going into more of the solo type fighter pilot flying. We were slowly gaining confidence in a great trainer, the SNJ. Formation, aerobatics, small field procedures, and even more of the combat formations such as the "Thatch Weave" invented by Commander Thatch during combat with the fleet early in WWII.

My next fifteen flights, flown during the period 2 July thru 9 July were solo. I was flying two, three, sometimes four flights per day. Each flight varied from one to two hours. All of them aerial gunnery runs over the water in the gulf! These were thrilling as we were firing at a long white sleeve towed by another plane. Practice involved overhead diving turns with "20 mils lead" in the aiming circle on our windscreen! Different colored bullets counted our hits! Four of these flights in five hours were taxing! We did not mind as each flight brought our *GOLD WINGS CLOSER*!

Several South American flight students suddenly joined us at Kingsville. They were friendly, fun loving and playing to their own band. I was sitting in my plane, parked next to a South American cadet. He was preparing for flight in his SNJ. I was waiting for taxi instructions from the control tower when I heard over the radio a message from the South American *"WATER TOWER, WATER TOWER, PREPARE FOR TAKE OFF!" WITH THAT HE PROMPTLY TAXIED HIS PLANE OUT ONTO THE TAXI WAY AND PROCEEDED TO TAKE OFF!"* I made certain I did not move until he was in the air!

You could sense that the Pacific War was going tough, as the need for pilots seemed to be increasing. We were flying almost every day and there were more hours per flight. From 11-13 July I completed five more hours of instrument flight. On 13 July, I returned to the solo flights and logged flights of three hours per flight for a total of fifteen hours in the air in five days. We were busy. They added night flying to the syllabus on the 19th, which was a thrill on a moonlit night over the gulf.

The rest of July, the pace of flying remained hurried and intense. From the 23rd up to the 30th, I had between two and three fights a day. Another two, two-hour night flights were on the schedule for 22 and 28 July. Again, the syllabus was changed and about every type of combat flight predicted for the future was covered. I was living a dream. You cannot imagine the confidence, ability, and maturing that was building up in my mind and body!

At the end of July, I knew that the commission as a 2nd Lt in the *USMCR and the GOLD WINGS* had to be just around the corner. August 1st and the pace did not let up. My cadet flight program still had hurdles to complete. There were additional gunnery runs over the Texas coast, formation flights, cross country flights, and the final instrument check ride to establish my position on the low frequency section and the A and N quadrants on the beam into Alice, Texas.

Fourteen flights remained on my required schedule to complete before the final instrument ride with Ensign Dow. Three on August 1st, three on August 3rd, two on August 4th, four gunnery runs on August 5th, one on August 6th and finally, two on August 7th. Each day was tougher for me to go to sleep at night. Now, for the instrument check ride with Ensign Dow. It was a typically hot and muggy day. I had just completed a solo flight when Ensign Dow came up to me and asked "Do you want to fly your final instrument check now in order to graduate the next Tuesday?" I excitedly answered, "You bet! Let's grab a cold drink!" I gulped a large amount of water, grabbed my parachute and scrambled to the plane!

We took off, the hood put into place, and I was flying on instruments. Ensign Dow accomplished all sorts of unusual flight positions and it was my job to take the controls and to recover back to straight and level flight! "Needle-ball, air speed on the instrument was quickly utilized! Now we went low frequency using the A-N beam to find the *ALICE BEAM* to fly to Alice, Texas. I was just turning onto the solid sound of the beam, and I needed to belch! *WOW, WHAT A MISTAKE*! I promptly "upchucked" all over the hood and over my instructor's cockpit in front of me! Double horrors! There go my *GOLD WINGS*! Dow's reaction was human and controlled. He told me over the mike," Relax, you have had a good check ride! " You cannot imagine my relief and happiness. I will always remember Ensign Dow's courtesy and understanding! He was an example of a fine officer and a great teacher.

The preparations for the big graduation ceremonies were now put into place. I had the weekend to do a million things before the big day, AUGUST 11th, 1943, 10 AM! A trip to the paymasters' office, and the finishing touches to the several uniforms and items required for my new status in life! We no longer were wearing Navy uniforms. The Marine Corps had adopted the Eisenhower style of Marine greens, very sharp and comfortable. This meant we had to use our new uniform allowance before our graduation ceremony.

Phone calls to mom and dad, sisters and to all my relatives! Packing for my next move, I had about two weeks leave time in route to my next duty station, NAS Jackson, Florida. My logbook now showed I had completed 245 hours flight time. My constant buddy, 2nd Lt. to be Ralph Lagoni and me now had special permission to use the base Officer's Club. We had many different decisions to make. Should we use the total time we were due to fly home, OR should we decide to save money and meet in New Orleans and see what Bourbon Street had to offer. Lagoni did not graduate until Thursday, August 13 so we had to arrange to meet in New Orleans. It turns out that had we made the decision to fly home instead of going to New Orleans, we would have saved a LOT of $$$! However, had we followed the sensible path we would not have had nearly the good times, or the memories we would re-live for the rest of our lives!

Tuesday, August 11th arrived and in a memorable event, I was commissioned as a 2nd Lt., USMCR. The ceremony ended, we were dismissed, and I headed for my room. While going up the sidewalk, I met several enlisted Navy sailors. One of them threw me a salty salute, and I immediately followed custom by thanking him with a dollar bill. Memorable! I called the folks and told them I was now wearing the coveted *"WINGS OF GOLD."*

That afternoon one of my Navy cadet friends, now a new Ensign in the US Navy, asked me to be best man at his wedding. Of course, I said yes, and Andy Anderson married that afternoon. I kissed the bride, wished them well, and headed for the train depot for the train to New Orleans. I have never heard from or received any news of Anderson to date.

I checked into the Roosevelt Hotel in New Orleans and waited for Lagoni's arrival the next day. There was a large display in the lobby heralding the traditional "FAMOUS RAMOS GIN FIZZ!" Lagoni and I made certain that we would taste and recommend that libation during our four-day stay, to all who cared. The days and nights past fast and I had to get my sharp new light brown gabardine uniform sent to the cleaners twice due to my "jitter-bugging" dancing activity in the humid atmosphere of the "gin mills on Bourbon Street"!

Lagoni met a beautiful, sweet Navy enlisted young lady; I met her moderately "attractive" friend, which was par for the course. We had supper and danced and never saw them again. The stay in New Orleans became a shorter party than we originally expected as the money rapidly disappeared. Ralph's orders were for Miami, mine were for Operational Flight Training, Jacksonville, Florida. We wished each other well and hoped to meet again at MARINE CORPS AIR STATION (MCAS), EL TORO, CALIFORNIA.

Chapter 6   Operational Flight Training

August 1943

The Naval Air Station at Green Cove Springs, Florida, was a small operational training facility about 20 miles from the commercial airport in St. Augustine, and NAS Jacksonville.

After checking in and proceeding to our new quarters, we found that living here we would have the best housing to date. Buildings were new; we enjoyed very nice single rooms with new furniture and shared bath. Things were looking up. The shock of being a commissioned officer was slowly changing. In addition, the paychecks were much larger! The first days were filled with indoctrination to all the regulations, schedules and descriptions of the various classes we would have from time to time. They issued all types of flight gear to us.

About 30 young pilots made up our Operational Class. I recognized one, Lt. Wellwood from Sheridan, Wyoming. Very few of the guys had autos so most of us would have to get the bus schedule to Jacksonville, the only city of any size. After viewing our first flight schedule it was evident that we were not here for fun, and every day would have from one to three or four hours of flying. We would spend time in the altitude chamber where we would learn the symptoms of oxygen depletion while flying above 15,000 feet. It was amazing the first time you felt the effects in the chamber. Later on, we would have the feeling of a dark shade slowly pulling down over your eyes as if you were pulling excessive G's. This was insurance time in the training!

All of us were excited about the fact that soon we would be flying the airplane that had become famous in the CACTUS AIR FORCE during COMBAT in GUADALCANAL. We were days away from checking out in a famous fighter of which we were in awe! At that time, we had no real idea of what to expect from this plane. This was a time of REALITY flight training!

F4F Grumman Wildcat
In flight February 1942.
Official U.S. Navy Photograph, Naval History and
Heritage Command collection

Top speed: 320 mph (290 knots)
Range; 830 mi Service Ceiling 34,000 ft.
Rate of climb: 2200 ft/min
Armament: 6 - 0.50 mm machine-guns 3/wing

Now you can see why all of us tender fighter pilots were anxious to climb into this cockpit! We were now going to be flying a real combat aircraft. Speed, real guns, oxygen training, and 30 turns of a crazy hand crank to extend and retract the landing gear! There were plenty of serious actions to learn in and out of the cockpit. The most tedious was operating the landing gear!

August 24th, the first flight on the new airfield, the prelude to what we had been waiting for! Of all things, instrument refresher and familiarization flight with Lt. Bodell under the hood with me putting him in all the unusual position recoveries! I was in the back seat of the SNJ #26758 for one and one-half hours. All went well, and we waited for my turn the following day!

On August 26th, I strapped into the cockpit of the F4F WILDCAT, pictured above! I started the engine by firing a shotgun shell that would spin the propeller until the engine caught hold. Taxi into the position as per ground control orders, checked the two magnetos; tower says "permission to go!" Eighteen hundred horses of power and away we roll. Who hit me in the butt? The next realization was climbing 2200 ft/min to a cruising altitude of 12,000 ft. Now I could relax a little and enjoy the view of landscape, ocean and beach in the distance. WOW! After almost an hour, it was time to prepare for my first landing. The WILDCAT had a very narrow landing gear and a tendency to quickly try to ground loop after you start the rollout on the runway! This was going through my mind as I gradually let down and greased the Cat on the runway! Hoorah! Number one accomplished! Congratulations from my instructor and now go around and repeat the whole scenario. Another hour in the air and my maiden voyage was in the logbook.

On August 27th it was the same routine to accomplish for another three flights. Each one, however, brought more confidence and maturity as a pilot. This was the schedule for the next three days. On the 30th, I had one more of the same, but then a flight up to the altitude layer that would require a short time in an oxygen mask! Thus ended August.

One of the most interesting phases of Ops training was FIELD CARRIER LANDINGS! One runway had a replica of a landing deck of a carrier, with the position of the landing signal officer in the proper space. This is where this officer stands with two paddles in hand to signal certain action from the pilot. Satisfactory speed, alignment, altitude, cut to land, or frantically waiving the paddles to "bolder" or to add throttle and go around for another approach. Combine this with the dangerous presence of the possibility of reaching stalling speed and with the presence of tall trees surrounding the runway, the increased probability for dangerous situations to occur was evident. Add to all of the above, the speed of the carrier was not part of the scenario! This plus flying one or two knots above stalling speed before a cut to land was "hairy" to say the least!

Our schedule for the next three to four days of flying: 7:00 AM breakfast, then one hour of actual footage of film showing real crashes and bolders (wave off) of carrier landing operations. We then moved to the WILDCAT and saddled up for two hours of flying thrills! This was the Navy way of adding maturity and responsibility to young aspiring fighter pilots! YEAOW MAN!

September 1943

By late August, as I scrolled through my Logbook, I discovered that I had 295 hours logged in training flights! The status of the war was clearly affecting the tempo of our training. It was speeding up. The action in the Southwest Pacific was creating a need for more fighter and dive-bomber pilots.

The last week of August, we had been flying hard every day, including Saturday. Flights during that time were spent learning how to fly the WILDCAT. Starting in September, it became combat tactics for real! This included some local formation, but mainly section tactics (two & four planes), bombing and gunnery runs on a tow sleeve. The gunnery flights were most fun as they were at high altitude, and on oxygen; these overhead runs would have a tendency to "black you out" if you pulled too many G's. You had to be very careful with the older F4F-1 WILDCATS that came back from the CACTUS AIR FORCE. The CURTIS ELECTRIC PROPELLERS would go into "high pitch", which resulted in losing thrust and difficulty in retaining altitude! This was a no-no, especially if you were too far out over the Atlantic! They maintained you could "toggle" the pitch, but that was not always the case! We flew all of our gunnery runs east of here, from St. Augustine east over the Atlantic Ocean.

It was a bright and sunny day on September 1st and in 295 hours of flying I had never scratched an airplane, UNTIL TODAY!

We had taken off on the very long SE runway and completed our third gunnery run. We returned to St. Augustine Airport and asked the tower for landing instructions. We expected the long SE runway, but for some unknown reason they gave us the short East-West runway, which crossed the main highway and their were many high tension wires that surrounded the coastal railroad.

Now, fat dumb and happy enters the picture. I check my landing procedures, make my approach behind the leader of our flight and proceed. Suddenly, the plane ahead of me, well into his landing, BLOWS A TIRE! This of course puts me into emergency procedures...CRANKING UP THE 30 TURNS OF THE WHEELS! All is going well, and I am cleared for another hairy run over the wires, etc. I have the sensation of the control stick wobbling all over the cockpit. My confidence is complete, and I succeed in getting the wild steed onto the runway. Suddenly, I noticed the indicator was still showing about 40 knots of speed. I immediately unlock the tail wheel and ground loop the plane. I was sliding onto the beach sand, towards the Atlantic Ocean. As I heard the crash truck roaring up on the runway, it occurs to me that I had forgotten my landing procedure of lowering my FLAPS! I knew the next day I would have to attend an ACCIDENT REPORT meeting! Lucky for me I met with the famous Commander Thatch, inventor of the THATCH WEAVE! Fortunately for me, he asks, "Son, perchance did you not forget to lower your Flaps? I IMMEDIATELY SURRENDERED!" Lucky for me, the famous Navy Pilot remembered once being new to the Navy Flight Program!

The first two weeks of September were filled with gunnery and bombing runs. Formation flying is learning the "symphony and concentration" of the Thatch Weave. This was the "waltz" of formation flying. Two planes were a Section – four to a Flight! The Weave was the system of keeping your "six" (your back area) clear of Japanese Zero fighters! We were learning the combat methods used by the Navy fighter pilots in the Pacific Theater. We were building confidence in and respect for our flight partners. More serious life insurance!

This portion of Navy Flight Training focused on a precision technique requiring your ability to fly the WILDCAT and eventually the MARINE F4U's! It required a lot of practice and for two weeks in early September, two to three hours of saddling-up in your FM WILDCAT daily!

After two weeks of daily flying, bombing, strafing, and night flying, we finally got Saturday and Sunday liberty to bus up to Jacksonville. We needed to find out if beer and "jitter-bugging" had not been forgotten! Hoo-rah! Some things never change!

I can remember one night; we ran into some Navy Nurses. It was a party! Some how one of the nurses had a real interest in Marine fighter pilots and GOLD WINGS! For some reason, she liked them more than the Navy Nurse wings she had on her uniform. Later in the evening she had appropriated more than one set of the GOLD WINGS! She also had an auto and graciously offered four of us transportation back to our base. How the guard at the entry gate never noticed the collection of wings, she had on her uniform, and didn't pull us all out of the car, we will never know!

From September 21st to the 29th we were flying more hours each day, until finally another bus to Jacksonville and a couple days of fun! My Logbook now had 291 hours in the air.

October 1943

Florida weather had now cooled a bit, and life was much more comfortable. The schedule changed somewhat with the addition of a flight instructor who flew along with a two-plane section, or four-plane flight. They then monitored and graded the precision accomplishments of each group of planes as they performed their assignments. At one stage my group had Major Ohleric, a pilot who, after three years with the ground Marines at Greenland, had been transferred into flight training. Unfortunately, he was not the best pilot in the air. It was bad enough that we, behind his back, nicknamed him, "THE BLUE FLAME!" The reason I have mentioned this is because two years later he joined VMF-114. Every time he joined up as "Tail-end Charlie" on a squadron flight, it was a circus. Major Stout, our CO, questioned me as to "where in hell did this guy come from?" He was at the time a Lt Colonel, assigned to our squadron, but under Stout's command. This was an unusual situation in the USMC. He was fortunately not around very long!

October arrived with a big schedule! I just thumbed through my logbook, and we were busy with the most flights in one month to date. Every day we logged three, four, and sometimes five hops. A lot of these were only one hour. Most of those were gunnery runs over the Atlantic from St. Augustine. After four flights, you were very tired.

Also, we started night flying. We had a couple of flights when a big HARVEST MOON would creep up just coming slowly out of the water to light up the whole sky! It was breath taking. We enjoyed those flights! Flights during dark nights were not so hot!

There were WACS stationed at Daytona Beach, Florida, and we always let them know we were in the air by "buzzing" their quarters. If it happened to be a night mission, we could get a little lower going west right on the water and pulling up fast over the beach to hide the numbers on our planes. That did not always please their commanding officers. It did not stop us however!

We were slowly adding up the hours in our Logbooks and realizing our next assignment could not be too far away! Sixty flights in thirty days was a record for me.

The last six days of October I logged eight hours of night flying and a mixed bag of different types of time in the WILDCAT. On my last flight at night I witnessed a unique accident. The pilot who followed me in to land either forgot his wheels or there was a malfunction, which caused his landing gear to collapse. The WILDCAT had a Fuel Dump Valve directly midline of the fuselage. As the plane skidded along the runway, a slow burning line of flame moved up behind the cockpit, an explosion would occur if it caught up with the damaged valve! Fortunately the young pilot saw what was about to happen, and he immediately exited the cockpit and ran as fast as he could. RESULT, SCRATCH ONE WILDCAT, SAVE ONE PILOT! Exciting fire!

I had grown to enjoy this unique little plane. I felt I was ready for my next assignment, which had to be in an advanced fighter. My confidence and experience had given me the ability to handle whatever came my way! Cocky yes, but I also realized there were no "old and bold pilots!"

Bring on my next assignment. The Logbook now read over 360 hours. I anxiously went to the office to find out what awaited me! Wow! 30 days travel and leave time before reporting to MARINE CORPS AIR STATION, EL TORO, CALIFORNIA! I did not know for sure, but my thoughts told me, it had to be the F4U-CORSAIR!

I called my parents and sisters in Pocatello, Idaho, booked a flight to Cheyenne, Wyoming and planned a short stop in Laramie to visit some old friends at the University on my way to Pocatello. Life was very good now!

Chapter 7 Advanced Fighter Training, F4U-CORSAIR

December 1943, El Toro

Upon completion of the first phase of operations training in Florida, I headed for Pocatello, Idaho where my parents lived. En route I stopped in Laramie, Wyoming to see some friends who were still in college.

Arriving in Laramie I was eager to go to the Student Union and see many old friends who had not yet entered the service. Naturally, I was extremely proud to appear in my Class A USMC uniform, complete with the gold bars of a second lieutenant and even more proudly my *GOLD WINGS*! The campus was not over flowing with male students as an extremely large number of young men had answered Uncle Sam's call to arms. It did not take long for me to be surrounded by a number of friends and a couple of female students who admired my uniform and understood my accomplishments. How hard it was to remain humble and proud at the same time.

My former girl friend, Katie Swanton, had pledged *KAPPA KAPPA GAMMA SORORITY* and become the campus queen. She had to be back to her sorority house by 9 PM. So my visit was much shorter than I wanted. It turned out to be just as well as I later discovered she was corresponding with duplicate letters to me, and another boyfriend who was in the European Theater while I was at Peleliu. How soon they forget! He was not lucky, as on his first mission as a B-17 bombardier he was shot down and became a prisoner of war. My plan was a short visit in Laramie. My social time was spent at a campus favorite, the Plaza Bar. How the beer did flow!

I had planned on meeting my sister, Jeanne, in Laramie. She was living in Kansas at the time. The Union Pacific Railroad came through and I met her at the station. Together we experienced an extremely unusual wartime trip by rail to Pocatello in an "1890

Passenger Rail Car" that was lit by an oil lamp! Her husband, Eldon, was currently a flight instructor in the Army Air Corps. I could look forward to a Daniel family reunion!

My visit home was a wonderful reunion and my parents were impressed with my new wings, gold bars, and snappy U.S. Marine uniform. My father was extremely pleased to take his "Fighter Pilot" son to the local *ELKS CLUB*. Only too soon, my leave time was running out. My flight to California was scheduled for 11 PM. At 9 PM my dad suddenly feigned a bad shoulder pain and had to go to bed. I could not blame him for not being able to say goodbye. He could not help but be very concerned about what I would soon be facing. At the time I had trouble completely realizing what my mom and dad were thinking, with their only son facing combat in the very near future.

The Daniel Family
From left to right, Bottom: Arlene, Dad Top: Mother, Me, Jeanne

My new assignment took me to the Marine Corps Air Station in El Toro, California. It was here I was to check out in the powerful new F4U CORSAIR, the *"PREMIER COMBAT FIGHTER"* in operation. It was a 2,000 horse powered demon with a climb rate of 3,000 feet per minute. ***The Japanese military soon knew the Corsair as "Whistling Death."*** Getting to know and then to control this powerful fighter was quite a challenge for a 20 year old USMC fighter pilot.

I could not at the time realize what was ahead of me. I knew it was what I wanted and I was ready for the challenge. U S Marine Corps Air Station El Toro was a brand new base, teeming with serious training going on, night and day! I'm not certain that I realized how exciting my next few months would be! My first day, I met up with my great friend, Ralph Lagoni. He had completed operational training a few days before me in Florida. True to form, he already had met a blonde with a Ford convertible!

We had suddenly realized the meaning of what it was to be a *MARINE FLIGHT OFFICER* on a real operating base. We were issued the flight gear normal for combat fliers. The shock was that a .45 caliber pistol, complete with leather holster and ammunition was ours! The first thing a Marine does "as the old Corps say," is to "flame grain the holster" with cordovan polish.

By now a group of young pilots, the threesome of Daniel, Lagoni, and Bob Roy, had renewed their friendship and week or two of indoctrination had been completed. It was a beautiful Sunday and the three some had accomplished forming a six some with three lovely young ladies, Ginny, Maxi, and Pitt. We arranged for them to join us, for a Sunday evening at the very posh "officers club" at six PM! In the meantime, the young "Gryrenes" had time to venture into the hills close to El Toro and fire their pistols! All went well until one happened to note it was past time to meet the "faire damsels!" By the time we made it back to the club, the young ladies were being well taken care of by "thoughtful Marines" at the bar. Needless to say, the six some was close to becoming a threesome!" As young Marine fighter pilot in Southern California we realized we were in the "land of Milk and Honey.... Cold Milk and Hot Honeys!"

Long Beach Naval Officers Club

14 December 1943

Before getting near the Corsair I had a short flight in the SNJ-4 to get the "lay of the land" of the local area. I was able to casually look the area over for about an hour.

The fact that we were scheduled to fly the premier fighter plane in Marine Corps Aviation meant a great deal of time on the ground learning the "to do's and not to do's." The flight manual's take off and landing procedures, power settings, cockpit instruments, and oxygen systems and more proved to be very time consuming.

Before we actually sat in the cockpit for a blindfold session touching each instrument, we were to spend an afternoon at the end of a runway, actually watching planes touching down, especially the Corsairs. It was here we witnessed a tragedy! Four of us were sitting in a Ford convertible with top folded down to give us a close view. A Corsair roared over us to touch down! Closely following him was a SBD Douglas dive bomber. Horribly we watched as he came too close to the "prop wash", lost control, struck the surface of the runway, cart wheeled, and crashed! Right before our eyes we witnessed the death of a young Marine pilot. Boy, this was one tough indoctrination!! Yes, accidents do happen! After watching the ambulance, fire trucks, and crash crews start the clean up, we adjourned to the O-Club to calm our nerves.

16 December 1943 F4U-1 #13203 (The #13 has always been my lucky number.)

Bright and early that morning we went to the flight line for the next scheduled introduction to the magnificent F4U-1 (bird-cage) Corsair. *A BIG FIGHTER!* First was the pre-flight inspection. The big prop was pulled through several times to oil the engine. The mechanic then inserted the starter cartridge, jumped down off the wing, signaled all clear, and then came the delicate part, gently moving the throttle, a big cloud of smoke and loud bangs as the engine struggled to start. Then the roar of 2000 horsepower straining to go into action. *I AM ACTUALLY ABOUT READY TO TAKE THIS MIGHTY BIRD INTO THE SKY!*

I called Ground Control for taxi clearance, taxi into position to check the magnetos that provide the spark ignition to engine. After checking the drop in both "mag's" it is clear to go. The tower gives you clearance to take off position, *OK TO GO!* Throttle forward, seconds later, "who hit me in the butt?" Suddenly you are airborne, climbing at 130 knots and 3,000 feet a second! WOW, a fantastic view. Altitude 12 thousand feet, air speed 180 knots, the Pacific Ocean and beach below, and Los Angeles and the Santa Anna mountains in the distance; it was a sensational view. Among other things, I had to check oil pressure, the carburetor-cylinder head temperature, fuel pressure, rpm, and air speed. You check every dial in the cockpit randomly! Carefully you turn more sharply, tightly, and feel the mighty horse rise up and drop down! Hard to relax but I'm getting the feel. I realized this plane is a wonderful machine, but also that you had better take it easy, learn its complete capabilities and limitation and proceed with caution for a number of hours! Normally a new pilot would fly this baby for 10-12 hours before you attempting any acrobatic maneuvers.

December 16th and 17th were familiarization flights doing touch and go take offs and landings. We did not vary from the carrier approach method. You must call the tower to obtain the runway heading, traffic information, execute the landing check-off list, and mentally say to yourself **GUMP *(GAS, UNDERCARRIAGE, MIXTURE, POWER)*.** "GUMP" is the acronym that can never be forgotten as it serves to protect you during all future landings.

You have already put down the necessary flaps and the wheels from the undercarriage. God forbid if you execute a wheels *up* landing having forgotten to lower the wheels. *Wheels up*, a very nasty term on your flight record!

The above procedure, readies you on your down wind leg to then pick out the spot where you want to touchdown. You slowly lose altitude on the turn to the runway where you will cut the power and touch down in a three point position, main wheels and tail wheel all landing in unison! You can now take a deep breath, slow your speed by touching the brakes gently, and start a side-to-side taxi to park. You have no clear sight forward because of the 15-foot nose of the Corsair straight ahead. You have now completed a good landing, *which is the definition of any landing!*

The next five days saw five more familiarization flights for a total of six hours demonstrating your knowledge and ability to handle your new challenges! Section tactics were now "for real" versions of combat flying. We were now in the real world of "getting ready!"

December 31st

New Years Eve turned out to be another tragic date, the second fatal accident to occur that month. It all started very casually. Six pilots were free to now "chase tails" in the air! Actually, it was a case of too much, too soon! I and five other new Corsair pilots decided we would have fun, roaring though the beautiful cumulus cloud formations. All went super until the lead plane started a "follow the leader loop." The mistake he made was the amount of speed he used to start the maneuver. He was at least 50 to 100 knots too slow! I was number three in the parade and as I approached the upper stage of the loop, I realized I did not have enough speed to get over the top. I immediately slowly turned off to my right side and aborted the loop. I was sure the pilot following me would do the same. I was *horrified* when I saw him try to complete the loop! He did not have nearly enough speed, proceeded to stall and went into the dreaded '*DEADMAN'S DIVE*" an inverted spin into the ground on the ranch below! 2nd Lt. Erich Jont, Chicago, Illinois was killed instantly.

He made an unbelievable hole in the ground. A medic, who was assigned to the accident, later showed us a half dollar coin that had a quarter imbedded into it. That was in his pocket when he hit! This together with seeing the hole his crash made convinced us of the power of a Corsair crash! The whole incident was a result of attempting too much too soon! I later notice in my logbook that the 31st of December was the date my roommate did not survive a water landing while the two of us were ferrying Corsairs to Guadalcanal. The 31st day of the month was not my day to be flying!

1 January 1944

We celebrated the New Year at the El Toro Officers Club and got ready to get back into the "saddle" with a new schedule of combat tactics. Our new instructors were mostly captains recently returned from combat in the SW Pacific. Several of them were Aces with five or more Zeros shot down! They were a great group, friendly, very knowledgeable, impressive fighter pilots! When they gave instructions, you listened intently. Two or three of them were winners of the Congressional Medal of Honor. 2 January to 10 January we flew Section Tactics, bombing and gunnery missions over Catalina Island. A great view of the Pacific Ocean!

There were three flights on January 11th and 12th, and two of them were night flights. What a view up to Los Angeles and the millions of lights of a metropolis. This night was the time I flew through a cloud and came out up side down. I experienced a slight case of vertigo and the lights of Los Angeles and the night stars were reversed. Which was up and which was down? I first noticed the junk from the floor of the cockpit was scattering all over me. Quick reference and a belief in "needle ball and airspeed" and I was back to straight and level. A memorable night!

The next ten days were filled with oxygen flight familiarization, gunnery, and division and section tactics. This training was eight planes executing the "Thatch Weave" (two flights of four) over bombers. This represented a new beat in the training waltz. We also did one night of touch and go landings and air work from the 20th thru the 31st of January. In January, I completed 30 flights, one additional flight for night tactics, and added to the logbook which now showed a total of 416 hours flying! Never once did we complain of being overworked!

One night Lagoni and I wound up dancing and having a couple of drinks with two nice young ladies. Surprisingly we befriended them well enough that we were invited to their house as the evening grew late. We had little notice of how the evening would come to a close! They lived in a quite, nice small home that had a very strict landlady. I guess the four of us got a little loud and roused the composure of the landlady. The next thing we knew she was at the back door yelling that she had locked the doors and was calling the police. We knew that it was necessary that we vacate the premises immediately. Lagoni, being short fused, got rid of a screen on a side window and we scrambled out hearing the approaching sirens in the distance. Neither of us had a car but we knew a main road was not too far away and we could flag a taxi or catch a bus back to base. It happened to be a very dark night and the quickest way to safety was through the many orange tree groves in the Santa Ana area. In our haste we neglected to notice our escape path would take us through muddy rows of orange trees. We escaped but had officer's trousers that were ready for the dry cleaners. This made the automobile in the next paragraph a wonderful addition to our entertainment!

In spite of a daily flight schedule, we found time to enjoy a little nightlife in Hollywood and LA. Our group of 2nd Lts even came into the possession of a 1927 LaSalle Limousine. This limo was designed for a chauffer in the front compartment who communicated to the back seat via a wire. The back compartment had flowerpots over the doors. We talked our plane mechanics into welding a waterproof tank on the floor for ice to cool beer in route to LA and the Palladium nightclub and dance hall. We even had a "duty roster" indicating who was the designated driver and therefore not allowed to have liquor that evening! The driver's steering wheel was huge. This proved to be a magnificent machine to sooth the rigors of learning to fly the Corsair! I will write about the disposition of said amusement vehicle before we went aboard the Savo Island aircraft carrier in San Diego.

We always had a daily schedule posted the night prior so we knew if our nightlife was cleared before the next day of flying! This made it possible to see in person such celebrities as the trombone player, Tommy Dorsey and singer Helen O'Connell, Louis "Satchmo" Armstrong, and the Nat King Cole Trio! They had just appeared on the scene at a small bar in LA. A few weeks later they were starring at The Trocadero on national radio, and years later on TV.

February 1944

It seemed like the intensity of our training was gradually moving into more serious and purposeful operations. Our instructors constantly explained in detail exactly why mistakes would get us into trouble and errors were corrected. Each flight was thoroughly briefed before and after we landed. Each day we realized more and more that we were not playing a game. Division tactics involved a

49

four-plane formation executing very close movements. Gunnery flights involved rolling the plane over on its back, picking out a target sleeve, with a high speed high *G's (INTENSE PRESSURE)* diving turns to get the proper 20 mils lead on your target! The ammunition (*50 Cal. machine guns*) was painted different colors to identify hits! The duration of each intense training event was generally one and one half hours. Two or three of these flights in a day were tiring to say the least.

On the ninth of February, I had three one-hour day and a two one-hour night flights training on division tactics. This was a good day's work. On 13 February I had two flights of "dogfighting!" This was tremendous fun soaring through big cumulous clouds and simulating the shoot down of a Zero. This was as close as you could get to the real fight. Very exciting! Then we had one more high altitude flight over 20 thousand feet for one plus hours on oxygen.

My month of February totaled 27 flights and thirty-six plus hours of the different flight training to bring my total hours of training to 452 hours.

Fortunately before completing my time at El Toro, I had the opportunity to let my parents know that my time for shipping out to somewhere in the Pacific Theater would come soon!
They immediately made reservations for an immediate train trip to Southern California and sent me their itinerary. I had made close friends with my plane mechanics and one offered me the use of his car! This was a great example of the respect the men on the flight line had for their pilots. This made the long weekend with my visiting parents possible.

I met them at the LA Union Pacific train station for the start of a wonderful three-day visit. The first day my number one priority was, naturally, to take them for a visit to the flight line and an introduction to a Marine F4U Corsair fighter. My parents were overwhelmed by a close visit to one of many big planes on the flight line! As we approached the first Corsair, my mother informed me *"I'M NOT LEAVING UNTIL I SIT IN THE*

COCKPIT OF THIS PLANE!" I immediately had a big decision to make, as to how to get her into that cockpit! My two plane mechanics quickly solved it by getting two ladders. We somehow got her into the pilot seat and she started touching the instruments and asking questions! This went on for several minutes as my father stood on the wing listening. Finally, mom crossed her arms, took a deep sigh, and said *"OK, BUDDY, I THINK YOU KNOW WHAT YOU ARE DOING. I GUESS I WILL LET THE MARINE CORPS SEND YOU OVERSEAS!"* I informed her that I would give her decision to the Commandant of the Corps and he would be duly impressed!

We had an opportunity to visit my father's sister who had married a very successful man and lived in a very upscale section of Beverly Hills. Sister Helen was impressed and thrilled by our visit. The three days went by too quickly as we had a wonderful and impressive visit. I kissed them fondly good-bye, not knowing if and when I would see them again! I returned Sergeant Goody's auto, full of gas, unharmed, with sincere appreciation for his thoughtfulness.

I felt that my time to be getting orders to go somewhere overseas had to be not far away. One reason that led me to this conclusion was a decision by the Commanding Officer of the training unit. He had decided the young fighter pilots in training at MCAS El Toro might be having too much fun at the expense of their physical training. So, he ordered two USMC Drill Sergeants from USMC Recruit Battalion San Diego to come to MCAS El Toro and initiate a program of Physical Training, Monday through Friday at 0700 hours. The following 2nd Lts (the list included 2nd Lt Daniel) will report minus any recognition of rank! I fortunately went through only two days of this misery before I received my orders to report for an overseas assignment!

March 1944

Ralph Lagoni had just been ordered to fighter squadron VMF 122 and sent to El Centro, California. Our paths were not to cross until

51

several months later in combat at Peleliu. Two flights on 3rd and 5th March would complete my flight training at MCAS El Toro!

On the 10th of March we were ordered to our unit headquarters. About 22 pilots were assembled for information and dates that we were to report to MCAS Miramar in San Diego and prepare to go aboard a carrier, to deploy to somewhere in the Pacific Theater for assignment to a fighter squadron.

Fighter Training Unit 41/MCAS El Toro 1943

Chapter 8   USS Savo Island CVE #78

April 1944

We had a lot of things to get squared away. Phone calls to parents, packing the things we would take with us–only one suitcase and footlocker. Two days were allowed for us to report to Miramar to wait for assignment. The four of us that owned the limo had managed to receive quite a large amount of automobile gas coupons, so we hoped our stay in San Diego would be a holiday for us. This was true and we took advantage of the time to acquaint ourselves with the beauty of the San Diego area especially the beach and party areas of La Jolla.

One memorable event happened during our stay at Miramar. From time to time at happy hour at the O-Club we would observe groups of pilots who had received orders to ship out. They would be in the process of having a final drink and saying good-bye to their wives, or girl friends. Eventually three or four of our group would migrate to another party bar in La Jolla, and we noticed a small group of the wives of the departed pilots appeared, available to join any male that would approach them. This 20 year old fighter pilot made up his mind that matrimony for him would be put off for quite a time after fighting in WWII had ceased! It was hard to believe.

Finally, after spinning our wheels for almost two weeks we were informed that in two days we were to report to building # 28 to load up on a truck and leave for North Island to board a carrier. 0630 was reporting time. We did not know which carrier, or where it would be bound.

The night before we had to board the truck and head for North Island we had dinner and a party to celebrate our last night in the USA. Suddenly we remembered we had to do something with our limo. On our way back to MCAS Miramar, we came upon a Marine sergeant "hitch hiking" a short distance from the gate. I was driving so I made a command decision! I said to the Sergeant

"Sarg, how much money do you have in your pocket?" Looking interested he answered, "about $50 dollars!" I then made my pitch. "Would you be interested in paying that and receiving three hundred gallons in gas chits?" Gas was rationed and each of us had been issued this in total amount of chits. He was hilarious in his answer in the affirmative! We then drove by the Officer of the Day's (OD) office, certified the title, and had him drive us to pick up our gear. I still wonder what happed to our limo? Had he held on to it a few years he would have been a well to do Sergeant.

The truck picked us up and drove us to the receiving gate to go aboard the US SAVO ISLAND CVE #78, a smaller "JEEP" carrier. As we boarded we notice they were preparing to load several Corsair fighter aircraft aboard the carrier deck. These would be ferried to our destination, wherever that might be. Our going aboard this carrier included the time honored procedure of saluting the "OD," asking permission to board and then following the sailor who directed us to our home for the next 28 days. I was designated the "Billeting Officer" for this group and as such I assigned each man to his room. A few of us had small cabins. I made certain I had that! Life aboard a carrier was indeed a wonderful experience. Clean sheets, clothing was laundered for you. Even your shoes were shined if you so desired.

Navy enlisted sailors, most from the Philippines, were friendly, courteous and most efficient. Dining was in the Officers Mess with tablecloths, napkins and seating designated by your serial number. 02809 seated to the right of 02810. Very prestigious and *NAVY PROTOCAL*!

The "gangplank" was pulled in, all kind of bells and whistles and verbal commands sounded and the carrier was moving. We knew not where we were headed, but were assured we would find out later on. It was a strange and new feeling, realizing we were on our way to the combat area. We slowly sailed out of the North Island area, saying goodbye to the Point Loma hills and the beautiful area of San Diego. The time was early afternoon and we had time to explore the carrier deck, the hanger deck with elevators, and all the interesting equipment necessary for operations. We were in a new world, amazed and curious. Most amazing was the pilot's ready room. Here we found an air-conditioned room with beautiful leather recliners and every thing to satisfy a pilot's needs. We would fantasize how busy it would be when the future might bring aerial combat to CVE #78 operations.

When we were two or three days out the sound system ordered our group to assemble in the ready room and the AIR BOSS briefed us on what we could expect for the next twenty five or twenty six days. CVE#78 was on a "shake down" trip to deliver the Corsair Fighters to Espiritu Santos in the New Hebrides Islands. This of course was news to us. Submarines on patrol in the area we happened to be sailing would escort us from time to time. The Hawaiian Islands were by passed. Our path would take us close to Tahiti, but we could only see it from a distance. Surprising to us was the fact that most of the time we were alone at sea. Hopefully, our path would be in the areas in which no Japanese ships, submarines or patrols were operating.

The fantail (back of the ship) was home for the big gun. From time to time we had life jacket drills and access areas we would go to for lifeboats. One day with no warning, the gun on the fantail was fired, shaking our billeting area wildly, and it scared the hell out of us. We were sure an attack from a Japanese submarine was under way!

During the 28 days we had a lot of time to look around and memorize the location of all of the ladders, the small walkways and the pathways we had to navigate. One thing was evident; we were all rookies to the rhythms of life on a carrier. This was a small deck carrier that did not have all of the luxurious living conditions available on today's nuclear carriers. However, the food was great and available to us 24 hours a day. Movies, all kinds of reading material, and card games were available in the Ready Room. Also exercising, basketball and weight lifting equipment could be found on the hanger deck.

I found that in the evening, forward to the bow of the ship, under the hanger deck, watching the flying fish was most enjoyable. It was cool, comfortable and the stargazing was unbelievable.

The number of shooting stars, the galaxies, and the Milky Way in all of its splendor. The Little Dipper, the Big Dipper, the entire sky in such splendor as you would never see in the USA. The South Pacific is a constantly changing fascinating mélange of strange phosphorescent lights, flying fish and all manner of exotic creatures. Only in the middle of the ocean, away from the lights of civilization could this be seen. I spent many an evening on the bow of the carrier mesmerized by the opportunity to enjoy this wonderful sight, brought to me by joining the Marine Corps.

Midway through our journey we were crossed the Equator. This event cued a huge celebration that involved most of the crew of CVE#78! This time honored party goes back to the very start of the U. S. Navy's traditions.

April 1944

The Shellback-Polywog Festival

I cannot say if *this* was rational, civil, acceptable, and honorable adult activity or not. It just happens because it always *has* in Naval history! I'm sure that every healthy, dedicated, ambitious future fighter pilot accepted the challenge because to turn it down just did not make sense! Your pride would not allow it! It out did any collegiate fraternity hazing!

It was a bright and sunny day, the water was calm, and the carrier was cruising at about 15 knots. The carrier deck was cleared and a large tank of water was being filled with all kinds of leftovers from the wardroom kitchen. A large chair covered with the trappings of royalty was placed at one end of the tank. At the other end they had made a platform with a droppable chair like apparatus. The horns sounded and King Neptune and Queen Nefertiti took their places along with their Royal Court of (royal bearers) Shellbacks. On one side of the tank a Chief Petty Officer was properly attired, but with his large belly exposed as if he was 8+ months pregnant. All of the Polywogs (the pilots who had never been inducted) were lined up, each waiting to approach the bench one at a time. First they had to approach the Royal Baby and kiss his stomach. One at a time a Polywog climbed upon the chair bench to be questioned by King Neptune. After they answered three questions, if answered correctly, they were hailed and accepted to the Royalty. If they did not answer correctly, which happened most of the time, a bell rang and they were dumped into the tank containing all the garbage! I was lucky. Why, I know not, but I was not dumped into the tank! Before nightfall you were recognized as a member of the Royal Court of Shellbacks! You were issued a nice card as evidence!

It took a day or two to recover from the crazy day when we became a SHELLBACK! Over one-half of our journey was completed by now. Every day was almost the same routine. The one thing that was apparent was that life aboard a carrier without any flying could become boring. However, we always enjoyed the food and the wonderful way it was served. We enjoyed clean sheets and a comfortable bed with no rain or storms to mar our passage. In our future we would live not like the Navy, but like Marines, lucky to have a pyramidal tent with a sharp coral floor and fighting typhoon winds with heavy rains that would stream down the pole of our tents! In the future we would think, "Oh to be aboard the SAVO ISLAND!" All of us were looking forward to arriving at a "south sea island" as all of the books and movies portrayed. We would have the experience ahead of us, but now each day was a day of wondering. Then suddenly one day, with the early morning sun beating down, far on the horizon...the New Hebrides Islands became visible – a small speck. After breakfast, a trip to the front of the carrier brought a more complete picture into view. We were safe and sound and about to make port! Excitement was consuming us, as our imaginary thoughts about South Sea Islands were about to come true. We were at Turtle Bay, Espiritu Santos, with a French Plantation, coconut trees, an Officers Club and a mess hall on the beautiful bay! It was all to be enjoyed, but only for a few months!

Chapter 9   Espiritu Santos, Turtle Bay, New Hebrides Islands

April 1944

Finally, it was time to leave the carrier. We saluted the officer of the day, asked permission to depart the ship, and looked for the truck to carry us to *Turtle Bay*, the landing strip on *Espiritu Santos*. A Captain Richards, who happened to be from Cody, Wyoming, met us. He was quite friendly to me and said that his younger brother was a Marine major, also flying a Corsair somewhere in the Pacific.

He informed us our next week would be in a program of "HOW TO SURVIVE IF LOST IN THE JUNGLE!" Training was located on an island, *Efate*, about 50 miles south of Turtle Bay. We would work with a native who was very talented with a big knife. It was similar to an American corn knife. We would learn how to open a coconut and live on its milk and meat; and we would scrounge in the jungle for snakes, berries, and other edible items!

As a result of the native's expertise with the knife suddenly pilots came up with the idea to use our bayonet for our knife to open coconuts. It was, as bayonets go, much reduced in size and much sharper than normal. These "pilot bayonets" were to be used while flying when, unexpectedly, boat packs in the parachute cushions inflated due to excess G-pressures created by violent combat moves. The inflated boat packs would cause the control stick to be moved forward and result in excessive control problems. Not a good thing to happen in the middle of combat. The knives, fastened to our leg, enabled pilots to resolve this problem.

Bill Paine, Tuffy Thomas, Bob Roy, and I were practicing opening coconuts with the sharply pointed bayonets. Bill, (a graduate of the renowned Slippery Rock University) made a jab at the coconut and missed it. He immediately looked at the palm of his other hand to see the sharp point of the bayonet had stabbed clear through his palm to emerge on the other side. It didn't take long to get him to the field hospital. He had a tough time living down this surgical move!

Time in the jungle was good for our confidence. Navy had an R&R area located quite a distance from our tents. They served cold beer from 1600 to 1800 hours. This made drinking a beer a fast "drink down" performance. In order to accomplish a trip to this area, we had to find a driver and a vehicle to transport six of us to the beer shack! The first day back from the jungle, we were thirsty. Mission accomplished in locating a driver, but it was a tough ride as roads in Efate were not good. By the time to return to base arrived, we had consumed a full load of beer, and the sun was about to disappear! We arrived to our tent area and dispersed to tents. En route one of pilots, in the darkness, encountered a bomb crater full of water from a recent rain. We were able to pull him out and help him to a shower!

When it was finally time to return to Turtle Bay we were all ready, as we had not flown a plane for some time. Check in was completed and we found that our quarters consisted of Dallas Huts. These were very comfortable, manufactured type construction, with each housing two pilots. Our showers were outdoors, but not bad. We had arrived in what was to be our *South Sea Island Paradise*! It was on a former French coconut plantation with a beautiful lagoon complete with a small rectangular pier. The Officer's Club was open from 1130 to 1300 hours for lunch and 1600 to 2000 hours for supper and recreation. This metal type facility had a panoramic view of the beautiful lagoon.

On the backside of Turtle Bay there was a 2500 ft. mountain with tall trees and jungle. The runway was built from Coral Rock, was comparably short but very safe for takeoff out towards the bay. Corsairs were suitable, but required one's complete concentration on both landing and takeoff procedures!

Espiritu Santos was the rest and reorganization area for all operations in the *Solomon Islands* starting with the invasion of *Guadalcanal*. It had been improved upon and was now a very comfortable area, with roads to all areas of the island. The French still operated a restaurant that was within driving distance from our area. Fine steaks and good wine were readily available. Bottled wine was served from used coca cola bottles and at times would bring on "uncomfortable" dysentery trips the next day!

Larger planes operated on the other side of the island with two long runways (Bomber I and Bomber II) capable of handling any of the larger bombers. The US Navy's Carrier Aviation Service Unit had runway operations at a separate field. I will tell of my work there as a Test Pilot later. Checked in, good quarters, good food, large supply of good beer, we were set to go.

Replacement Squadron #41 was the operational unit assigned to our group for flight operations while we waited to be assigned into a combat squadron. Combat squadron operations would form here. The Marine Corps plan was that pilots, after squadron organization and training would go "up the slot" into combat for six weeks, go to Australia or New Zealand on R&R (Rest & Recuperation), return to fill any vacancies and repeat this same cycle for two additional six week combat tours and then, hopefully, return stateside. First lieutenants would be promoted to captain and their service would move on. This was the Corps' plan; this was what was *supposed to happen*! Unfortunately, as the progress of the war revealed, my squadron, VMF-114, was in for a different destiny! More on that as we progress.

April 27th 1944

I was finally ready to climb back into a Corsair. #56026 was assigned to me for my first flight in a long time. Back in the saddle again! Four of us pilots logged one and one/half hours in division tactics and familiarization that day and it was good to be back in the air. All too soon it was time to land.

The first time we turned into the final approach to Turtle Bay's runway proved interesting! We approached a beautiful runway that had been built straight out onto the bay. The coral strip ran down from a sloping mountain covered with tall pine trees. As we turned into our final approach air speed was a few knots above stalling speed. We passed over a drainage culvert cut out of a coral roadway. As we passed over the culvert we were almost done flying, and started to drop onto the runway at close to 80 knots, stall speed. If our speed was excessive, we faced a difficult choice! Either make a hard turn and then brace for the resulting crash or ride the bird into the bay! What a great arrival to Turtle Bay! Our Naval Aviation Flight Program had prepared us well!

May Day arrived and on the 3rd and 4th I flew three flights in the 41st Squadron. I could see that it could possibly turn into the same old routine type of job. I had the opportunity to see if I could obtain a test pilot job with a *Navy Carrier Aircraft Service Unit*. This I did with a lot of enthusiasm. I was thus able to fill the void of waiting for a combat squadron spot.

From the 6th thru the 24th of May I was involved in testing an addition to the Corsair's water injection equipment, an addition newly added to the engines of all of the new planes brought into the Solomon Islands Theater of Operations. The new equipment added a 14 gallon $H2O$ tank, which, in an emergency situation, pilot could receive an instant burst of power and add 15 knots of speed to the Corsair by adding water to the fuel. This would give our pilots another advantage over Japanese fighter aircraft. We checked this move at sea level and at altitudes of 16,000 and 22,000 feet. Two to three flights a day were scheduled for the 16 new Corsairs that were being tested during this timeframe.

Two interesting events occurred doing this period. The Navy gave the New Zealand Air Force six new Corsairs. The New Zealand Squadron Commander arrived flying a vintage P-40 fighter, his personal plane. It was his pride and joy, and held together with bailing wire! Five of his pilots had joined him and I was assigned to give these six men their cockpit check-out on the "do's and don'ts" from both the manual and from my experience flying the "Bent-Wing Bird!" We met at the flight line where six brand new beautiful Corsairs were parked, ready to soar into the sky. I proceeded with the hour-long presentation. I answered all of their many questions. My main concern was to impress on them the necessity to log eight or ten hours in the big fighter before inverting in flight while trying their aerobatic maneuvers. Corsairs at this time were noted for going into an *inverted spin* very suddenly and with little warning! Most of the time this mistake proved fatal. We all shook hands, thanked each other, and bid adieu!

Perhaps forty or so minutes later, I was busily engaged at 16,000 feet having finished my check operation. I glanced in the mirror and noticed six Corsairs flying in trail and racing through the sky in obvious hilarity! They finally approached me at my altitude, still flying in trail, and then preceded to do slow rolls around me! Needless to say, I was stunned. The sixth finished a perfect roll; they all then wagged their wings in salute and dived away, continuing their wild ride! I realized that the "Kiwis" were indeed a wild and reckless, but talented group of excellent pilots!

Years later while my wife, Connie and I were visiting Christchurch, New Zealand, we visited a veterans club and noticed a large picture of a beautiful Corsair on the bar room wall. The bar tender told us that we had just missed a group of retired New Zealand pilots who get together every evening or so for a pint, reliving old, but bigger, stories of their flying days. I've often wondered if we had just missed the group that I briefed that wild day.

It was a normal day of water injection testing and I had just landed and was exiting my Corsair. As I glanced over the tail of the aircraft, a Jeep was approaching. I noticed a full colonel was driving, and he and a tall thin fellow were approaching me. I remember thinking, "WOW, the guy with the colonel must be important because Marine colonels never drive their own Jeeps!" The passenger was dressed in regular khakis and had U. S. insignias pinned on his collar points. He was quite friendly and asked me several questions regarding the performance of the Corsair. I was at ease and answered his questions as best I could. After about thirty minutes he thanked me, shook hands, and he and the colonel departed. On our way back to our quarters Bernie Bernhardt said to me, "Colonel Lindbergh sure seemed like a friendly gentleman!"

"COLONEL LINDBERGH, WHERE DID YOU SEE HIM?"
"YOU DUMMY, YOU HAVE BEEN TALKING TO HIM FOR
THIRTY MINUTES!!" I honestly never expected to see the famous
pilot. He stayed with us in the area for almost six days, working
with our mechanics and giving informational advice to all the
Corsair pilots on operating the *BIG BIRD*! Having him around for
that period of time was a fantastic experience. He even signed my
"short snorter dollar bill!" The last days in May were occupied
with completing my stint with the *CASU (carrier aircraft service
unit)* and some refresher instrument flying. A couple of division
tactic flights and then one terrible event!

30th May 1944

That afternoon the pilot pool headquarters assigned Lt. Olmstead
and me to pick up two Corsairs on the following morning and to
ferry them to Henderson Field, Guadalcanal. We were quite
excited, as this was a five and one-half hour, overwater, and 580
mile flight! We would be escorting a big Curtis Commando
transport. Olmstead had a supply of scotch, so we opened a bottle
and discussed the next morning's flight. He asks me "Danny, what
would you do in the event of an engine failure, say 100 miles or so
into our flight? My answer "I would jump because we had
emergency equipment, and the fact that Air Sea Rescue, with help
from the Commando escort, would find me!" His answer to his
own question was "I would try a water landing due to being scared
to death to bail-out over water!" I admit that I was startled with his
decision.

31st May 1944

Early in the morning we went to the flight line and picked up the
two assigned Corsairs. #49904 was the serial number of my plane.
Olmstead's number I did not know! Each plane had a big 265
gallon belly tank attached to the under side of the plane. We did
not address that on our previous night's discussion. We joined the
crew of the Curtis Commando, completed our pre-flight checks,
took off and circled to join up with the escort plane.

Sunny skies, perfect weather report all the way to destination Guadalcanal. We had checked all conversation with our accompanying transport and were cruising comfortably just less than an hour from take off. I had just checked all of my instrument readings, glancing at Olmstead, when suddenly a puff of smoke came out of the cowling of his plane and his propeller froze in position! My body stiffened as I realized we had an emergency situation. Our conversation of the night before suddenly became a reality. With the big belly tank in the centerline of his fuselage, it had to *be dropped immediately*. I felt he would not attempt a water landing, but I told him we had to drop that tank! He said he was trying, but it would not release!

We dove and pulled G's, but to no avail. We were now gradually losing altitude. He appeared to be frozen! I called for him to jettison his cockpit hood, put down his flaps, and concentrate on finding a smooth wave to hit. I called him to prepare to water land, as I would call out his air speed, gradually slowing for the final wave. I accompanied him down as close to the water as I dared. The God awful time now arrived, he hit the water and his plane dove vertically into the sea! Assured that he could not survive, I frantically called the Commando, and searched the water for oil slicks, or some wreckage. I could find nothing but the circle where he hit. After circling some twenty minutes, the Commando command pilot radio pilot radioed for me to return to Santos! With a heavy heart and still in dismay and shock I confirmed departure, and returned.

I safely landed at Turtle Bay and sought the proper command to confirm and make the accident report. I had not prepared myself for what had to now be done! Making the report and surveying his clothing and all of his belongings was a traumatic assignment. I had difficulty in putting this tragedy out of my mind. First, I wrote my condolences to his parents in Seattle, figured out a decent check for the scotch that remained, sealed and sent the letter and decided that the sun would come up in the east in the morning. I sincerely felt that Olmstead would have agreed with my scotch decision. Life goes on!

I checked my logbook and realized that it was on the 31st day of the month at El Toro when we lost Eric Jont to his terrible accident. I decided that was a bad day to be flying! Coincidence?

June 1944

On the 2nd of June I was assigned to fly Corsair #49004 unaccompanied from Santos to Guadalcanal. This was the same plane I had flown on the 31st when we lost Olmstead! Sometimes cowboys who are thrown off a bucking horse and land badly are forced by their friends to get back on a horse as soon as possible. This is to ensure they won't shy away from ever riding again. Sometimes in life you have to get back on the horse. Guess what? I would be tested! I think it was just a happening, or was it? The flight to Guadalcanal was 4.5 hours over water. It was a tiring flight, with me fighting the thoughts of what had happened. Thankfully, I landed safe and sound.

6 June 1944

At 7:30 AM I woke up, bright eyed and bushy tailed. I went to breakfast; not knowing this day would be the biggest and most memorable day in my career.

Our Adjutant Officer found me and told me I was to report to Major Stout, Commander of VMF- 114. I thanked him and proceeded to the major's tent. I saluted; he invited me to sit down. He then proceeded to tell me he was going to choose a wingman (the position to fly on his wing on combat flights). My reaction was to almost fall out of my chair. I realized this was the man I had met at the Homecoming football game in Laramie in 1941! He informed me he thought I was from Wyoming and he was prejudiced for UW students. I reminded him that I had worked with his brother Jack at the Student Union. He then informed me that we were going to fly some gunnery runs today and that if I could fly and shoot worth a damn, I would be his wingman! He added that we would bet a beer a hole on the tow sleeve and that the beer could only be consumed upon arrival back in Laramie's Plaza Bar!

Holy Cow! Here was one of the USMC's famous *ACES*, having received the highest US Navy's combat medal, the Navy Cross while flying in Guadalcanal's Cactus Air Force! He had shot down six Japanese Zeros. This lieutenant would probably owe him a truckload of beer by day's end! Luckily, I must have won the bet. Before we parted that day, I was no longer a replacement pilot but a member of VMF-114 and Cowboy's wingman until he was shot down at Koror.

As I look back, the history of VMF-114 is a very powerful story of the hurried Corsair training. Marine Corps Air Station El Toro became a vital component of Marine Aviation in early 1943. Located south of Santa Ana, California, it grew rapidly and soon became a vital USMC operational base. The war in the Pacific was forcing the rapid organization of new squadrons and the rapid production of fighter airplanes. The fighter that was soon to become the premier fighter airplane in the Marine inventory was the beautiful and powerful gull winged F4U, known as the Corsair, and lovingly called Bent Wing Bird, Hose Nose, along with many other nicknames. It was a powerful plane with a R-2800 Pratt & Whitney engine that produced 2500 HP of takeoff thrust, a 3000 foot a minute climb rate and a speed of 426 MPH at 30,000 feet. In flight the fifteen-foot propeller, located several feet in front of the cockpit, along with the gull wings that pulled beautiful streamers off the wing tips produced a magnificent picture in flight.

Chance-Vaught Aviation in Connecticut introduced the first Corsair model to the USMC inventory in early 1943. This resulted in the formation of several new squadrons, such as VMF-114 (V-heavier than air), (M-Marine), (F- Fighter). VMF-114 was formed on 16 July 1943 at MCAS El Toro. Stout was named the commanding officer and was the only captain in Marine Corps history to command a squadron. The squadron departed early to *Ewa, Hawaii* for further training. Several accidents and three pilot fatalities ensued during the training. Tad Gage was killed while attempting an emergency landing, Robert "Rags" Smith crashed on a gunnery run and Bob Meyes died in a mid-air collision.

On 18 December 1943 the squadron deployed to *Midway Island* and conducted further Corsair training. Pilots enjoyed training in "Gooney Bird" flights and tumbles! This was the primary athletic and spare time activity on the tiny island. In February '44 the squadron was ordered to return to Hawaii for a short month of training before loading a transport ship for the long trip to Espiritu Santos, the rear area where Marine Aviation squadrons prepared for combat. VMF-114 pilots were minimally prepared for combat hours in the Corsair, even with the additional training that was conducted at Turtle Bay.

The squadron soon departed for *Green Island*, a Marine Air strip in the northern Solomon Islands, north of the Japanese stronghold of *Rabaul*. This was their introduction to combat and it would prove costly. Combat missions were flown in the vicinity of Rabaul. This area was the "hot bed" of Japanese aviation. The untested squadron would lose nine pilots during the initial combat tour of VMF-114. Bill Hobbs and James Parmalee disappeared on a pre-dawn CAP (combat air patrol) from Green Island in bad weather. Walter Telep crashed during dive-bombing practice when he suffered target fixation, and Giles Smith was shot down on strafing runs at Rabaul. Finally, Robert Brown died when crash-landing at Green Island. Additionally, four pilots, whose names are unknown to me, took off one morning and were apparently lost during bad weather and were never recovered.

The pilots of VMF-114 paid a big price in combat prior to their R&R in Sidney, Australia. While in Sydney, the pilots decided to design a squadron logo to recreate the hand that Wild Bill Hickok held in a poker game the night he was shot in the back in a saloon in Lead, South Dakota. A bloody hand, Aces and Eights separated by a Four, indicating VMF-114, now known as the *"Death Dealers!"*

I joined the squadron about the time 114 returned from Sydney. Jack Conger, Wally Weber and Bob Peebles, a trio of pilots welcomed me and it did not take long for us to become life long friends! Conger was our operational officer, a veteran of the

Cactus Air Force, and the first American pilot to shoot down ten *Japanese Zeros* at Guadalcanal.

6 June 1944

During my first flight as Cowboy's wingman I was, I must admit, a little bit nervous! Our mission briefing was quick. We were to be a division of four planes, Stout in the lead, Daniel in the wing position, Pete Hansen, #3 section leader, and Don Francke #4 (tail end Charlie). Cowboy was a great leader, demanding, forceful, and understanding. He was a magician in the air, a master of tactics. It was indeed a privilege and honor to fly with him. He briefed after every flight and if you had screwed up, you bore the brunt of his corrections. Each flight, as we returned to base, we joined up in close formation, and as we came to turn on our final, we broke to the left abruptly pulling beautiful "streamers" of mist! Anyone looking up in the air knew VMF-114 was arriving!

From the 6th of June to the 10th we flew radar calibration, and strafing using mid-board guns. We practiced scramble alerts with radar intercepts, division tactics (Thatch Weaves) and after six days and eight flights, finally a couple of days off. We had a skeet range to practice shooting shotguns and understanding 20 mills lead. 20 mills (mills are the angles of lead to a target) was the size of the circle etched on our windscreen; this circle was used to determine the amount of lead to use when engaging the tow target or…a Japanese Zero! Unfortunately we never saw any Zeros, damn it.

All had gone very well until one morning we conducted engine check flights. As I was on the down wind leg of the approach to my landing we experienced another tragedy. A fellow pilot, Stu Wessman, had just become airborne when his port (left) wing suddenly folded and he crashed into the water not too far from the end of the runway. He was killed instantly. The accident investigation determined the wing-fold was the result of hydraulic failure that caused a large bolt to fail and this failure caused the wing to fold upon takeoff. A pre-flight procedure was instituted that prevented any future accidents.

Our days were busy when flying; the flights were intense for a couple of hours. But we still had plenty of time to relax and tend to our household duties, daily physical exercises and time to read, write letters etc. It was not the most fancy South Sea Island paradise, but it was close.

We spent our off hours swimming. There was as a boardwalk that went down to a small pier that was close to our area. Pete Hansen had smuggled a Great Dane puppy on his flight back from Australia. We enjoyed watching this huge pup, all legs, trying to learn to swim. Torpedo Squadron 8 had a pet pig that could beat swimmers in the group back to the beach after they threw it off the pier! One of the guys had the cutest little Scotch terrier. Each day at eleven o'clock the mess hall opened for lunch hour and this little dog beat every one to the door. He was anxious for his daily issue of beer that was waiting for him at the door. He would drain that issue of beer and waddle back to his home to doze and await the four o'clock opening of the mess hall in the afternoon.

Time to break into our boat project! Two bright Westerners, Daniel from Wyoming and John Bernhart from Utah decided to build an outrigger boat. We scrounged up a used 260-gallon belly tank, had a two-man cockpit cut out of it, and started. We somehow obtained the following items: a used parachute for use as a sail, some pipe and cord, two hollowed out 100-pound bombs, some length of steel pipe, blue paint and a sprayer. Most of the pilots were very interested in the project. With the help of our maintenance men we finished the project and alerted everyone to the launching of the project. We christened the outrigger boat, but sans name, with a bottle of beer! A reasonable crowd assembled for the big event. We shoved off successfully into the lagoon and floated blissfully away, but found we could not turn the boat to the right or left. We had a full windblown sail, but what was the problem? I pushed one of the outrigger bombs into the water, only to damn near overturn the boat. We were on the verge of sinking it. Someone in the crowd shouted, *"You don't have a centerboard, dummies!"* How did we not know that our problem, the missing piece of board, was a necessary component to turning the boat? After correcting that flaw we sailed merrily all over the lagoon, until some dummy sank it while both of us were on a flight! End of the Westerners sailing mission!

The clouds of combat were constantly over us, and it was only a matter of time. Who knew how soon? From 13 June to the 20th we were flying more division tactics (ranging from dog fighting to bomber escort, (Thatch Weaves), radar interception and calibration, two hour plus attack problems, gunnery on tow sleeves, high altitude oxygen and conducting test flights after maintenance work was accomplished on any planes.

On the 20th I was finally assigned to fly as the pilot pulling the tow sleeve for other pilots to fire live ammunition at the sleeve! What a menacing machine the Corsair was at it fired real ammunition, while you hoped to heaven the pilots did not make a mistake and misjudge their 20 mills lead. It was exciting!

I also had time for a fun flight in the SNJ-4 with Lt. Blain in the rear cockpit. I hoped I did not make him sick while I showed him slow rolls, loops, a slow roll at the top of a loop, and a little inverted flight. He was a happy lieutenant when we finished.

The month of June flew by as flying aerial gunnery completed the last week; it was my turn to shoot! I had eight gunnery flights out over the water from 22 to 29 June 1944. It was a total of eleven hours spent firing on the tow sleeve. This involved overhead runs flying high above the tow target, then turning over on your back to dive down while keeping the target in your sights, finally firing your guns and looking for your tracers hitting the sleeve! The noses of the tracer rounds were painted unique colors for each plane–and this established an accounting of each pilot's accuracy. Diving like this on the target sleeves actually created heavy G's that produced terrific pressures on your body. If, while diving the plane, you developed what looked like a dark window shade gradually coming down over your vision, you were pulling too many G's and were about to blackout. It was necessary to immediately pull out of your dive or risk going unconscious! Your plane had developed great speed during these dives to engage the target sleeves and this speed enabled the plane to then climb at over 3000 ft. per minute back to your original altitude. This procedure was vital to learning how to stay alive in aerial combat! Your firing circle sight in mills is also used when varying the angle of attack in your dive. You could not practice a straight in approach towards the target, as the tracers would hit the pilot's plane towing the target. It was normal for the tow pilot to be very apprehensive!

Target gunnery flights were generally no more than two hours in duration as they were tough on the pilots and used a lot of ammunition. For some reason, I cannot remember that we were ever briefed as to the number of target hits each pilot received. I know that if we had missed entirely we would have been told!

July 1944

We had heavy rains at times at Turtle Bay. This negated some of our flying schedule. No flights appear in my log until the 7th of July. SNJ #09862 was used that day as one of our mechanics wanted a flight. Hatcher and I enjoyed two hours of fun, aerobatics and sight seeing. He did not complain after we landed! Evidently the word spread as to the availability of joy rides in the SNJ as on the 9th, Sergeant Carlson requested a ride in SNJ #09862. For almost two hours we repeated the aerial fun and as with Hatcher, he survived the aerobatics!

On the 8th I was introduced to the famous Navy carrier fighter plane, the HELLCAT (F6F-3). The Hellcat was a thrill as the flight characteristics of this plane were similar to the Corsairs in certain ways. Once again I had to learn electrical, hydraulic, fuel and oil, air cooler system and memorize emergency systems, prop and mixture control, gear handle (or wheels up and down controls), aileron, rudder trim tabs and all of the dials on the front of the instrument panel. All these things I had memorized before flying the Corsair.

The Hellcat had the same power plant, similar speed, and much more stable flight reactions. It was much easier to fly but not quite as spectacular as the Corsair. I would log several hours in the plane during my military career.

For the first time on the 10th of July, I experienced flying the Corsair *under the hood*! This means after take off and gaining altitude I fastened a canvas hood so that I simulated complete instrument flying. I relied on "the dials and my radio!" Fortunately I had a chase plane flying on my wing for safety. *This was really a new experience for me!*

On the 12th and the 15th our Corsairs were introduced to practice Glide Bombing, targeting for hits with 500 and 1000-pound bombs. On the 17th we performed Intercept Problems against the F6F Hellcat. This was realistic training. We did not fly again, probably due to weather, until the 28th when I finished up the month with five test hops checking the mechanical results of our technical teams. My logbook now showed a total of 560 hours in the air.

August 1944

Oh happy day! On the 1st of August we took delivery of several brand new FG-2 CORSAIRS! These were F4U's manufactured by Grumman Aviation. # 14016 was assigned to Lt. Daniel, *Cowboy Stout's wingman.* This made several of the original lieutenants in VMF-114 a little jealous. They did not manifest this openly, but the feeling was there, under the surface. For two days it was mine to test hop and work out any deficiencies it might have. I noticed a thing or two that needed to be fixed, but I flew two hours on August 1st making #016 mine! Flying the Skipper's wing has its perks! On the 2nd I had a gunnery flight in the new FG (*Corsair made by Goodyear and Grumman).* That night we had our first flight under a million stars! Wow, in the islands was that different! A little spooky at first, but spectacular!

Another gunnery run on the 3rd, before climbing back in #016, for another two test hops' making certain all was well! It was again my turn to tow gunnery run before getting my #016 for another test on the 5th. Skip Bombing was scheduled for the 8th and 9th. To Skip

Bomb the pilot approaches the target low on the water, keeping the target in the gun sight until just before he drops his bomb, hoping it would skip into the middle of a ship and explode! We actually had the opportunity to do this on an actual strike in combat with myself leading and putting a bomb about 200 feet in the air over the middle of the ship! Stout followed my lead as did Hansen, both making the same mistake! Our hero, Don Franke, placed his bomb in the middle of the ship. Hence his name Don, the skip bomb ACE! We never had this opportunity again.

We were now feeling that departure from Santos was not too far off. The following few days were filled with division tactics, squadron tactics, and escort tactics (Thatch Weaving above bombers). These last seven flights insured that Corsair #016 was officially Lt. Daniel's plane to fly the wingman slot on Major Cowboy Stout!

On the 28th of August we practiced fighter tactics and on the 31st flew formation flights to Efate and back.

September 1944

On the 1st of September a squadron flight from Turtle Bay to Ambryn and return. The 4th of September was our final Squadron Tactics flight as on that same day we received our departure order! We were all very excited and anxious to go! Early the 6th we were briefed that 24 VMF-114 Corsairs would depart for Henderson Field Guadalcanal. This meant that ten of our pilots would not leave with the first group. We now spent our final day at Turtle Bay checking flight gear, packing our foot lockers, and going over our final departure to Guadalcanal and the unknown, but combat was definitely in our near future. I am thrilled that #016 will fly wing on Cowboy en route and in combat!

VMF 114   INSIGNIA

"THE DEATH DEALERS"

Origin and Significance

After the rejection of many designs, the personnel of VMF 114 voted unanimously for an idea conceived by Lt. J. K. Wallace and Lt. J. L. Parmelee. It was designed and executed by Lt. Parmelee. It seemed to fit everyone's frame of mind and express the squadron's intent both well and aptly. The insignia was the famous "Death Hand" that Wild Bill Hickok held when he was killed at Deadwood, South Dakota. The notorious aces and eights were arranged so that the cards ran Ace, Ace, Four, Eight, and Eight. Thus the first three cards also represent the squadron numeral, 114.

The idea, of course, was death to the enemy so it had to be our game, dealer's choice and the sky's the limit. That is the story behind our lurid insignia — one of the most colorful in the Corps and the origin of the squadron name "The Death Dealers."

Chapter 10   Flight to Peleliu

6 September 1944

We received a flight briefing at 0600 hours and departed to the flight line carrying what little we were able to strap down behind our seats in the cockpit. My plane captain put my parachute into the seat. After completing the ground pre-flight inspection of #016, I climbed into the cockpit. Becknell and Goodie, my plane captains, whom I trusted entirely, assured me they have completed their checks. They will be with me before and after every flight I will take in #016. *From now until we return to the states my life while flying depends on their efficiency!*

I do my on-board pre-flight procedure, checking every system, six degree rudder settings, aileron, elevator, fuel settings, radio check, oxygen system, all instruments on the front panel, seat position and go through GUMP (gas, under carriage, mixture, power). Then I received a thumbs up from Goodie, fire the cartridge starter, and my 2500 horsepower Pratt & Whitney engine roars! I now watch for Cowboy to start his take off movement to the area where we check the magnetos (electrical system which maintains spark to fire the cylinders to function). The tower clears us for take off and one by one we roar down the runway developing the power for a three thousand feet per minute climb rate and lift off.

Cowboy starts a slow turn to the right that allows me to snuggle up close to his wing and wait for Hansen and Franke to join up. Now, we take a 302-degree magnetic heading on our gyrocompass to start the 548 nautical mile journey to Henderson Field. It is a beautiful clear sky with no signs of any weather. Our final destination however remains unknown to us. It was a 1040 hours time of departure.

24 Corsairs were escorted by five RC-5s from VMR-952. Six Corsairs flew on each Commando, three on each side of the big transport. Five extra pilots and eight men (NCOs and enlisted) were passengers on the RC-5s. That order was followed to *Emirau.*

Flying on the left of the first RC-5, Major Stout, Lt. Daniel, and Lt. Neiswanger. Flying on the right were Lieutenants Mosca, Zabel, and Sullivan.

I had been to Guadalcanal on a couple of previous occasions but most of our 24 pilots had not. Our destination was on the lower right of and within a few miles of the three other islands within the island group. It was known from the previous battle to be a very uncomfortable place. Large rains at times made it almost uninhabitable. As a result of almost constant rainy weather it was necessary to put steel planking, known as Marsden Matting, on the runway and taxiways. If you slid or wandered off the matting you sunk into knee-deep mud. Quite often the roughness of the matting planks would lead to tire blowouts, which could be very dangerous on your roll out. Mosquitoes and tropical fevers also plagued the island. We were happy to RON (remain overnight) there for only one night. Our flight time had been 3.8 hours, which was a moderate time in the air. Twenty-four of us checked into the BOQ's (bachelor officers quarters) for the night. Cold beer and modest food was readily available.

The best laid plans…a storms delayed our departure. Reveille was bright and early the morning of the 8th. We learned that a storm front lay between us and our next stop, *Bougainville*. However, our weather office predicted it would not be a problem. Boy did they ever SNAFU on that prediction! Our takeoff time was delayed but not cancelled. After waiting a couple of hours, off we went into the wild blue! 80 miles out we suddenly ran into a serious tropical storm that reached down almost to the water and rose to sixty or more miles high! Evidently Cowboy and our "hell for leather' fearless operation officer Jack Conger, having battled storms earlier in the Cactus Air Force at Guadalcanal, decided we could make our way through the front. We were flying to Bougainville with a group of four big twin engine Curtis Commandos (R4D) from Marine Transport Squadron VMR-952. Cowboy's group of six Corsairs quickly joined up with one of the beasts with three planes on each side, flying very close to each other, together we all entered into the storm. Cowboy had the lead with Daniel on his wing and Franke was third on the port wing of the first R4D.

76

Weber was on the starboard wing with Hansen on his wing and Zabel followed third.

I remember Cowboy, as we entered radioing, **"SUCK 'EM UP BOYS, CUDDLE UP CLOSE! WE ARE IN FOR A WILD RIDE!"** At first it was not too bad. But as we penetrated the front the turbulence increased markedly. We had a full combat load; the airspeed at which Corsairs stalled out was **88** knots. The R4D's were warned they had to maintain at least 100 knots climb rate to prevent this from happening. It was raining horizontally so hard you could hardly see past the windscreen or the side windows of the cockpit. Most pilot's respect and fear vertigo in weather. Your senses become disoriented! I was flying as close as possible to Stout's plane! My altimeter never registered much over 200 feet above the water. Off and on we would get a glimpse of clear vision for seconds. I dare not panic or waiver from what I was doing. I must have had a death grip on my elevator stick as the next morning I could hardly open and close my hand.

On we went for over an hour in this storm and suddenly broke into the *eye of the storm*. It was just like I had been told. It was clear blue sky as high as you could see with beautiful sunshine and clear blue water below. Now it was possible for us to circle and refresh our nerves. As we regrouped we heard Zip Zabel screaming into his mike, "I've lost you, lost you, I'm still on the dials!" Cowboy radioed "Danny, if he doesn't brake into the open soon we are going to have to go back in and get him"! Who me? Colonel Lindbergh? Not I! **It was only a thought**. Just as Cowboy finished, Zip broke into the eye and was screaming, I see you, I see you! I took a deep breath of thanks!

Soon we realized that we had to go back into the storm! We had been successful to date, WHY NOT! Leave us go! Another forty-five or so minutes we battled on and finally broke out of the storm and in the far distance could see Bougainville. Needless to say, our supply of ice-cold beer was guzzled with delight that night as we thanked our lucky stars. Cowboy and Conger were right! 24 happy VMF-114 pilots were safe and sound.

The Japanese were still active in the close areas of Bougainville. It was necessary for us not to wander happy and stray too far from our perimeter. Again we were in tents and the rain was pelting the top and sides of the canvas. We could hear the big guns roaring and the bursts of their ammunition. We were finally on the edge of the conflict.

Information that we had been waiting for was given to us that we would fly on in the morning to the island of *Emirau*, which was another three hour flight. This was the place where we would await our final orders into combat. This was the staging area for the Marine Corsairs that had been doing such a great job of shooting down the Japanese fighters from the islands of *New Britain*, *Kavieng*, and the stronghold of Rabaul. The famous Marine Ace, Joe Foss and his squadron, were operating from the runways of Emirau. Our VMF-114 pilots enjoyed meeting the famous pilot. He was a partner of Cowboy, Conger and Bastian in all the action of the Cactus Air Force at Guadalcanal. Graciously, he offered his refrigerator to Cowboy's division to cool our beer supply. Foss's pilots adored him. In the O-Club, if he crossed his legs, they did as well. If a cigar was in his mouth, they had one as well!

We did not fly too much during our short stay at Emirau, logging only one-hour of flight time for engine tests.

After a morning rain, "Gabby" Gesner, our head mechanic, was taking me to the flight line in a jeep. After turning sharply on a sharp corner I was ejected from the seat and found myself sliding under the front wheels of a large 2½ ton truck. I suffered coral cuts and it tore the cover handle of my .45 caliber pistol to bits. Later as I related the incident to Cowboy he told me to pop him in the nose. I wanted to but refused. Years later x-rays indicated I had suffered a fractured spine.

With the arrival of the Corsair into the war, Marine Air had slowly eliminated Japanese air power in the Solomon Islands. This chain was comprised of the *Russell Islands, Torokina, Munda, Vella Lavella*, Bougainville and finally, Rabaul. This made it unlikely we were going to see any Japanese planes at Emirau. The efficiency of the Corsair and ability of the pilots had eliminated Japanese air power in the area.

By the summer of 1944, advances against the Japanese in the Pacific were happening as planned. MacArthur was thinking and planning about his return to the Philippines. There was a fight between Nimitz and MacArthur as Admiral Nimitz recommended against MacArthur's plan. President Roosevelt flew to Hawaii to settle the argument. Nimitz felt that *Peleliu* should be canceled but MacArthur got his way. The *Battle of Peleliu*, deemed to be important by MacArthur to protect his flank eroded into a terrible mistake, costing almost 11,000 casualties on both sides. Initially, Major General Rupertus told the invasion Marines of the 1st Division, "This will be a cake walk ending in three to four days!" It turned out to be a 70 day disaster! Old men make decisions that young men pay the price for! No one in the Marine Corps realized this was going to be the price until it was too late. Had Admiral Nimitz taken Admiral Halsey's advice to cancel Peleliu and *Yap*, VMF-114 would have gone to the *Philippines* and our world would have been much different.

On September 15th 1944, word was received that the invasion of Peleliu had begun. Alas, it was evident we were going to participate in this battle! *Palau* was a group of about 200 small islands stretching north/north east for some 200 miles. Peleliu was the largest of two sister islands. The island of *Angaur* was the other. The beaches on the southwest side of Peleliu were deceitfully dangerous for tract landing vehicles. 2 by 3 miles in size, the island had ridges and cavernous deep ditches of coral rock. These ridges hid some 300 caves that were interconnected by passageways excavated out of the coral rock. There were living areas and combat positions with large guns protected by steel doors. When the doors were opened the Japanese guns were pointed directly at the invasion beaches. Navy battleships fired hundreds of shells on these positions, but failed to eliminate most of these positions! After three days of shelling the Navy left for the Philippines, telling the Marines that they had neutralized the targets! This mistaken conclusion resulted in unbearable causalities, deaths, and misery for the Marine Infantry! Finally, we were going to support our Marines in CODE NAME STALEMATE!

VMF-114 waited until the runways were secured and in condition for aerial operations, then received orders to complete their exodus and move to battle. At 0800 hours on the 24th of September 1944 we saddled up 24 Corsairs and departed Emirau for stop number one, a less than 2 hour flight to the tiny island of *Pityiliu* in the *Admiralty Islands* group. VMF-114 arrived there to refuel and to RON. The fuel I received here created some problems for me later on. All of the flight hours inserted in my flight log from now on would be made in red ink to indicate flight hours in the combat arena!

The morning of 25 September 1944 wound up to be our longest time in the air, almost four hours, in route to *Owi Island* on the east coast of *New Guinea*, in the *Schouten Group of Islands*. The US Army Air Corps was based here and supporting a large military hospital treating casualties from the action in the Philippines. The stay in Owi enabled me to meet a Greek Air Force pilot who later helped VMF-114 make beer run flights to *Hollandia*, New Guinea.

Right after we took off and headed for the island of Owi, oil suddenly started creeping over my windscreen. It was getting heavier rapidly, so I called Stout and told him I was having a rocker box leak (the box over the top of a piston.) This happened at times in the Corsair. Because we had a long flight, I requested to return to have it fixed. I landed and the ground crew immediately fixed the problem and in short order I was able to catch up with Stout, still in fight. This was a minor incident on the long 3.7 hour flight to Owi.

Excitement grew and adrenalin was flowing on the morning of the 26th. As each mile went by we realized the last chapter on our trail to combat was nearing the end. Estimated time to target, Peleliu, was about three and one half hours. The flight was tailor made with smooth air prevailing. As we came closer we could see cloud formations over the Palua Islands. We had learned in most of our operations over water that siting these cloud formations was a good indicator of landmass.

Almost on cue, Stout called to confirm our location and arrival time to Jungle Tower and requested permission for landing instructions. They answered immediately instructing us to remain under 200 FEET altitude as *they were shelling Bloody Nose Ridge* by our runway! This really *GOT OUR ATTENTION!* As we approached we could see the guns placed not far from what would be our tent locations. Doing our normal *"Burst and Pull Streamers," we alerted the 1ˢᵗ Marine Division that the Corsairs of VMF-114 had arrived.*

All 24 Corsairs arrived in good shape. The howitzers were firing their large shells towards the caves on Bloody Nose Ridge. Marine infantry was busy fighting the ten thousand Japanese that were holed up in these caves. Peleliu looked to us like it was on a planet in another universe. Almost all of the trees had been blown to shreds or splintered into pieces. The surface, nothing but coral rock, was also blown apart. We had been warned of snipers and we could hear large shells blasting, creating massive holes and generating lots of smoke. In the distance stretcher-bearers were trying to bring dead and wounded Marines down the coral precipices. It was a horrible battle and we were on the perimeter, 1500 yards from the action. What I'm describing was continuous round the clock horror.

We gathered what we were able to bring with us, and jumped on a truck to be taken to our assigned tent area. Four pilots each would live for months in 16 square foot pyramidal tents. My tent mates were Sam "Irish Leprechaun" Porter, a short happy Irishman who always had an Irish "morning" quip and Larry Marshall, our Intelligence Officer, who every morning would go for his run. He was a Harvard graduate, 42 years young, and nicknamed "Menopause Marshall." His favorite saying was "how he missed his lovely wife" every rainy morning! Ray Durham was the back up football quarterback for the famous Frank Albert's Stanford Cardinals! He became a medical doctor and died at a young age. He is the one who somehow obtained a Jap skull, boiled it and studied it in his spare time! HELLO! We would sleep on canvas cots, and eat and drink from mess kits and metal cups. It was not the Peleliu Hilton. It would take several days for our troops to set up mess tent facilities and hot meals etc. We were lucky! Marines on Bloody Nose Ridge were surviving on little or no water, with most of what they had ruined by oil in the barrels.

After sunset the darkness was really weird. Star shells were lighting all types of areas, creating shadowy figures and unreal pictures. Movement in the area was dangerous as Jap troops invaded some tent areas searching for food. Later, after we had scrounged enough wood to build a bed we put four by four pieces of wood and scraps of rubber tire tubing together to create a type of mattress and bed. Bug netting and poles formed our night protection against all sorts of insects. The weirdest sound as we tried to sleep was the scratching noise that large sand crabs made as they marched across the coral. Leather holsters for our .45 caliber pistols were nailed to the bedposts for safety from Jap soldiers. It was necessary for us to use passwords to identity ourselves as we went to the "head," a military term for a urinal! We received the 24 hour password and response at reveille. The only casualties we suffered were the Scotty dog and the swimming pig. Unfortunately they could not remember the password answer in time.

27 September 1944, Cowboy's division took off early for over one hour of familiarization over the Palua group of islands. To the north were several "hogback types of small islands," uninhabited and beautiful to see from the air. They contained camouflaged Japanese radio listening posts, and their communication to the capitol, *Koror*. A bridge connected Koror to *Babelthuap*, the largest island of the group. At 25 miles long the island contained an airfield large enough for bombers to use. It had a message on the well bombed runways, "WELCOME YANKEES!" Further north, was a large beacon facility that also stationed Japanese anti-aircraft guns. We strafed that facility every mission we flew either going or coming. Now we looked forward to new missions, realizing that the Japanese would be shooting at us for real!

Chapter 11   The Battle of Peleliu

28 September 1944

VMF-114 wasted little time getting into action conducting what was to become it primary combat mission – close air support of ground troops. The invasion of Ngesebus Island just north of Peleliu was to be one of the first American amphibious assaults where the air support for the landing force came from Marine Air. In earlier landings, air support had come from Navy and sometimes Army aircraft. It was reported by Marines on the ground that much of the effectiveness of the Ngesebus invasion was due to the aviation under the command of Major "Cowboy" Stout.

As LTV's (Landing Vehicles Tanks) entered the water from Red shore, naval gunfire alerted Japanese forces prematurely to invasion troops, Stout's pilots immediately recognized the situation, restraining their strafing of Ngesebus until the LTVs were thirty yards from the beach. The Corsairs flew so low that the watching Marines Infantry expected some to shoot each other down by ricochets! This action shut the Japanese forces down, and Marine Forces were on the Japanese before they recovered from the shock of the strafing Corsairs!

The following are excerpts from E. B. Sledge's book <u>With the Old Breed</u> (Page 110).

"The Invasion Landing at Ngesebus Island, 28 September, 1944. "We boarded the tractors and tried to suppress our fear. Ships were firing on Ngesebus. We saw Marine F4U Corsair fighter planes approaching from the airfields to the south. "We gonna have lots of support on this one!"

"Our Am tracts moved to the water's edge and we waited for H hour as the thunderous pre-landing gunfire bombardment covered the island in smoke, flames, and dust. Corsairs from Marine Fighter Squadron VMF114 peeled off and began bombing and strafing the beach. The engines of the beautiful blue gull wing planes roared, whined, and strained as they dove and pulled out. They plastered the beach with 50 cal. machine guns. The effect was awesome, as dirt, sand, and debris spewed into the air! "Our Marine Pilots outdid themselves, and we cheered, yelled, and waived, raising our clenched fists to indicate our approval."

"Never during the war did we see fighter pilots take such risks by not pulling out of their dives until the last instant. We were certain, more than once, that a pilot was pulling out too late. But expert flyers that they were, they gave that beach a brutal pounding with out a mishap to plane or pilot. We talked about their spectacular flying even after the war ended. "[1]

Excerpt from VMF-114's 1944 AIRCRAFT LOGBOOK from 9-28-44: Two missions by the squadron were led by Stout, Daniel, Hansen and Francke.

Two excerpts from Lt. Daniel's Aviators Flight Logbook:
(1) 9-28-44   FG-1   14016   1.5 hours bombing and strafing for Ngesebus landing
(2) 9-28-44   FG-1   14016   1.5 hours bombing and strafing for Ngesebus landing

That afternoon we flew the first Combat Air Patrol (CAP) that Cowboy, Daniel, Weber and Francke had drawn. The mission of the Combat Air Patrol is to find and interdict any enemy air. At Peleliu, Japanese fighters were capable of and expected to attack Peleliu. We took off with oxygen masks in place and climbed to 25,000 feet and checked in with the Jungle Tower and our radar station for vectors (altitude and compass directional information). Our mental stage was on go as we hoped intercepts would occur. Combat Air Patrols would become rather boring, but we realized at no time could we let our readiness at this stage relax. By necessity, these are early bird flights to fly altitudes of more than 20,000 feet. They become dangerous if the weather deteriorates, as night flights do not have any lights to refer to and vertigo is quick to happen. Fortunately the weather had been good but typhoons and heavy rains remained a possibility.

On the 29th, my plane was due for safety checks, and I drew a different FG-1 #1492 for an observation hop followed by my first bombing flight. This was a 1000-pound bomb dive-bombing flight of .9 hours on the hills of Peleliu. Our tents and the runways were only 1500 yards from Bloody Nose Ridge. A similar flight on the 30th necessitated closely checking the pull out elevation. We dove from 16,000 feet and had to maintain at least 1000 feet of altitude for our pull out due to the high speeds the dive created! At no time did we use a dive brake.

Our first bombing run on Umurbrogal cave country was this 1000-pound bomb dive-bombing strike. This was the first of many attempts, and there was little more than 1500 yards of separation from takeoff to target. Because of the nature and location of the target, it was possibly the shortest bombing run in WWII. With pockets in the coral rock that could be compared to a stony bathtub there were some 300 or so caves that had two sides. There were precipitous craggy outer sides, and inside there were interconnected corridors with steel baffled doors that could be opened to create murderous fields of fire. The Marine Infantry was under three withering fields of fire from Bloody Nose Ridge!

October 1944

October was to be a busy month of flying. Two other squadrons, VFM-122 and VMF-321, arrived and finalized the MAG-11 Corsair operation. I flew 26 missions during that time. Our flight schedule was taking on a full bore of combat flights. My first flight on October 2nd was a bombing mission over Molucca Harbor. This was the first real ack-ack (anti-aircraft fire) we received. The Jap Aak-Ack guns were effective up to about 16,000 feet. Our initial dive would start at about that height. You could have shells bursting at different levels up to that height.

I was fascinated, looking at first glance, at what I called fireworks on the 4th! As you entered your dive the bursts came closer, and you realized this was real, and they were trying to kill you. The closer they came, the more realistic it was. Some of their fires were not too accurate, but as we did more bombing, they got better!

Point Princeton was the radar point from which we received our vectors on the Combat Air Patrols. Also on 2 October we had another Combat Air Patrol of about 3 hours. Once again there were a couple of errant vectors or "boogies" (possible targets) for us to chase down. In spite of that we were hopeful but disappointed! That afternoon, we bombed a big AK ship anchored in Molucca Harbor with 1000-pound bombs. Fast in, fast out. The Harbor was ringed with ack-ack fire. Later, we found their anti-aircraft fire was becoming more accurate as measured by the fact that we were sustaining more hits on our planes.

On 6 October, the Japanese anti-aircraft fire succeeded in tagging my plane with its most serious damage to date. I was initiated into the "club." It was my first "arrow up my butt" (slang for being hit seriously by anti-aircraft fire). Stout and I were attempting to locate a Float Plane that had been bothering us at night. We thought it could be found in Molucca Harbor and our only concern would be small arms fire. As we circled the harbor flying almost on the water, I suddenly experienced 40 mm explosive shells bursting off the port side of my plane. My plane was hit, and the shell entered the fuselage just aft of my cockpit and exploded directly behind my armor plating. It detonated my EMERGENCY IFF gear filling my cockpit with smoke. My first reaction was that I had a fire, and I hit my mike button and hollered, "I'M HIT!" Naturally my voice squeaked, and Stout never let me forget it. The shell exited the right side of the fuselage, causing one large and many smaller holes. It damaged some control wires but did not affect the control of the plane.

Safely back and parked, I climbed out to notice my two plane mechanics checking the side of the fuselage, and looking at a large area of scattered metal pieces. It was a mess, and they were chuckling as they checked the damage. I remember asking them, "What in the hell is so funny?" Before we departed on later combat flights, as we got close to the planes, Cowboy would casually say to me, "Boy I hope we don't have any "I'm Hits" on this flight!" I was told later that the plane I flew that day (not my F4U 016) was eventually cannibalized and surveyed out of the inventory due to the damage sustained. It was Sam Mantel's special plane. Sorry, Sam.

After lunch on the afternoon of my lucky day we flew a 3.6 hours combat air patrol above Kossel Passage, a few miles north of Babelthuap. It was a marvelous deep-water anchorage where all of the Western Pacific fleet that was not at Ulithi Atoll was located. It was also the location from which many PT Torpedo Boats operated. These well-armed and swift small attack vessels also received many requests from our pilots for a ride. Radar blips from Navy ships vectored us on this Combat Air Patrol.

VMF-114 was settling into days of relatively short, but important combat flights. We were always briefed before taking off and then debriefed by Intelligence Officers after completion. More time consuming than the regular combat flights. My next four flights were equally divided between barge sweeps (low over the water, searching in and out of small waterways) looking for small crafts to catch in the act of moving supplies and ammunition, or sometimes troops. You never knew what you might uncover. The other two missions were pinpoint bombing of the caves of Peleliu. These were very short as time from take off to target was as low as fifteen minutes. Marine Infantry covered the entrances to the caves with a circle of smoke. The center of the circle was the cave's entrance. The outer circle of the smoke signaled the location of friendly Marines. Tough and nerve racking? You bet! 500 and 1000-pound bombs are powerful. Out of necessity we became very precise.

Finally on the 8th of October Cowboy's flight of four Corsairs loaded 265-gallon tanks (which had been used as fuel tanks) with jellied gasoline (NAPALM) and dropped them on the cave entrances of Blood Nose Ridge. Holy Cow, what a deadly area of fire! Napalm either sucked the air out of caves or burned the occupants to death. Hence the squadron's jacket emblem, our symbol for the Death Dealers!

Nick Virgets, our champion boxer from Cajun Country Louisiana and New Orleans, was the first and only pilot to have a malfunction with a hung tank of Napalm. After trying everything he could do to drop it over water, he flew out where destroyers were positioned, called one of them and said, "You fellows better have a good supply of ice cream on board as I'm coming to see yah!" He bailed out and was picked up.

9 October   Another Lucky Day

About mid-morning, I was on my bunk reading a magazine when suddenly it felt as if the whole island had exploded. I looked out of my tent and saw that massive explosions were filling the sky with shrapnel of good size and billows of smoke. The Japanese were firing on the ammunition dump that our Marines had captured during the invasion. I quickly reached for my steel pot. Only my cardboard liner was available. Looking out, I found my pot, being used by Zip Zabel rinsing film. I dropped the film on the coral and started my dash for the foxhole some fifty yards away. As I approached the foxhole, both hands were fixing the steel pot on my head. I recall a hard bump on my head. Next thing I realized I awakened on a cot in the First Aid tent. They had ripped my shirt and were working on a wound on my shoulder. I was shaky, as one of the three men who were already in the fox hole when I got hit asked me if I wanted to see what it was that hit me. A large steel piece of what I later learned was a five by six inches, jagged sharp piece of the casing from a 1000-pound bomb! It was still hot, laying on a piece of board. Had it hit me three inches lower, it would have decapitated me! I still have it on my desk in Tucson. The next day the sympathy from my fellow pilots began "Yeah Danny, you are the only fighter pilot in Marine Corps history who ran a 100 yard dash chasing a piece of steel so you could get a PURPLE HEART! I finally answered saying, "Have your fun. After we arrive stateside, I will take this out, place it on the bar, and wait for the civilians to buy me Scotch!"

On the 14th of October we flew two more Napalm drops on Bloody Nose Ridge, as well as our first "Scramble Alert" flight. Alerts were defensive tactics to engage "Boogies" (radar images of Jap planes). Four or more Corsairs were always combat ready on the flight line. Each plane was manned by a pilot either sitting on the wing or in the cockpit, ready to take to the air immediately. Radar then vectored the plane to intercept the Boogie! We had one more alert on the 15th that was a second dry run on an actual radar blip. While sitting in #016 on the scramble alert, a Marine sergeant climbed up on my wing and wanted to shake my hand for the Napalm bombing runs we had made. He was limping from being hit in his leg a day or two previous. I asked him how long he had been overseas. He said this was his fifth invasion in over 35 months. He had the thousand-mile stare, and it almost scared me to look at him. He had been through Guadalcanal then sent to Melbourne, Australia for R&R. There several young Marines went AWOL (ABSENT WITHOUT LEAVE) thinking they had died and gone to heaven with beer and girls so plentiful! The Shore Patrol gathered the men up, and told them there would be two ways they would return stateside, "WHEN THE WAR WAS OVER, OR IN A WOODEN BOX"! He shook my hand, slid down off the wing, and gimped away hoping for hot food and a shower after nine days of combat! I will never forget his look!

On the 16th we flew the first Napalm attack on Mizuha Village, the Japanese troop barracks at Babelthuap Island. Ack-ack fire was dense for the first time from low level. Several planes arrived home with holes in the flaps or wings, and these were readily repaired using pasting material.

Our next bombing and strafing mission was a 550 miles each way flight over water to the Japanese held Island of Yap. Breakfast was early morning followed by a briefing to include the US Navy's DUMBO crew (PBY-5A FLYING BOATS). I will always remember this briefing. The Naval Aviators told us they would take off two and one half hours prior to us and circle at a half way point, then join us and follow us into the Yap area and that they would be at a point close enough to pick us up in the event of trouble. "Don't worry they said, we will find you and pick you up out of the water!" I'm sure there might have been a little of doubt in that statement, but later, as we observed their rescues they proved they were fearless and dedicated survival insurance. Our flights to Yap and return were usually four to five hours duration. Theirs were twice that length.

Weather was the first information provided at the briefing. The forecast to and from Yap was broken large cumulus clouds, also over the target. Winds were to be moderate from the northeast, and the ocean would be calm with moderate sea caps. All in all, a good trip weather wise. Three divisions, a total of 12 Corsairs, each loaded with a one thousand pound bomb midline under the fuselage. We would cruise at 16,000 feet, 21 inches power, 1850 RPM (propeller revolutions per minute). This would give us a cruise speed of 240 knots, with 50 gallons per hour consumed. The main tank had 265 gallons, and there were 57 gallons in each wing tank. The gyrocompass heading was 58 degrees, and you could guess at your wind drift if you had one, by observing the wave caps on the water. Cowboy would lead the strafing and bombing runs. The anti-aircraft was tough, and you had to go in at top speed and try to outguess guns firing at you. When you got hit on your wings from machine guns, it was like someone stitching on a sewing machine. Small arms fire got to be routine as we had self-sealing gas tanks. That was a lifesaver if they hit you in one of those tanks. After 20 to thirty minutes over the target, we were happy to clear out and hear from DUMBO on our way back to JUNGLE TOWER! Total time of the mission was 3.7 hours. You were happy to have no one in trouble and to see cloud formations over the Palau Islands. We all made it safely!

The first flight on the 19th was a short one hour Napalm bombing the jagged cliffs of Bloody Nose Ridge. That afternoon was a 2.3 hour Combat Air Patrol. The 20th was again hitting the caves of Bloody Nose, two short trips dropping the napalm bombs to help the Marines having one helluva day on the coral cliffs!

My logbook shows that we had three days in a row off after having two trips per day. October 24th was a 1.3 hour trip north to Babelthuap to bomb the Ngardmau supply area. That afternoon, Stout and I spent 1.5 hours looking for activity to strafe on a Barge Sweep around the islands of Palau. We did find one small boat camouflaged to look like a fast pleasure boat. We passed it over feeling it might be a trap for low-level gunfire. Not worth the risk. The Marine Corps would never believe or be happy with our story.

On the 26th, we flew two flights. There was a short one hour barge sweep flight along the shores of Babelthuap looking for where the Japanese were moving small barges to transfer ammunition and supplies. Usually where small waterways emptied into coastal waters. These areas were always well camouflaged, as were the small arms locations. That afternoon Cowboy and I bombed a troop area, Airai off the east shore of Babelthuap. It was a short flight of one hour. On these flights, fuel and speed were no problem. On the 27th October, we started a big fire with a napalm run on Ngardmau, a Japanese troop and storage area. We engaged some small anti-aircraft fire as we strafed.

On the 28th my reliable #016 developed rough engine pops upon take off. Three Corsairs circled as I returned to our area to pick up another bird, #0192 to rejoin Cowboy, Pete Hansen and Don Franke to fly a short two hour Combat Air Patrol.

VMF-114 finished October with another Napalm run on Bloody Nose Ridge. The "predicted two to four day invasion" is now into almost it's fiftieth day of hell for the Marine Infantry! They are fighting as only the Marines fight, killing Japanese at a horrible rate, but suffering terrible casualties and unbelievable fighting conditions. My heart goes out to them!

VMF-114 had concentrated the majority of their combat sorties on Peleliu's Bloody Nose Ridge with Napalm. Still the Marines, in spite of tremendous effort, were moving slowly through the coral rock caves, with well-placed Japanese machine gun and mortar fire effectively causing mounting casualties. The famed 1st Marine Division had suffered casualties of 90% in one company. A division of Army infantry was gradually being called into action from Anguar Island, an island already secured.

One thing I neglected to mention earlier was the midnight raid that gave Captain Wally Weber and Lt. Daniel a challenge! That was to obtain a metal frame, originally from a bakery tent that was to become a historic bar and officer's club for VMF-114. Pete Hansen had artistic ability and painted a wondrous backdrop for the bar of a Varga type nude. I have a poster of this infamous rendering in my den in Tucson, Arizona. Each side of the interior of the club was about four feet in height making patrons of the bar bend down to sit in a small chair at a small table. It was created for midgets!

From the time it was put into operation the club served the squadron well! Many a poker game started there. Visiting Army Air Corp pilots would RON on their missions to and from the Philippines taking wounded back to the hospital at Owi. They appreciated the hospitality our "club" offered them. In fact, it was there I made a contact for our beer trips to Hollandia, New Guinea. It served us well until the frame was given back to the bakers when we moved to MAG-11's new bar.

MAG-11 (Marine Aircraft Group) had fashioned three Dallas Huts put together like a capital T. On the night of the dedication (30 October 1944) one of the sober pilots exchanged military cover (hats) with a two star general. They both celebrated the exchange! Magnificent Champagne was available for $1.00/bottle, and it guaranteed a monster hangover!! The bar was built on a small cliff edge overlooking the ocean. The next morning two pilots from VMF-114 were found sleeping at the bottom of the cliff, with solid hangovers, but very happy!

November 1944

The last couple of days in October my #016 bird had been acting up and was in for engine timing work. The 1st of November saw it back in action with Napalm bombing runs on Bloody Nose. The 4th was a 1000-pound bomb dive on Ngargal Island. After a two hour barge sweep on the 5th, I had to fly #016 on three more test hops to help Sergeant Goodie, my mechanic, work out the bugs. I guess I had been treating it too tough! We bombed the Japanese ammunition dump on Ngargal Island again on the 6th. Guess we missed something on the 4th!

The night bombings of Ngergong on the 9th and 10th was unusual because we didn't have much light. I was getting a little worried about old #016 as I had to take another test hop for an hour on the 11th. Ken Wallace did not return from a strafing mission this day.

No one saw it happen! Amazingly his plane, in pieces, was found in 2006 identified by the Bureau of Aeronautics Records. It was hidden in dense jungle. He was the first pilot we lost on this combat tour.

Another boring Combat Air Patrol for almost three hours including the briefing on the 12th, followed by a day off from flying on the 13th. The schedule on the 14th included another barge sweep and strafed along either side of Babelthuap. At the north end of the island was the lighthouse I mentioned earlier. We performed the usual strafing of it as we turned south along the shore.

Fortunately, we had a day off on the 15th but on the 16th we conducted a four-hour bomb strike mission to Yap and back. We had the normal (Dumbo mission) PBY-5A flying ahead of us to meet and follow us home. The weather was cloudy, and there were some rain squalls en route, the target loomed ahead of us from about 80 miles from Yap. We carried a 1000-pound bomb and a full ammo load in our wing guns. We dove through more flack than we had experienced before, and our strafing runs were hot due to more machine gun fire from Jap gun positions. Right after our last run, Herb Mosca, our proud representative from the famous "Slippery Rock University," had taken an explosive round in the ammo case of his starboard wing. As we headed further back, it was terrifying, as fire and the bursting ammo from his wing became more serious. The fire slowly burned out, Herb said a few rosaries and made it back to Jungle Tower Peleliu. Luck was with us. DUMBO WAS THERE!

On the 18th of November a strafing mission was scheduled in the area of Koror, the capitol city of the Palau's. The well known Battery Hill and Molucca Harbor was the home of hot anti-aircraft fire. Carefully we did not get too close to that area while strafing some enemy Jap barracks. On the way back to Peleliu the weather was turning bad as typhoons were forecast for late evening. During the night the winds and rain were pelting our area.

Fortunately, we had secured the planes and also our tents for the terrible weather. Horizontal rain battered us for the better part of the next three days. Lightning was busting during the night, and about four inches of water soaked the floor of our tent. We had the lucky tent, as the wind did not blow us down. For the last night of the storm, our home had about ten visitors huddled up and partially dry. If a piss call was necessary you pulled the Navy waterproof upper jacket on, grabbed a small roll of T-paper, tucked it under your arm, and headed for what was left of our heads (toilets in USMC language). All that was left of most of them was a bench and a hole (already full of water). This was not South Sea Island luxury!

Dawn on the 22nd brought broken clouds and a little sunshine. This provided some much needed time to repair to our living areas. Our Corsairs had weathered the storm, so I had a one hour test hop of #016! On the 23rd, there was another barge sweep for two hours.

November 26th featured yet another 3.5 hour scheduled Yap Island strike. The briefing followed an early breakfast of SOS (MILITARY LINGO): Ground beef-powdered eggs and gravy! Yap Island was roughly 550 miles northeast of Peleliu. Yap Island was originally scheduled to be an assault and capture, but those plans were cancelled and it was relegated to three fighter squadrons from MAG-11 bombing the runways at set intervals. Normally we would go there in flights of four Corsairs, each with 1000-pound bombs. VMF-114 would be scheduled to create large craters in their runways once a week. We bombed and strafed the runways, housing, gun batteries, and did so while dodging anti-aircraft fire. We lost Lt. Bob Spain, who was hit flying in Bob Peebles division. "Peeb" received a radio message that Bob was bailing out, but he was never able to find him. That was a tough loss as he was one of the most popular personalities in the squadron. Weather squalls bothered us on the way home; Cowboy's division arrived Jungle Tower unharmed! Two days off followed.

I have not yet mentioned the Air-Sea Rescue Equipment that we had on every flight, as our biggest safety needs being not over land but water. Longer flights were 300 to 500 miles over open seas. On every flight we wore a life preserver (inflatable-type Mark IV), called a "Mae West." Fighter Pilots sat on their chutes that included a pack and an assortment of practical things you hope you would never have to use. Lumpy to sit on, they included an inflatable life raft of Signal yellow color visible for miles, a whistle, and a patch kit for holes you hoped you never had to repair. There were emergency rations, hooks and line for fishing, a flashlight and a metal disk with a hole to be used to signal Air Sea Rescue. In addition I carried a first aid kit, a holstered .36 mm pistol, with two packs of tracer bullets. In view of the atrocities the Japs inflicted on American pilots at Chi-chi-jima, Koror, and the Philippines, most of us determined we would not be captured!

November ended with another barge sweep strafing any of the small barges moving ammo and military equipment to the Jap forces. My last flight of the month was a 3.2 hour special CAP (combat air patrol) off of Kossol Passage. This was a large area north of Babelthuap. Fast PT boats, large flying amphibious PBY-5A and other Navy equipment operated out of this large area of calm ocean water. Evidently their radar station was receiving some blips showing possible Jap operations.

The invasion of Peleliu had lingered a lot longer than expected, and the cost in wounded and killed to the 1st Marine Division had been beyond imagination. Water problems and the terrain of Bloody Nose Ridge were still horrendous. VMF-114 was starting to feel the effects of missions that were tedious and not rewarding for the potential cost. Living conditions and boredom were starting to be felt by the pilots. No one could complain, because whenever we were tired, the plight of our wounded Marine Infantry ensured that any thoughts of our conditions were forgotten!

An extract from HyperWar; USMC Monograph – The Assault on Peleliu. ""Perhaps the most significant aspect of Marine Aviation's participation in the Peleliu campaign was the opportunity afforded for perfecting the practice and techniques of that Corps specialty, Close Air Support. It had been relegated to a secondary role owing to the protracted employment of aviation in the neutralization missions in the Solomon's, Bismarck's and Marshalls. The splendid close air support made the shore-to-assault one of the most effective operations of its kind in the Pacific. Dive bombing with pin point precision, and strafing at tree top levels, pilots of VMF-114 so stunned the defenders that the Japanese, in well manned, well prepared beach installations were incapable of opposing the landing. Throughout all the subsequent fighting on Peleliu, the Marine fighters of all the squadrons continued to display great daring, ingenuity, professional skill and an eagerness to cooperate that raised the morale of the ground troops immeasurably. Not only did the Marines, who were happy to be working with their own brothers, appreciate the aviators, but so did the Army's 81st Division Wildcats as well, who seldom made an attack without calling for air support."[2]

Descriptions of the initial days of the invasion of Peleliu (Code Name Stalemate) often refer to "a battle like no other in United States Marine Corp History." Passages from Brotherhood of Heroes, by Bill Sloan, described the battle and are quoted in the next few paragraphs. They are an attempt to clear up the fact that men survived in spite of complete deterioration and the disaster of pre-invasion intelligence reports regarding the Japanese beach defenses caves and numbers of the enemy.

An extract from his chapter, Sea of Chaos and Isle of Fire, ""The Pacific seemed to be holding it's breath! It was Friday September 15th, 1944 D-DAY AT PELELIU! Every thing about the Amphibious Assault was neatly diagramed on planes maps and charts. D-Day looked simple enough to General Rupertus that he made the "infamous announcement" to the troops it will be 3-4 days and a cake walk!"

"Three Infantry Regiments of the First Marine Division were assigned beach objectives. 0800, LSTs moved into attack positions. By noon, "Confusion, Chaos, Death seemed to be everywhere. Even the white beaches were turning red with Marine Blood!" Now before the first wave of assault forces landed, their Am tracts came under heavy fire and once ashore, found themselves "caught in the jaws of a giant meat grinder!"

"In reality, most of the 500+ men lost so far on D-Day by the Marine Infantry were already dead or wounded, roughly one/sixth of its strength. Truth was the entire beach head was in danger of collapsing. It was only mid-afternoon and the Marines still on the beach had aged immensely."

"At no junction in its history had the USMC faced a darker, more desperate period than the first two days on Peleliu. AM of D-day Colonel "Chesty" Puller's First Marines had lost close to 1,000 men. By 08:30 on September 17th, 48 hours after the regiment had come ashore, one out of three of his Marines had been killed or put out of action."

"BLOODY NOSE RIDGE–"70 more days of Hills, Horrors and Heroes! Once the air strip and the Point were captured, Five Brothers, Five Sisters, Horseshoe Basin, nothing but coral hills, ravines, some 300 caves faced the valiant Marine Infantry. Japanese bunkers, positioned so that they could control machine gun and sniper fire from all angles, established staggering causalities and agonizing progress for the overworked Marine Infantry."

"The D-Day debacle, coupled with terrible decisions by Senior Command Officers in Pacific Command Headquarters down to the First Marine Division, including Regimental Commander's, had completely failed in their pre-invasion Intelligence. This included the majority estimates of casualties (KIA's, Wounded, Equipment and Days in Combat) involved in OPERATION STALEMATE 28 September 1944.""[3]

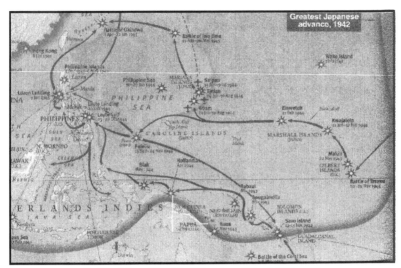

Battle Map, Pacific Theater, World War II
(Map Provided by Tom Campbell)

Corsair dropping Napalm on Bloody Nose Ridge

Lt. Daniel awarded the Purple Heart, Oct. 1944

Chapter 12   The Invasion of Peleliu Drags On

December 1944

VMF-114 had now spent 77 days in combat on Peleliu and I had flown 82 hours of combat time.

The island had been declared neutralized, but fierce fighting continued. Hand to hand combat, mostly at night, continued to claim the lives of many Marines. We had two pilots KIA, and several had been wounded during three water landings (they were rescued by the great Navy PBY-5A crews). One of our pilots, Gus Sonnenberg, had successfully bailed out as well as surviving a water landing! He was a part of a four plane sweep on the west side of Babelthuap and in his own words, "We had burned two warehouses, a line of trucks … light AA broke out all around me, before I could even jinx, fire had broken out in my engine and oil flew all over the windscreen. With 2000 ft. of altitude, there was no time to deliberate. I decided to bail out. I had sufficient power to cross the bay and cleared the land. Suddenly the controls failed; I took advantage of the plane's upside-down attitude, popped my belts, and dropped out at 1500 ft. I swam to the reef and found coral, but it was not perfect cover for machine gun fire coming across the water. I deflated my Mae West and lay deep in the water. Lt. K.F. Brissette, USNR, from Patrol Squadron 54 rescued me in 30 minutes!" Flight Surgeon Riordon, from Kansas City, Kansas bought him a beer. "Doc, you are going to ground me?" "Naw" answered Riordon, "just like bein' thrown from a horse, you get right back on!" Less than a week later, Gus was flying the same area. Maybe, the same gunner hit him again. No fire, but no power. He had enough speed to make a water landing. This time, only fifteen minutes elapsed and DUMBO once again picked him up. They carry six packs of Lejon's 100 proof brandies for emergencies. Like I said before, after the second event in seven days, Gus was bombed by the time he returned to his tent! He had consumed all six three-ounce bottles. He was quite happy.

My first flight in December was a test hop in #016. I then learned that that my buddy, Rob Roy, was in VMF-315, stationed at Roti Peninsula, Guam. On 3 December, with Cowboy's permission, I boarded R4D-5 and had a 5.5 hour flight to Guam. Lt. Johnson graciously allowed me to take the right seat on this long flight. What a great reunion with Rob. I had a tour of Guam, visiting the happy time bars and restaurants available there. Four days away from combat. I had not seen him since El Toro. After the war, he visited me in Laramie, Wyoming on his way to the Corsair Races in Wisconsin. Unfortunately, he was killed in a crash at the races. On the 6th, I boarded R4D-94 for a two-hour flight to Ulithi Atoll. LT. Tinker again allowed me the right seat for the two hour flight to Peleliu. It was a short R&R to regain health and attitude!

I did not fly again until on December 9th for a Barge Sweep around the shores and jungle on Babelthuap. These had become low level search and destroy missions. The enemy had large caliber .40 mm guns hidden around truck placements. VMF-122 and VMF-321 were also flying strikes. The Japanese forces numbered over ten thousand on the main islands.

On the 11th, the mission was a 1000-pound dive-bombing run on the airstrip at Babelthuap. Anti-aircraft guns were plentiful around this target. For these attacks, we would start our dive at about 14,000 feet, release the bomb at 6,000 feet and make sure we were out of the dive at 1,500 feet. Grey outs (g-force pulls) were common and dangerous. The real danger in dive bombing and air to ground attacks was "target fixation" or "target hypnosis." It may seem strange to non-pilots or civilian pilots, but fighter pilots can concentrate so intently on the electronic circle ring site that he becomes unaware of the speed with which he is closing on his target, and he flies right into it.

The 12th of December proved to be an interesting dawn CAP. Cowboy, Daniel, Hansen, and Francke achieved our cruise altitude before sunrise and all was going well. When the light from pre-dawn vision appeared I was in my normal position on Cowboy's wing. I looked over at Cowboy's plane and noticed his tail wheel was dropping down. This was an indication of the loss of hydraulic fluid and this would probably negate his ability to lower his wheels for landing. I radioed him, and his answer was, "Ignore it, Daniel, we will blow them down if necessary." Well, later as we were returning, he unsuccessfully engaged the blow down cartridge wheel movement. He then tried to pump them down, again no movement. He executed a dive and pulled up hard, again with no result! It was now evident that he would have to land wheels up! No pilot looks forward to this. However, a surprising number of pilots do it accidently! We are approaching Jungle Tower and Cowboy obtains clearance for me, and for planes three and four to land in advance of Stout as he was going to have to land wheels up. I go ahead and proceed to lead the flight in. As I am well into pre-stall speed, thank God the enlisted Marine, in a jeep parked close to start of the runway, fired his Very pistol and a red missile (the emergency signal to abort landing) crossed into my vision. As I, in desperation slam on my throttle to maximum power, thankful for the 6 degrees right rudder full engagement, and several "Hail Mary's" I barely gain enough airspeed to pull out of the landing. I take stock of the situation and realize that in spite of being a DUMBO, I will safely set my Corsair down. Engrossed in the situation with Cowboy, I had forgotten to use my landing checklist (GUMP)! A thousand thoughts go through my mind. What would happen to me after working the wheels down procedures with Cowboy, which resulted in him having to execute a wheels up landing, to have me crash land WHEELS UP IN FRONT OF HIM! How could I thank that Marine with the Very pistol?

14th-another Barge Sweep, 15th-test hop in #085 plane, the 16th and 17th were days off. On the 18th I had a Dawn CAP and Test Hop in #199. I guess I am helping the mechanics test the Corsairs that have been hit often. On the 19th I was back in #016 and we dive-bombed a Storage Dump on Babelthuap with 1000 lb. bombs. There was moderate to heavy flak but no serious Corsair damage.

Christmas is just around the corner, but we will finish the year with a very busy schedule. Scheduled Barge Sweep on Christmas Eve. These missions look simple on print but believe me they are not! We are taking fire on everyone and pilots are lucky to not have to pay a price. Where is Santa? We did not fly on Christmas and the day after. We celebrated and after Svare and Hansen made a trip out to a Swedish Merchant Marine ship with a supply of booze. They returned with three turkeys! HOORAH, great dinner for the pilots on Christmas Day! The rest of the story is that Cowboy saw the turkeys and said, "Wait a minute boys, that turkey is going to be turkey hash to feed the pilots and 300 enlisted Marines! END OF STORY, that was the kind of Skipper he was!

We were back in the saddle on the 27th. Major Stout and Lts Daniel, Hansen and Francke were briefed for a flight to Ulithi Atoll. He had met with an Air Corps Captain who was also scheduled to fly there in a P-38 twin engine, equipped with multi-photo and radio equipment. I was the only pilot in the flight that happened to have been to Ulithi. It was a great idea as he was going to navigate us there. The gyrocompass heading was 58 degrees to destination and we joined up and headed out! Early on at altitude my compass kept heading off of course. I called Cowboy; he answered, "Something must be wrong with your compass. The captain has a radio beam tuned in on Ulithi." Later Cowboy radioed, "There it is." We saw some land below the broken cloud cover. Suddenly flak and the sound of airbursts were heard. Cowboy immediately contacted the P-38 pilot and told him we were off course. He admitted that he must have beamed a Japanese radio station. Stout radioed "Ok boys, relax. Let's circle and I'll figure out where we are!" To the P-38 pilot, "If you want to follow us, OK!" "Francke, climb on up, see if you can get a vector on IFF for Ulithi. If you can't and anyone runs out of fuel, we will water land, tie our rafts together, and they will find us!" Always the optimist! We soon had a vector. All had enough fuel and soon we were landing at Ulithi. We forgave the captain as he was headed stateside on an emergency situation with his wife. Hope he made it in time.

We checked into the BOQ and RON'd (remained overnight) in Ulithi. Soon after we landed we received a timely briefing with information on the enemy. Japanese Bettys were overflying Guam and were intent on bombing the 7th Fleet, which was preparing to move closer to Japanese strongholds in the Pacific. Several large carriers and their support ships were gathered in the Ulithi Atoll.

The atoll was a huge area, capable of handling the large number of warships in the 7th Fleet. Our mission was a fighter sweep to hopefully find Japanese planes preparing on the small island of Woleai, 400 miles southeast of Ulithi. Early on the morning of the 30th of December, we loaded our Corsairs with maximum fuel in the main tank, and wing tanks, plus added the 295 gallon belly tanks centerline on the Corsairs. This would give us time to fly to Woleai, spend time over the target and then return to Ulithi.

Major Cowboy Stout, wingman Lt. Danny Daniel, Section leader, Lt. Pete Hansen and the tail end charley, Lt. Don Francke, were all extremely anxious as they climbed into their Corsair fighters. We were preparing to intercept Japanese Zero's, destroy Betty bombers and strafe hangers on Woleai. Weather forecasts to and from our destination were good. The ocean was calm, and whitecaps were visible. We were going to fly at an altitude that did not need oxygen masks. We would put the masks on when closer to the target. The belly tank fuel was used and in the event there were hostile planes to engage we would jettison the tanks. After two hours, we could see the island in the distance and prepared to encounter some resistance. Cowboy told us to drop our belly tanks and go into combat formation, altitude and spread out latterly into the Thatch Weave maneuver in case of Japanese intercepts. None occurred. Hells bells we were disappointed!

Not seeing activity on the island, and with no enemy planes visible, we dove, strafed and received some resistance. We started several fires and explosions and continued to do as much damage to installations as possible. Cowboy was upset as he expected Guadalcanal type resistance as it was in his Cactus Air Force days. The rest of just felt disappointment.

We returned at cruising speeds greater than normal, as fuel was no problem. 3.1 hours after leaving we were back on the ground at Ulithi. The after action briefing was disappointing for us, but we satisfied higher ups. On New Years Day, December 31, 1944, we returned to Peleliu and then conducted a strike on Yap Island, giving some quick strafing and receiving normal flak. Flight time total for the entire mission was 8.5 hours, covering in excess of 1600 miles.

December featured one big move for Second Lieutenant Daniel as I was promoted to First Lieutenant. OORAH!!

So long 1944, certainly hope 1945 will be a better year!!

Chapter 13 A New Year, Same Old War

January 1945

After the end of December, the three squadrons that had been on Peleliu since September had flown so many barge sweeps, MAG-11 headquarters colonels were having a tough time coming up with targets that had not been hit several times. They were satisfying FMF PAC (Fleet Marine Force Pacific) by dreaming up strikes that were not worth the practice Japanese gunners were having on the Corsair pilots. It was a "stalemate" that was properly named! The Palau Islands conflict had a strangle hold on the thousands of Japanese troops on Babelthuap and in the caves of Peleliu.

The officers that had experienced flying with the Cactus Air Force, Stout, Bastian, Conger and some enlisted were real warriors with a fierce hatred for Japanese and everything they stood for in this war. The pilots were not expressing any of the negative thoughts about our missions, but keeping it to themselves.

Island hopping had secured the Solomans, Bougainville, Rabaul, New Guinea, the Mariana Islands, and "King" MacArthur was returning to the Philippines. The colonels (O-6) in Pacific Headquarters' were chasing they're "stars" for promotion to flag officer (general/admiral) by eliminating every Japanese starving in the Palua's. In spite of these facts, every Marine in Peleliu was fiercely following their orders. The pilots in VMF-114 had said hello to Marine pilots headed for the Philippines and hello again as they returned on their way back to the USA. Our three combat tours of six weeks were no longer SOP (Standard Operating Procedure)! We did not realize our tour on Peleliu was only half over.

It was a New Year, but the same old war was starting to drag on. Nevertheless, the overall mental state of the pilots of VMF-114 was good. The biggest problem was the boredom of the same mission sets plus the questions surrounding why the Marine Infantry had to continue to suffer tremendous unnecessary

106

casualties. WHY? We felt that the island of Peleliu was now bypassed for all reasonable intents and purposes. There were thousands of Japanese troops holed up who were, unfortunately for both sides, dedicated to giving their life up for the emperor!

We tried not to think about the strikes that were ordered, but we couldn't help but think were about the low value these strikes achieved versus the high cost in lives. The "juice wasn't worth the squeeze."

Back to the war! On 2 thru 8 January we once again bombed Ngatpang's shores searching for hidden smaller vessels, and conducted three barge sweeps on the island of Babelthuap. This large island was covered with thick jungle that hid Japanese equipment, ammunition, supplies and troops. The hungry troops were even growing food gardens. Barges were now only moving at night. They had stopped using tracer ammunition, 7 mm and larger, because tracers readily revealed their gun emplacements. Flashes you could spot but by the time you saw them at low level you were either hit or they had missed. Stout had been the leader on most all of the strafing runs. We soon realized that the Japanese gunners were trace setting their guns on our number one Corsair and firing on the number two, my plane! I was being hit more than was Stout. Cowboy said, "Ok Daniel, you lead the next strafing run and I will fly number two!" He was always thinking of his pilots.

The barge sweeps we conducted from the 10th thru the 16th were all with bombs plus strafing.

I mentioned earlier that I had befriended a Greek Army Air Corps captain, Captain Pelakos, at our small O-club. On 10 January, returning from the Philippines he RON'd at Peleliu and had cleared the flight for me to accompany him to Hollandia on a BEER RUN. Cowboy readily signed a request slip for me to take on the trip to obtain six hundred cases of beer at the Navy Depot in Hollandia. Early on 11 January, in a big Curtis Commando, C-46, Capt. Palakos, Lt. Littman, and me departed for Hollandia, New Guinea. 5.6 hours later we arrived at the strip at Hollandia, which was located on a high hill. We had a view of "King" McArthur's mansion on the hill. We were able to enlist the services of Master Sergeant Williams, who readily consented to provide a deuce and one/half ton truck, and agreed to ride "shotgun" from the US Navy Depot back up the hill with the 600 cases of beer, minus a few six packs, to load on our plane.

We were able on the early morning of 14 January to accomplish the loading and 7 hours later, after unloading 100 cases for the nurses and men at the beautiful officers club at Biak, we successfully returned to Peleliu with almost 500 cases for the thirsty men of VMF-114. Cowboy made sure the EM's (enlisted men) received a big share of the beer.

On January 17th, a typhoon reared its angry head for the second time. Fortunately, for this one we were somewhat better prepared. Our planes weathered the storm, but the pilots suffered. Lightning bolts were popping all over the area. Two parachute riggers living in tents near us suffered direct hits, killing one of them. Several inches of water were rolling through our tents. I had a metal cover from a bomb serving as a small stool. I was seated on said stool when lightning struck near us, and I could see a streak of an electric current run down a tent pole near me and into the water. It knocked me off the stool, but luckily did nothing but scared the hell out of me. I tossed the stool out in a HURRY! Our tent held up well again with the exception of the running water. The toilet facilities suffered the usual typhoon damage and, as a result we suffered a level of discomfort. K rations and soup were the meals of the day during the strong winds and horizontal rain.

Throughout the Peleliu experience, the three men who shared this South Sea Island paradise in the tent with me went through it all together. Ray Durham, the future medical doctor, died prematurely in the late 1990s. The "little Leprechaun," Sam Porter, died in 1991. "Menopause" Larry Marshall, the Boston Financial wizard, our Intelligence Officer, who listened patiently to fighter pilots briefing about the same trucks that were destroyed fifty times! Well, Larry was over 40 years old when he joined the squadron. We 21 year old pilots thought that someone of 40 years was ancient! Larry returned stateside early in April '45. After the war, he told us, "You can trash that "Menopause" crap. My wonderful wife and I went on a 2nd honeymoon and 9 months later we had a 9 pound baby boy! I always loved spending rainy days with her!" This wonderful man passed away in 1989.

On the 21st, the weather cleared and we conducted yet another barge sweep and sat through a briefing for another run at YAP on the 23rd.

On the 23rd, we made the three and one half hour flight to Yap Island. This strike was a 1000-pound bomb on centerline, dive-bombing mission. Eight more big holes in the middle of their runways! We received more ack-ack, and we made sure we pulled out of our dives at proper altitude and avoided target fixation! This strike was definitely no SWEEP. The Navy PBY-5A (DUMBO) was protective insurance with us again! Again we successfully accomplished another long round-trip overwater trip with no casualties. We did, however, receive more gaping wing and aileron holes to paste!

On the 24th and 25th there were barge sweeps with bombs. We were eliminating supplies, ammunition, and hindering the movement of Japanese trucks and troops. On the 27th, another dusk combat air patrol responding to radar blips for the radar controllers. This was a night landing return, but no hydraulic leaks.

A C-46 Curtis Commando taxied up to its parking area, and the crew started to step down the ramp. This was a flight from the Philippines to take wounded back to the hospital in Owi. As luck would have it, Major Jack Conger was driving his jeep to the O Club. A very nice looking, beautifully endowed flight nurse smiled at him as he casually asked if she would like some refreshments. She was trapped as she said yes. One thing led to another, as did the refreshments freely poured at the Club.

After acknowledging he was a Corsair pilot, she smilingly said, "I would do anything to get a ride in a Corsair!" The magic words and Jack told her "he would have to sit on her lap, and no parachutes could be used." She immediately said, "when and

109

where do I meet you!" "Let's go!" said Jack and he quickly grabbed her hand, and off they went to his Corsair, #736! After about an hour, they taxied back to our revetment area. We met them and noticed red clay on the leading edge of the Corsair wings. On their approach to the must strafe lighthouse on north Babelthuap, Jack explained they had spotted four Jap soldiers, and he was so low that his bullets kicked up red clay. She was wildly excited and told us what a wonderful gunner Jack was as he had hit the lighthouse with every shot! Indeed, a master gunner! After a couple of cool drinks at the club, they retired to his tent. We could not imagine what happened.

Two more sweeps on the 28th and 30th would close out the action in January 1945. On one of these, an Australian spotter related information regarding a high-ranking Japanese officer's headquarters. We had missed it due to its excellent camouflage. On one of the above sweeps we were able to destroy this target using our six 50 caliber wing guns. Things were slowing down, but the Jap anti-aircraft hits were becoming much more accurate because of all their practice on us! My logbook now showed 21 more hours of combat flying. It was slow month for flying, and fortunately, no KIA's (killed in action)!

February 1945

Good old #14016, my FG-1! This airplane, with thanks to Sergeants Becknell and Goodie, had served me very well. This was due to the excellent adherence to all engine hour checks, the constant checking of every system and the fact that these two men were dedicated excellent mechanics. They each were responsible for a twelve hour duty shift each day. To date I had never stepped into or out of the cockpit, no matter the time of day or night, when they were not by the side of the cockpit to greet me! I had the utmost confidence that they were my best life insurance policy! My first two flights in February were test hops for work done on #016 by my mechanics and radar calibration took up the next two flights on the 3rd.

Now, I will tell you, Marine enlisted men were allotted a maximum of one beer per day. No reference was made as to the exact amount of Seagram's Canadian whiskey that was rationed. Lt. Ralph Lagoni from VMF-122 and my life long buddy happened to have been the squadron officer in charge of VMF-122's whiskey allotment when they shipped out of San Diego. It turns out that his squadron had mistakenly received a double allotment, and that was about to be corrected. He came to me with an offer I could not refuse. He would see that I would receive a case and one/half of Seagram's VO whiskey for an $18.00 donation to their kitty. Don't ask WHY OR HOW! I rapidly agreed and received said allotment. I immediately reached out to my contact in the Seabee outfit and got him to build a steel cage to store said booze, with me being the sole key holder. Naturally my lifestyle changed immediately. Many items were now available for an exchange, such as steak sandwiches late in the evening from the Seabee's kitchen! Even Becknell and Goodie were not denied a quiet request when my tent flap was raised. I wondered if I might have future success in the liquor business!

A short pre-dawn CAP (1.4 hours) occupied my day on February 5th. Another bombing barge sweep on 6th, prior to an early morning Yap strike on the 8th. The Japanese badly treated natives on the island, and their presence made strafing the island difficult for us. Additionally, Yap was a small island, so the ack-ack fire was concentrated and tough on the three squadrons from Peleliu making the almost six hour flight over water. VMFs-114, 122 and 321 have all suffered KIAs in strikes against what was an already by-passed island. Once again, in spite of the long, tiring flights, the PBY-5A squadrons operating out of Kossel Passage had given us outstanding support and had outstanding success in saving Marine pilots. After the first briefing upon arrival at Peleliu, their pilots reiterated, "Boy's, just get those wounded birds in the water and we will get you out." They did, and we were thrilled to see them on station.

Marine Corps records show the PBY'S fantastic records. Lt. Dick Rash, 114's world-class swimmer from San Diego University, had four instances when they proved their efficiency. Rash was shot down twice and twice picked up by Dumbo on 114's Green Island combat tour. Our Peleliu squadron records tell the story of another two times Rash used the Navy to survive trouble again. His third incident was after successful water landing when he swam over to be pulled out by a nearby Navy vessel. The fourth incident, after bailing out, he was picked up by a PBY-5A. This is a real challenge in rough seas with heavy swells! Dick Rash was one different fighter pilot. He must have had lungs with the air capacity of a whale. He collected "cat-eyes," which are a multi colored small shellfish that were used to make a pretty wristband. He would stay under water longer than any swimmer I ever saw. He was always in tremendous physical condition. He retired as a full colonel, was still flying Marine fighter aircraft at age 52 and in 1981 rode his motorcycle to one of VMF-114's reunions from San Diego, California to Tucson, Arizona.

On the 3rd of February, I took #49905 up for a radar calibration. I must have had temporary trouble, as I was airborne only .4 of an hour. I changed to #14018, a newer FG-1, for a 1.4 hour flight.

The 5th of February I flew #14018 on an early dawn CAP for two hours and we were back "home" for coffee. The 6th found me back in my #016, and we flew another bombing barge sweep up and down the coasts of Babelthuap. We found a truck dump to bomb. The morning of February 8th there was an early briefing as intelligence came up with activity on YAP that necessitated another 3.7 hours over water to that island and back. The good 'ole PBY-5A was on station two hours before we took off, would circle and wait for us again to make our trip home. This time, our "tail-end Charlie" didn't dodge a Japanese gun and got his starboard (right) wing stitched! That was the sound he heard as machine gun fire hit him! Hansen looked him over and determined he could make it back to Jungle Tower (Peleliu). YAP had collected too many KIA's, but it wasn't going to get our "Charlie" that day.

Then for four days straight we flew two barge sweep bombing missions. This was followed by a short dawn CAP in #14052, and .6 hour test hop in #016. Our time in the air has been reduced. In a

112

way, this is too bad because when you are flying you are too busy to become bored.

The 17th was a longer 2.5 hours dusk CAP. Radar had received some unusual radar blips, and that put us in the air at dusk and brought us back for a night landing. Cannot afford to make a mistake at night.

There was another beer run on 18th of February. Captain Connelly, from the Army Air Corps, was at Peleliu to RON. He contacted me as the logistics unit in Biak had approved another run to Hollandia, New Guinea. I joined him early on the 19th, this time as co-pilot in the Curtis Commando C-46. Four hours later we touched down at Biak, off the East Coast of New Guinea, home of the big Army hospital serving the wounded from the Philippines. The hospital had a large number of staff nurses and doctors. The pilots stationed there had a beautiful officer's club. It was built on the beach, with parachutes hanging from the ceiling of the dance floor overlooking the surf. The only thing lacking was a supply of beer or alcoholic beverages. The usual payment for the use of their planes was a gift of 100 cases of beer and a few bottles of fine whiskey donated by the pilots of VMF-114.

Early on the morning of the 20th, Captain Smith and I climbed into the Cockpit of C-46 #XA-378 for the 2 hour flight to Hollandia. Once again I was in the co-pilot's seat. We landed atop the high hill and taxied to our stop overlooking MacArthur's palace. We again looked for M/Sgt Williams, negotiated the same contract as before for truck and shotgun protection, and moved on down to the US Navy Depot. Williams and crew helped load 600 cases of beer, sans a few six packs, onto our Curtis Commando #XA-378. We thanked MSgt Williams and took off headed for the 2 hour flight back to Biak. Needless to say, we had a real reception party awaiting us. We unloaded our exchange cases, went to the BOQ, showered, changed our flight suits and readied for dinner, dancing, and a party with newfound friends. The timing was great for all in attendance, moonlight dancing, and all! Wonderful, no WAR!

On the 22nd, I ate breakfast at 0800 and was back in the saddle with Captain Smith, my new friend. Again, I was copilot on C46-#XO377 for the 3.5 hour flight to Peleliu. My dreamland experience had ended! We radioed ahead of our arrival. A flight of four beautiful FG-1 Corsairs were making mock gunnery runs on the C-46. It was a thrill for the Army pilots to see, as well as frightening if you envisioned the real thing. What an experience!

We delivered the beer and gave Lt. Harshberger the responsibility for equal distribution to pilots and our EM's (enlisted men). Later, after we lost Cowboy, LtCol Ohleric, the Blue Flame, took over for a short time and pulled out the manual listing one beer per man per day for enlisted. In spite of Ohleric's rank, the Group Colonel overruled his stupid decision.

After my vacation to Biak, I was more than ready to climb back into #016, but it was in for check engine time. On the 26th and 27th we had barge sweeps in #14183 with 500-pound bombs. We were able to spot camouflaged Japanese troop areas in the jungle as well as some hidden trucks. Our bombs started fires and the flying debris in was evidence of our bomb hits.

February ended with #016 going back in for a final check after one hour of flight checking.

Chapter 14   Loss of Our Leader

March 1945

**Wyoming Alumni Lt."Bud" Daniel & Major "Cowboy" Robert Stout,
USMC - Peleliu, SW Pacific Jan 1945
Ready for a combat mission with VMF 114 in their F4U Corsairs**

Before going into the events of March, I wanted to describe the last flight we had on the afternoon of 28 February. We found several footbridges in a couple of Japanese areas on the big island. Our ammunition officers wanted to get rid of some 100-pound bombs. So Cowboy decided to oblige with this flight. When the ammo boys put those small bombs on the centerline of the Corsairs, they looked like firecrackers compared to what we had been carrying. Delivery on this flight would be from a low altitude due to the size of the footbridges. We only had one shot per plane with the bombs. Stout, Daniel and Hansen were successful in each destroying a footbridge. Now it was time for the skip-bombing expert, Don Francke to do his stuff. Knowing what he would hear if he missed,

115

the determination to hit home was uppermost on his mind. He went into his approach, concentrating on his release, ignoring the coconut trees that were close to the bridge. Everything was perfect except his approach to the final tree on his escape path. He hit the tree with the starboard tip of the wing. I swear that I observed his plane to turn horizontally around with pieces of the tree flying all over the area. Somehow he was able to control his plane and fly it carefully to base. Upon inspection, his wing tip produced several pounds of coconut wood. He was noticeably quiet when asked how this came to be.

Beware the "Ides of March." March 1945 was destined to be the worst month in the squadron's history.

For the first three days of March Cowboy's flight did not have a flight on the schedule. Evidently this was the time that the three squadron commanders and the MAG-11 Colonels and staff were busy formulating plans for the strikes they had received from the Pacific Headquarters in Hawaii.

On the third of March, 1st Lt. Ken Wallace was killed as he flew into a hill on a strafing run on machine gun locations. He was killed instantly, but his flight's pilots did not witness his crash. Ken had been warned about flying too low on strikes after tree leaves had been found in his wing gun ports. The crash site and his plane were found by a group of individuals who return every year to the Palau Islands to search for the remains of missing pilots. Pat Scannon, a medical doctor from the San Francisco Bay Area and a group called Bent Prop go to Peleliu and search the jungles every March. 1st Lieutenant Wallace's crash site was found in 2012 by the identification of Federal Bureau of Aeronautics numbers put on every plane manufactured.

On the evening of the third, we had a briefing on a strike for the morning of the fourth. In retrospect, I am flabbergasted that the officers of the command and staff could have dreamed up such a SNAFU! I realize I am now ninety years of age, and that was 68 years ago, which just goes to make it more difficult to imagine. I wonder if they (PAC HAWAII) were thinking how they had screwed up at Peleliu and wanted to somehow make up for it!

The picture was that three fighter squadrons, VMF-114, VMF-122 and VMF-321 were to each schedule four different combat strikes of six, four plane divisions, and were to plan these strikes at two hour intervals of delivery. VMF-114 was to fly low-level NAPALM bomb deliveries at sun up by 24 planes, followed at 0900 with another mission of 1000-pound bombs on the same area. This was to be repeated at 1300 and 1600 hours. We were to destroy the capital, Koror! Stout then gave us the following brief, summed up as, "We all would fly right on the water north along the "hog-back islands" to a point directly east of "Battery Hill." We would then turn left, approaching the target from a position coming straight out of the sun, then jump over the hill and release napalm.

Cowboy and Daniel flew abreast, directly over the middle of the Battery Hill gun locations! There was a 300-foot escarpment that guarded Koror from the east. The only ones surprised were the two of us. We were well over 300 knots air speed, but the complete area erupted with fire. It seemed that a dark curtain of "triple A" ack-ack covered the target as we approached. At that speed, it seemed like everything happened at the same time.

Suddenly, as we dropped our napalm, I saw Cowboy's right wing start to move up over his cockpit, and his plane start to move down towards the water of Molucca Harbor! The concussion from a shell blast bounced my plane up and to the right. As I controlled to level the plane's attitude, my immediate thought was, "COWBOY IS DOWN!"

His loss to me was not believable. Suddenly my life seemed to be shattered. My instincts must have taken over as I headed away from the anti-aircraft fire.

Controlling my plane and looking back, my thoughts turned wildly to the loss of Cowboy! I can vaguely remember, as we circled trying to join up for a search of the area, Conger telling me to go back to base. This was all a blur to me. So many things made the loss of Cowboy so needless. Major Tucker was on the island to relieve Cowboy, but he refused to leave before all his pilots had been sent home. Also, Major General James T. "Nuts" Moore told me in Hawaii, as I was on my way home, that he had offered a slot to Cowboy on a new carrier but that Cowboy declined. Two years after the war ended search teams found Stout's plane with his remains in the cockpit near the vicinity where I estimated he went down.

I vaguely remember landing and going into the ready room after the accident. I do recall the group commander consoling and telling me that, in time, I would be able to manage his loss. Also, something about tomorrow you will be on your way to Sydney for R&R.

My logbook also tells me I flew another mission that day scheduled for 1300 hours. This was to be my last flight in my good 'ole F4U #016! If I made that strike, it is not in my memory! I must have as I can remember that Lt. Brown, from VMF-321 was hit, and in spite of a severe wound in his left thigh, he bailed out. As his chute popped, he was floating down into a fiery cauldron. He maneuvered his chute and landed in a narrow channel of water between Koror and Babelthuap. As Lt. Commander Memer maneuvered his PBM, he saw Brown in the water and said to his co-pilot, "that guy is a goner if we don't pick him up." The Corsairs called the Dumbo and said that they would form a circle and support his landing with gunfire while they landed to pick up Lt. Brown. They succeeded throwing him a line, but he was too weak to hold on. This resulted in the PBM having to maneuver again to get Brown out of the water. Intense fire of all kinds was blanketing the flying boat as the co-pilot got out of his seat, went aft to the blister on the side of the PBM and reached out and hauled Brown to safety as they struggled to get airborne to complete this incredible rescue! That evening I went over to VMF-122's O-Club, where my buddy Lagoni tried his best to cheer me up, when who would walk into the club but the two Navy pilots who had succeeded in the miraculous rescue of that afternoon. I recognized "Mose" Landers, a high school classmate of mine from Natrona

County High School in Casper, Wyoming. My friend Lt (j.g.) "Mose" Landers was the co-pilot who rescued Lt. Brown! A few more scotches were called for during this personal reunion! It did a bit to cheer up my loss. Seeing him would not happen again in a million years, especially on the day our Wyoming Cowboy was shot down.

My logbook showed the last flight on March 4th, after Cowboy went down, was the last flight I took in #14016. After we had returned to the states, our squadron was reassigned to Okinawa. I hope the aircraft continued to perform for whoever flew it well. Becknell and Goodie, my mechanics, returned to the states.

The thoughts of seeing Cowboy on his last ride will never be erased from my memory. The loss was so personal and heart wrenching; I didn't think I could ever make sense of this damn battle that took the lives of so many. My training dictated I had to be ready for the days ahead.

On 7 March 1945, "Blackie" David, Anderson, "Andy 1", "Wink" Balzer and I boarded R4D #8905 for a five hours flight to Hollandia, New Guinea. This time it was not a beer run flight. OOH-RA, it was the first leg an R&R to Sydney, Australia! Andy 1 was so skinny from weight loss due to the "jungle rot" he had suffered that the others on the flight thought it was "a medevac" flight! He did not let that keep him from loving his time in Sydney. Andy was killed bailing out over the mountains east of El Toro, California shortly after the end of WWII.

As the flight climbed, I tried to relax and get some sleep. Normally sleep comes easily for me in the air, but thoughts of Cowboy's wing flying up and his plane dropping into the swamp kept entering my mind. I kept thinking how? How could it happen? Such a tragic price to pay for a lousy strike that should have never been! I must try to try to put the present on top of the past!
I CANNOT UNDO MARCH 4TH!

On the 8th of March, we flew from Hollandia to Finchhaven, a four hour trip. We taxied into a spot and parked next to where an

Army B-25 light bomber was about to park. The shutdown procedure on that plane included the pilot shoving the twin handles of the engines into the cut off position. Also, this procedure opened the bomb-bay doors centerline of the plane. They were parked on the steel Marsden Matting that covered a muddy area. Upon loading the plane, they evidently had not adequately secured the cargo, several bottles of premium whiskey. The command pilot had a horrible look on his face as GI's nearby scrambled to scrape as much of the liquid as possible into their steel pots. The poor pilot, destined to be a Lieutenant for the rest of his career looked very unhappy.

Leaving Finchhaven, it was five and one half hours to the very northern tip of Australia, Townsville. We were greeted there by the "dollies of the Red Cross", serving cold beverages and cookies. We refueled the R4D #263663 for a four and one half hour night flight to Brisbane, Australia. Ten hours on our way, but we were far from unhappy. We checked into a very famous hotel there that had been MacArthur's HQ's at one time. We would stay two nights there, before moving on to Sydney by train.

As we had time to look around we discovered that Brisbane was a very beautiful city. It was a most enjoyable time staying in a quaint room with excellent white sheets and a great hot shower! Civilization was indeed something after months in combat at Peleliu. The first morning's breakfast was steak and eggs, Australia's finest! Tough choices were when to have a "Bloody-Mary" or the "Aussie's" great cold beer! We had at least two weeks of "heaven" to live it up before thinking of returning to Peleliu. "Wink" Balzer was my partner and constant companion. He was Conger's wingman, about the same size, and a similar personality as myself. He turned out to be a perfect choice.

The first night in the "pub" Wink and I were enjoying a beer when a US Marine approached me and ask me to accompany him out on the long porch surrounding the hotel. Four "Aussie" soldiers had threatened him. They were not too friendly as their pals were in Europe and the women on their home soil were infatuated with and treated too well by the US military. Taking my best USMC stance, and the command attitude of a USMC Boot Camp Drill Sergeant, I said that if they touched this man I would see to it that the USMC would make them wish they were in a new world. The Aussie soldiers saluted and departed. I was glad they could not see my knees shaking. My crowning performance!

We awakened the morning of the 10th, a little sorry that we had to leave Brisbane, but looked forward to boarding an English Style train car with compartments seating six on each side and an entrance in the middle. Oddly enough, the train stopped for about 20 minutes at each station stop. Our new friend, a warm and friendly grandmother, taking her 18-year-old granddaughter to college in Sydney, was fascinated by the American Marine pilots in snazzy green uniforms with gold Naval Aviator wings. She made it very plain she was not going to have any US Marine alone with her granddaughter. This was to be how it was for 22 hours en route to Sydney. She was a doll, and each time the train would pull into another station, she would awaken one of us, asking if we had a desire to replenish our beer supply. The daylight hours were spent in seeing the land that would remind one of a picture of western Colorado, Arizona, and New Mexico's terrain. In the early morning, we arrived in Sydney and said goodbye and wished the best of luck to this wonderful lady and her grandchild! I think she might have wished to take one of us home with her. We were a day late arriving in Sydney; the train ride was worth missing a day!

It was the morning of March 11th when we arrived in Sydney and were met by Marines charged with greeting visiting Marine pilots. They were really organized. There was excellent news for us concerning the facilities we could rent for our visit. Marines had taken over a four-story apartment house located in beautiful Rose Bay. Balzer and I would share a third story apartment with five-rooms, two bedrooms and a balcony overlooking Rose Bay on the east. There was also a balcony on the west side overlooking the Australian Golf Course. Had we died and gone to heaven?

Blackie and Andy1 would have similar accommodations on the 2nd floor. After we had surveyed the "digs", we emptied our parachute bags that contained several cartons of American cigarettes and toilet paper. Toilet paper there was like American "butcher" paper. Advice we had received before we left Peleliu was to hide the main roll! Lady guests were prone to stealing the roll. Cigarettes were great bartering items for almost everything, shave and haircut to booze! A package was valuable. I did not even smoke.

We had a big laugh at the message each of us had on our bed the first morning they cleaned and refreshed the rooms. It read, "We love you Yankee Blokes, we want you to have a wonderful and meaningful stay, but if you have a lady guest overnight, please do not toss your overcoats under the bed. Thank you!" What in the world? Their word for CONDOMS! This brought a big laugh!

The Australian Hotel's barbershop was a must stop on most of the mornings. Shaves were a luxury. Balzer and I showered, dressed in our green uniforms, opened an "Aussie" beer and discussed our targets for the evening! We had recommendations on a few good "hunting" areas in downtown Sydney. We found "The Rocks" was the best. Streetcars and taxis were cheap with a package of cigarettes. Wink outlined his plans to me for each morning, noon and night. He amazed me with his plans to make up for the lonely hours on the islands. I told him if success was in his program; he better watch as he went to open a window shade, or he might roll up with it. He did not listen.

On every main street in the center city they had stores that opened on to the main streets at the other end of the store. Cannot think of the name they called them. There was a store that had a bar and lounge on the second floor that opened about four in the afternoon. Our pre-party briefing info from the 'ole hands was to make sure you had a table staked out by opening time. The four of us made certain to use that schedule. At five PM the forty some tables were filling up with what we called "Junior Leaguers" (young ladies 21 to 25 years)! Sure enough, our scouts were correct. There was also a good band that arrived about 5:30 PM. Wink and I had no trouble dancing with several different candidates, also making sure we provided their drink of preference. After the warm up period, I saw a very delightful young lady dancing with an Army Air Force soldier, and I decided to shoot that buster down! Wink had made several warm up moves but had not yet decided to strike! I moved in on the young lady and ask her to dance, much to the bomber pilot's chagrin!

I introduced myself to Michelle, who had a melodic accent that turned out to be French. That to me was very interesting. You have to remember all of my excuses, a 22-year-old fighter pilot, fresh out of eight months in the Pacific jungles, trying to forget all my harsh memories of the past few days in the Palau Islands! We were ideal dancing partners, even good at "jitter-bugging!" By now Wink had also selected his partner for the evening. The four of us went to a delightful restaurant and finished off the delightful evening by hiring a taxi and delivering my date to her home, which was not too far from our apartment in Rose Bay. I returned to the apartment and left Wink to his own decision. We had separate bedrooms, so I did not worry about Wink, even though he was the youngest pilot in VMF-114! All I in all, a very nice introduction to the nightlife in Sydney! I had a hard time "playing it cool, as far as Michelle was in my thoughts. I did not want to rush into anything. It was tough.

I made sure that I had Michelle's phone number and address and promises of future dates before I bade her goodnight! I had no trouble having a great night sleeping in our great apartment in a very comfortable bed. Balzer made his appearance about ten AM for a cup of coffee in our kitchen, but only grunted when I ask him if he was satisfied with our evening's experience. We decided to go to a fine hotel for a breakfast of steak & eggs, plus a haircut and shave in their barbershop for the trade of a package of cigarettes!

We found several things out about the beautiful Australian city and what the citizenry preferred. If they liked a sport, it was their insanity for their football, boxing, horse racing, and even cricket. Baseball had not yet exploded. The atmosphere of the city was much like the middle thirties in the US. Most of the food was fresh, meats, eggs, vegetables, etc. Every restaurant had their specialties on display in the front windows, much like Europe. The people were wildly thankful for the United States Marine Corps.

We did not approve of that, NOT MUCH! They were convinced that we had save their bacon from the invading Japanese. Walking down the street, they would grab us, shake our hands, ask questions, invite us for tea, or want to converse about our homes in the USA.

Believe it or not, before we departed Sydney, we did shop for our relatives back home. Things like sheepskin rugs, Koala bears, all kinds of trinkets, animal statues, pictures, etc. Anything to remind you of the wonderful people of Australia! They have not changed much to today.

The third day in Sydney, after our daily trip to the barbershop for a very cheap but comfortable shave, the four of us gathered to discuss the things we would like to do. We decided to check into making a special visit to a British carrier, which was in the harbor.

HMS ILLUSTRIOUS welcomed us for lunch one day and also served a "wee bit" of refreshment! Brits allowed their pilots to consume booze on board. They gave us a tour of the ship. We discussed the dos and don'ts of flying Corsairs. We discussed the "clipped wings" of the British Corsairs aboard their carriers. They had several different words for various parts of the ship. The Marine pilots had a fun and interesting event with the Brits! It was not as luxurious as our US Navy carriers.

One afternoon there was a knock on the main door of our apartment. There was a man who had a peach basket full of something. He asked if Mr. Blackie lived here. We told him that, at the moment, he was not available but would be soon. Did he want us to handle his problem? He did not act if it was a problem at all, but he would appreciate if we would see to it that Mr. Blackie received his success from the horse track that day! He said we had honest faces and must be friends of Mr. Blackie. Blackie showed up and thanked us for looking out for him. The damn basket was full of Australian money! He never told us how much, but he did buy us a few "Foster's" beers.

Wink and I were determined not to miss a day of enjoying every second of our stay. We took a bus out to Bondi Bay, a pretty beach that was very popular with Australians. The weather was great as March is the fall "down under!" We had not planned on swimming, so we returned to our apartment to plan the evening events. We found that our two partners, Blackie and Andy I, had very different events to enjoy. Andy had been a child prodigy of the Minneapolis Symphony. His interests were different from Wink and mine's. Blackie David interests were much different, leaning towards boxing, weight lifting and soccer (the Aussie football). This did not eliminate our visits to the popular pubs! We settled in on the Foster's Lager. It seemed to fit our schedule, delivering a smooth party buzz, with no hangover. A good single malt scotch was also no bad thing.

We found Sydney to be a very vibrant and wonderful R&R answer for us and actually, for any red blooded young man. Even in the middle of 1945 the nightlife was equally as good as was Southern California's. The Koala bears were cute, the kangaroos amazing. You had to be very careful of them. You didn't want to get too close! The Australian Museum had been around over 100 years. We went through it hurriedly. The Opera House in Sydney Harbor was impressive from a distance. Kings Cross was wild and a place to bypass. Blackie David could protect Andy I there but not me. The bar and grill above the shopping stores was more my style. Also, The Rocks was good, as was the Steel Bar for oysters on the half shell for Wink and me.

On day 5, I finally succumbed and called Michelle. She was a little discouraged with me that I was so late in calling. This was a danger sign, but I ignored it and asked if she would like to meet me for lunch. Yes was the answer.

I mentioned the Steel Grill and she agreed. I told Balzer we would meet him on the second floor bar and lounge around 4:30 PM and he agreed. At lunch I had learned more about Michelle's life. She said she and her family had been able to get out of France just before the Germans stopped people from immigrating to Australia. That info explained her accent. She also had married and divorced

125

an Army major who had been on MacArthur's staff, but had been ordered back to the states. This move had brought on the divorce, and she appeared well settled. For me, it raised a red flag that I needed to handle. All went well, and the band was playing as Balzer had made an acquaintance with his choice for the evening. Another very attractive and personal Aussie gal! Supper for the four of us found us enjoying a very nice restaurant on the bay overlooking the bridge. Dinners were reasonably priced and very nicely served. We were definitely wondering what the poor were doing that evening. It was becoming evident that I had met the young lady that I would date during our stay. I was still very firm in my determination not to get seriously involved with any female as long as there was a war going on! Wink was flying high and certainly of the same opinion.

Cricket matches were the order of the afternoon on day six as we were interested in seeing how different it was from American baseball. We found it interesting; a sport destined to appeal to the British. Five PM found our group back at the original party stop dancing to a good band that was easy to enjoy.

The morning of the seventh day we realized the time in Sydney was flying by, and we took a minute to wonder if the guys back at Peleliu were any closer to being sent home. We voted not to ask.

The Australian Golf Course was just a short distance from our back porch. We decided to try it for lunch. I had an interesting chat with the golf manager. He informed me they had a fine scotch, which was gently moving back and forth in a wooden barrel in the lounge. We had to whirl a bit of it on our tongue. He was correct, as it tasted magnificent!

We had two things we wanted to be sure to enjoy during our stay. One was football as the Aussie's played the game. It was enjoyable to see the crowd and how completely they were involved as the game progressed. The other was horse racing. They ran in the opposite direction to the way it is run in the USA. The special boxes we were in had information on the betting displayed for all of the major tracks in the country. The fans loved to wager a coin or two on each race. Oh, by the way, the water in the toilet basin does flow in a different direction! Opposite to the direction it flows in the USA.

Rose Bay was a wonderful area to wander. There were many small shops and tea bars. They had so many of the British habits of life. I rapidly decided that if I could import American cigarettes, gum, and toilet paper, I would live handsomely "down-under!" There were so many things to do in the Sydney area that I suddenly realized that we had spent very little time with our fellow pilots Blackie David and ANDY 1! Not to worry!

Shopping downtown Sydney was interesting due to the quality and diversity of their items. Michelle agreed to help me shop and we spent time looking. I had to have one sheepskin, one koala bear and a kangaroo statue. She was a big help in deciding something for mom, dad and my sister Arlene. I did buy Michelle a nice bracelet.

Two days and nights remained for us in the land "down under!" I had not seen as much of Wink Balzer as I had the first few days. Evidently he was really working on the challenge of going up with "a window shade!"

I called the Marine desk that would have our departure schedule. The sergeant that answered my call did not seem to care about my question. Do we dare try to stay longer? What if VMF-114 had been slated to leave? Finally the schedule showed us departing on the 22nd on a Marine twin engine PBJ small bomber. The rear glass, formerly the rear gunner had been taken out. At altitude we were going to be colder than usual. We prepared for it.

Attention 114 pilots, 48 hours remain in paradise for you to enjoy! Let me ask, what would you do with 48 hours? For some it would be eat, drink and make Mary! OOPS, be merry! Not us, we are Marines!!

127

Those of us who were Virgos would organize the packing; do laundry, check and double check. Those of us who are Taurus would say, "To hell with it, let's party!

I know what the four of us did. We found the best club, dined and enjoyed to the wee hours. On our final afternoon and evening, we enjoyed seeing the bright lights of Sydney and joined up at the apartment to say goodbye and god speed. Michelle was the life of the party. Not being a big scotch drinker, after a couple she could not speak English, only French. She was really funny, until we had to say adios, when she cried and I did my best to explain what we still had to do in Peleliu! We parted forever friends that enjoyed a short time!

On the 22nd of March 1945, a Marine station wagon pulled up to our apartment building to load up four Marine pilots to get us started on our return to Peleliu. We had enjoyed a breakfast not far from our home for the time in Sydney. Daniel, Balzer, David and Anderson had done their best to make memories for a lifetime of our time in Australia, our several days in the wonderland "down under!" However, not a day went by that I was not reminded of the mission that led to Cowboy's death, and that we would all have to soon face combat without our leader.
Marine PBJ-1-C, #35008 with Lt. Mellette in the pilot seat was ready to depart on a 3.3 hour flight to Rockhampton, Australia. Four pilots had loaded and tied down their parachute bags, empty of cigarettes and toilet paper but loaded with gifts and items for relatives and friends. A shared item, personally packed with a case of Australian Beer for the EM's & officers who put our planes in the air and made our airplanes safe to fly.

When we landed and checked into our hotel, registration area and bar upon arrival was entirely empty with exception of staff. By the time we had cleaned up and were to gather at the bar, the tables were filled with young ladies. It seems the word had spread that four Marine fighter pilots were in town for the night. A division of Yankee soldiers had recently been completely ordered up the combat line. The Australian ladies knew how to laugh, live, and forget! We were not meant to rest on R&R!

Breakfast was early the morning before leaving Rockhampton on 23rd March 1945. We had a long seven hours flight to Emarui. Four Corsair pilots in the rear cabin, with cold fresh air blowing into the cabin. Was this penalty for our happy times in Sydney? Fortunately we had loaded up on blankets prior to leaving Sydney. Sleeping through what must have been a front, we did not desire to break out a bottle from the case of beer. This turned out to be a really wild ride!

A surprise awaited us when we got down to the flight line on the 24th. Could not believe it, our plane to Manus was a PBY-5A! Thank goodness it was a short flight of 1.7 hours with Navy Lt. Smith at the throttle. Straight and level, full bore on the throttle; this excellent plane cruised at 115 knots per hour. It would be blasphemy for us to complain as this plane has saved many Marine pilots, just in our squadron alone!

That same day we boarded R4D #17273, the same type of plane that delivers our mail, Lt. Rosenberg in charge and it was only 3.3 hours to Hollandia. This trip we were lucky and received a short tour of the king's palace. He (MacArthur) was wading ashore in a photo op on his return to the Philippines. We checked into the BOQ (bachelor officer quarters), had a drink and supper. We met the famous boxer Gene Tunney, who was touring the Pacific Theater giving boxing lessons and presenting physical training programs. We enjoyed another RON before returning to Peleliu.

On the 25th and in the same R4D with crew, 3.6 hours later, we landed at Jungle Tower and returned to our tents. The gang greeted us with the bad news; there was still no news on our relief pilots.

Back in the saddle, after returning from Sydney, I learned that Major Bob Tucker had assumed command of VMF-114 after the death of Stout. That same afternoon I had a 2.1 hour CAP, flying wing on Wally Weber, one of my 114 squadron heroes. I was a little concerned but after three or four minutes I was satisfied. It turned out to be a routine CAP.

The 26th and 27th were routine flights with 100-pound bombs on both flights. Evidently the ammo officer felt we were still overloaded with 100-pounders. On the 28th I took off on what was supposed to be a routine CAP, but after about 30 minutes my engine in Corsair #085 started missing and acting up and I returned to the field with an emergency landing. I did not wait to see what was wrong. I was a little agitated.

The night of 28th I had a little trouble sleeping. Early the morning of the 31st in Corsair # 052, about 50 minutes after take off, the same damn situation happened causing another emergency landing. Now the other pilots and I started wondering, was it I? I went to our flight surgeon, Doc Reardon, he checked me out, blood pressure, heart rate and all the other pre-flight medical procedures found me to be fine. This time I went down to the flight check line and found that the engine definitely needed some work. I was relieved, but I wondered about what the other pilots were thinking? That is the way March concluded.

April 1945

From April 1st and 2nd I had one barge sweep and 2.2 hours of engine time on F4U #14261. The 2nd was the day of my last trip to Ulithi; it was in Corsair #14208 for what reason I do not remember, as I have a return flight to Peleliu on R4D #00723 with 3.3 hours logged. I thinks our ops officer, signing my logbook, must have hit the go-go juice!

From April 1st and 2nd I had one barge sweep and 2.2 hours of engine time on F4U #14261. The 2nd was the day of my last trip to Ulithi; it was in Corsair #14208 for what reason I do not remember, as I have a return flight to Peleliu on R4D #00723 with

3.3 hours logged. Me thinks our ops officer, signing my logbook, must have been hitting the go-go juice!

From the 3rd to the 10th we did not fly. One dawn CAP on the 11th, a barge sweep on the 19th. On the 25th a 15 minute CAP, the 26th a gunnery flight, and on April 30th an altitude test in #76579. Tell me

130

what in the hell was going on with these crazy hops, some under AA fire? Obviously someone in Group Headquarters was mentally disturbed. Let us see what the month of *May* brings to la-la-land?

he enlisted in the Marine Reserve and in December was appointed an aviation cadet. He entered flight training in February at Pensacola, Florida and received his wings and commission September 19, 1941.

Lieutenant Stout arrived at Pearl Harbor February 2, 1942 and was assigned to VMF-212. In April his squadron sailed aboard USS Hornet and arrived in New Caledonia, remaining there until the Guadalcanal operation began in August. During the strenuous months of October and November, Stout was in the master of the action. In four fights against tremendous odds, Cowboy Stout shot down six Japanese planes, winning the Navy Cross.

Stout returned to the States and, as a captain, took command of VMF-114 in September 1943 at El Toro, California. When the squadron departed for Hawaii and onto Midway Stout became the only captain in Marine Corps history to command a fighter squadron in combat.

VMF-114 was assigned to MAG-14 at Green Island, and Cowboy led numerous fighter strikes against the heavily-defended bases at Rabaul and Kavieng. The squadron returned to Espiritu Santo in May and reorganized for the upcoming Palau campaign. In September 1944, Major Stout was the first Marine pilot to land at the newly-won strip on Peleliu. It was during this tour that Cowboy led one of the shortest bombing raids in history, when his flight dropped napalm bombs on Japanese positions in the caves at Bloody Nose Ridge -- less than 1,400 yards from the end of the runway.

In November of 1944, Bob Stout learned of his brother's death. Lieutenant Jack Stout was killed in a crash while on a war bond drive out of MCAS Cherry Point, North Carolina.

On March 4, 1945 Major Stout volunteered to lead four Corsair divisions against heavily fortified anti-aircraft positions on Battery Hill in the center of Koror Island. Stout's F4U was hit with explosive shells at extremely low altitude, and the Cowboy's ride was over. He crashed into Koror Harbor and was killed in action.

This plaque is made possible by the surviving pilots of VMF-114.

War record: 6 victories.
Decorations: Navy Cross, DFC, Air Medal with two gold stars, and the Purple Heart.

MAJOR ROBERT F. STOUT

Robert F. Stout was born at Bethany, Missouri on March 24, 1918. His father, Ernie, homesteaded a ranch near Fort Laramie, Wyoming, in the heart of the famous Oregon Trail country along the North Platte River. Young Robert thus grew up on a working ranch and acquired the nickname "Cowboy." He graduated from Ft. Laramie High School in 1936 and entered the University of Wyoming that fall.

In the spring of 1940, Cowboy applied for flight training with the Marine Corps reserve, having completed two years of Basic ROTC.

Major Stout, Cactus Air Force Ace/Guadalcanal
World War II American Fighter Aces Hall of Honor,
Museum of Flight, Seattle, WA

132

Chapter 15   **Back From the Pacific**

May 1945

We had to be on a short rope in May. On the 1st of May, I had an hour dawn CAP. The 4th and 6th saw some test hops. On the 8th, for some unknown godly reason, another one hour napalm strike. El Goofo, ring the bell!

THE BLOODY BATTLE OF PELELIU WAS OVER FOR THE PILOTS OF VMF-114 ON THE MORNING OF THE NINTH OF MAY 1945.

Now we had orders to fly home. We would leave in small groups of five to eight pilots. We all would go to Pearl Harbor; Hawaii first, and then gets a MATS (Military Air Transport Service) flight to Naval Air Station Alameda, California!

The Mott, Act One

Now for the first act of a story involving the "Mott", 1st Lt. Billy Martens, plus his buddy 1st Lt. "Duke" Gilchrist. On 10 May 1945, seven pilots of VMF-114 were gathered beside the runway, waiting to board the long awaited bird for home, a four-engine transport R4D would take us on the first leg of their flight to Hawaii. As we waited suddenly here came "the Mott" dragging his parachute bag and stopping a C-45 that he thought was going to Australia. He grabbed the wing and succeeded in hitchhiking a seat on board. He waved and shouted I'm heading for Sydney! We all thought, well goodbye to the Mott. Thus ended the first act.

My group bid goodbye to eight months of combat, typhoons, 125-degree heat on a two by four mile island of coral, death and destruction. The ugly toll, the sum result was 2,336 USMC KIA and 8450 wounded. On the Japanese side there was 10,695 KIA and 202 captured. All of this happened in eight months.

We climbed aboard the R4D with Lt. White commanding a 2.5 hours Peleliu-Anguar-Ulithi hop, then refueled for another 2.5 hours flight to Guam. At Guam, the BOQ facilities were good, and we were happy!

Early on the morning of the 11th, we met Lt. Pettyjohn for a 6 hours flight to Eniwetok. There it was raining cats and dogs so we stayed right on board with Pettyjohn's crew. Soon we were in the air again for a 2 hours flight on R5D #39159 to Kwajalein where we refueled and grabbed a food bag in preparation for a butt buster flight with the same crew, 9.5 hours to Johnson Island. We all had stretched out on a canvas seat or a blanket on the floor. We were not complaining as it was now dark, and every hour that passed was an hour closer to Hawaii.

We were finally on the last leg of our journey to Hawaii and swaying dancers and palm trees! We landed at Ford Island, the scene of the "day that would live in infamy!" As I was gathering my gear, a head poked thru the doorway and a most familiar voice, dripping in enmity, said, "Hi there! It was one of my dearest friends Phil "Flip" Samson! I had not seen him since our cadet days in Pasco, Washington!

Phil was Major General J.T. "Nuts" Moore's "go-fer" and chief pilot! The General, who was the commander of the Fleet Marine Force Pacific or FMFPac, had learned I was on this flight and his driver and Phil had been dispatched to pick me up and bring me to his headquarters. The two stars waved brightly on his personal car as we drove to his office. I thrilled to see "Flip" and very impressed with General Moore. He was like a "father" to Cowboy Stout, and wanted every detail of what had happened that frightful day on 4 March. He would find time to talk with me every day during the three days I spent with him and Phil. Living in the General's quarters and dining at his mess in the company of two generals, one admiral, six full colonels (eagles on collars) and a couple of lieutenant colonels, plus Phil and I was interesting! General Moore asked me if I was interested in a regular commission and a career in the Corps. I told him I would be completely interested if only I had completed college. With only one year completed, I felt it necessary to graduate from college. Little did I know at the time, both college and a career in the Corps would have been very much possible if I had only known that a program for this was going to initiated by the Corps less than a year after the end of the war. A big example of "if candy and nuts were …!" That was a big "if only" in my future life!

The Mott, Act Two

The original group of 114 pilots, minus the Mott, was gathered at the Ewa Officer's Club waiting to board MATS (Military Air Transport Service) at 2030 hours (8:30 PM) when lo and behold, who would come through the doors but the Mott! He had wound up in the Philippines, not Sydney, given the loadmaster of the "hiball," a special speed flight to Hawaii, a fifth of booze, and talked his way on the plane to catch-up with us. It was short-lived, however, as about the time of his third martini at the bar, a full colonel came into the club and forgot to take off his hat. It was a violation of military custom to fail to remove your cover when inside a building. The penance for doing this in a bar is the requirement to buy the house a drink! The Motts reaction to this oversight, "Hey buster, I'll take a martini!" What that got him was two big military policemen (MPs) putting him in handcuffs and rushing him out the door! Good-bye once more to the Mott. End of act two, and no flight for him to the US of A!

I was lucky to board a large PBY-5A, one with four bunks, for a 12 hours flight to NAS Alameda, California. A Navy commander boarded at the last minute and outranked me out of a bunk for the flight. A few hours later he graciously offered me the bunk for the remainder of the flight. As we approached the coast of California, gradually we could make out the Golden Gate and we knew, home at last was our cry!

Our foursome was hustled into a Navy station wagon for all of the routine business of processing back. The biggest item was clothing, as we had lost our uniforms in one of the typhoons. We were taxied over to a men's clothing store and measured for a complete new set of Marine Corps Greens to be fitted the next morning. What were we going to wear our first night on the wharf in San Francisco? Fortunately we were fitted in a set of khaki shirts and trousers and got permission from the Shore Patrol to wear those with our fight jackets with the DEATH DEALER patch in full view. That should help catch the eyes of a few ladies. In no time we were checked into the Alexander Hamilton Hotel, a small suite for two. We gave little thought as to the whereabouts of the Mott. The first thing Duke Gilchrist did was to remove his "Boondocker" flight boots and toss them out an open window from the sixth floor! This was the first act of a great night.

15 May 1945

The five of us, Duke, Gus, Wink, Bernie and I, located one of the best hot spot nightclubs in the Wharf area. We were quite a crew and obviously returning USMC Pacific vets. We were most graciously accepted, with one exception. The world's tallest midget, Danny, after a few courage building drinks of scotch and water, accepted a bet that I would not ask the vivacious Rita Haworth, who had graced the building with her presence, for a dance! I very gentlemanly approached her table, waited for the appropriate moment, and ask her if she would honor a combat Corsair USMC fighter pilot with a dance. She looked at me, with a look that would stun a Greek god, and said, "BUSTER, YOU DO NOT QUALIFY!" I smiled, departed for a table where "Wee Bonnie Baker", the diminutive, but well-known singer, was occupying. I ask her the same question; she almost jumped into my arms for a couple of dance numbers. I felt like throwing Rita a "finger!" That event made my night.

The very next night, the same crew, Duke Gilchrist, Bernie Barnhart, Gus Sonnenberg, Wink Balzer, and Danny Daniel were "teaching Riley" how to live! Who said Navy Waves were not attractive? We were in the posh Mural Room of the St. Francis Hotel.

Our group had seven days to report into NAS Miramar, California. San Francisco was in the midst of a multinational conference that was forming the United Nations. The headquarters of the conference was at the St. Francis Hotel. Our hotel was located just up the street from the St. Francis. Every time we turned around it seemed a "big wig in a limo" was arriving or holding up traffic. After two days, we decided to go on down to Los Angeles. First we had to spend some time in Lefty O'Doul's bar and grill. This is a must in a visit to San Francisco.

18 May 1945

Space was available to LA on the non-stop overnight SF-LA fancy streamliner. It was to leave SF at 6:30 PM and arrived at 7:30 AM in LA. It was a perfect schedule for our group. We all boarded and paired up in small cabins for trip to LA. This train was for executives and important persons connected with the war effort. The lounge car for beverages and small talk was two connected normal railroad cars. We found it to be very favorable for returning pilots from the Pacific. One of the infamous patrons was the big union executive who had been connected with the coal strike that screwed up barges unloading fuel at Peleliu. We did not try to start a conversation with him. A heavyset Irish US Navy chaplain befriended us quickly. He even made sure our beverage desires were also quickly and efficiently taken care of by the stewards. The conversation with the passengers was interesting and hospitable. We managed to get to our berths by midnight. In the early morning, we gathered up our gear and proceeded to the hotel that the Marines from El Toro patronized while on R&R from duty at MCAS EL Toro. We had no reason not to expect attached rooms that would facilitate afternoon planning sessions. We checked in the hotel and had our first planning meeting early in the afternoon. Our Philippine waiter, who remembered past Marine gatherings, had just delivered our first beer order.

The Mott, Act Three

We were comfortably sipping a beer, discussing various bar/lounges we could remember, when a knock came upon the door. I opened it and behold, standing there was the Mott! None of us could believe our eyes. Somehow, he had mesmerized the Marine colonel and the MP's into allowing him transportation on a

Holiday cruise ship from Hawaii to LA. Not only was he given first class accommodation, he had also met Barbara Stanwyck, the actress who had played the part of the famous rifle shot, Annie Oakley, in a 1935 shoot'em up cowboy movie. In fact, he had even conned her with a diamond, and they were engaged! I do not believe this myself, but so help me it is true! He lingered long enough to drink a couple of beers and said "see yah later!" and departed.

I had called my parents and relatives with an estimated schedule that would send me to Pocatello on leave. We all had no idea for sure what our future orders would be. We had been led to believe that we would have choice assignments.

We spent a couple of days in the LA area, renewing the fine times we had there while stationed at El Toro. I was anxious to get to Miramar to find where my new orders would take me. MCAS Miramar was a beehive of activity. Marine pilots were going in every direction with orders to new stations. Checking in was the usual set of activities, physicals, catching up on money that was due, etc. I finally got my new orders. I was to report on 15 July 1945 to Naval Air Ferry Squadron No. 3 at the U.S. Naval Air Station, San Pedro, California. This included travel and leave time. Also, information was given to me that I was cleared to wear on my uniform the ribbons for combat medals designating awards of the Distinguished Flying Cross, Air Medals with two gold stars, the Purple Heart, Presidential Citation, and various other ribbons. The actual medals would be given to me later. This information made me quite proud. I immediately added these ribbons to my uniform jacket!

I immediately called my parents to try to finalize my travel. My sister Jeanne's Army Air Corps husband was an instructor was stationed near LA. She would be able to meet me and travel by train with her new baby daughter, whom I had never seen. This turned out to be wild. Travel arrangements were completed, and I met her at the large Union Pacific railroad station in LA. Travel was difficult during WWII. We finally arranged upper and lower Pullman facilities for the two day trip to Pocatello, Idaho. My sister Jeanne, her one and one-half year old daughter, absolutely a beautiful, darling child and I made quite a threesome to the other passengers. I was, of course, in my Marine Green uniform with my gold pilot wings and new combat ribbons, and the three of us appeared to the other passengers to be a returning combat pilot - who had never seen his darling daughter, and his loving wife. Jeanne and I were just not able to express the actual situation, to all of the wonderful grandmothers and elder civilians on board the train. We finally decided just to enjoy the charade!

The welcoming party at the railroad depot in Pocatello, Idaho was anxiously awaiting the arrival of the train. I had been away for almost two years, and my young sister had changed into an attractive young lady. In addition to hugs and kisses from all, I who had never owned an automobile was anxiously awaiting the sight of the car my dad had picked for me.

26 May 1945

As we departed the station, I saw a big red Studebaker President. The smile on my dad's face made me realize, there was my car. Indeed it was. I could hardly wait to get behind the wheel! The car was in mint condition. He had accomplished a fine job.

My parents lived in two-bedroom apartment on the second floor. It proved to be a little crowded, but who cared. I was home safe and sound. Something hit me the next morning as I sat drinking a cup of coffee. I thought of the feelings my parents must have had, every time the phone rang, or every time the knock on the door sounded. They had received one telegram from the government stating that shrapnel had wounded me in the shoulder. No matter what I had written to them about my wound, they could not understand I was ok until they saw me in person. It had to be tough on them.

My father, a railroad dispatcher and avid member of the Elks Club of Pocatello, beamed as he wore my flight jacket during our evening journeys to the club. I think he slept in that jacket during my visit! I was thrilled that he was so proud of his fighter pilot son.

The evening I arrived, we unpacked my parachute bag, which now held the assorted items I wanted them to see. Japanese flying boots, several "gimmick" items from Seabees trades, pictures of Japanese soldiers, and precious to me, there was also three bottles of good Scotch whiskey. These I had carefully packed and carried all the way home to drink when Dad and I went fishing. They were left from my roommate's items after he was killed in the water-landing incident. My trunk would arrive later as it was being shipped home. It contained the heavy winter sheepskin flight apparel that was for some reason shipped to Peleliu. If we had been flying B-24 bombers we might have needed that gear!

Two weeks flew by and I enjoyed every minute with my family. I did, however, want to return to the campus at the University of Wyoming to see some friends who had not been called into service. Also, I had promised Ernie and Maude Stout that I would spend time with them, if, and when I returned to the USA. I had written to them after Cowboy showed me the telegram saying his younger brother, Jack, had been killed in a Corsair crash in the states in November '44. Of course I wrote after Cowboy was KIA, somehow expressing my thoughts. No expression of my sympathy could begin effectively to explain what he meant to his men, the pilots and crews of VMF-114.

I loaded up my red Studebaker President, kissed my mom, dad and sister, and promised that I would spend time with them before returning to California. It was a day's drive to Laramie, Wyoming. Boy, did I enjoy driving that car on my first trip! All went well, and I checked into my friends' WYO Motel, and headed for the Student Union to find old friends. Fighter pilot pride, gosh, it was tough to be humble! Very few of my 'ole girl friends were around. They had not waited for me – really?

For two days, I renewed old friendships at the Plaza Bar. Telling my bartending friend of the beer bet with Cowboy that was never to be! I was ready to be on my way! Driving over the summit, east of Laramie, on a May Day, I drove in snow so heavy the wipers would hardly sweep it off!

In Cheyenne I made a stop to say hello to Colonel Pat Murray, and then on to Torrington, and then to Fort Laramie to find the Stout's Ranch. I phoned to tell them I had arrived, got directions to the ranch, and as I was arriving, I stopped to calm my emotions.

The Stouts greeted me as if I had been born on their ranch. It had to be one of my toughest most emotional few minutes of my life. Can one imagine how tough it would be to give your country two of your three sons, killed serving our country? They had great memories of the times they spent with Cowboy after Guadalcanal. Also of the time they had been spent together, along with members of VMF-114 at El Toro, proudly as Cowboy took over the squadron. It was the first time in Marine Corps history that a captain had served as a squadron commander. Jack Conger had become almost a son to Ernie and Maude. We spent hours discussing everything I had enjoyed as a member of 114. I had brought all my photos of Cowboy with me, and we talked in detail about every second of the tragedy that took his life. It was indeed a return of every emotion I had felt during that horrible sequence.

Ernie Stout was a big and strong man who had endured the tough weather that a Wyoming cowboy must endure, not only during the homesteading era, but also the day to day managing of the good and bad times of Wyoming ranch life. He had a great sense of humor and enjoyed going to his favorite Fort Laramie bar for his favorite bottle of beer. We had a fine time sneaking away for men's discussions of life and times. I think Maude would have adopted me, even though I could barely ride a horse. The toughest moment in saying good-bye to Ernie and Maude after three days was when Ernie asked me if I would ever be interested in getting into the ranching business after the War. I was honored and amazed that he had asked me; and it hurt when I had to say no. Fortunately, for several years we were able to see each other when they visited Laramie to see relatives or for an athletic event. They were a wonderful example of a Wyoming ranching family!

I returned to Pocatello having fulfilled my desire to see if Wyoming had changed, after all I had seen and done in the two plus years away. It had not, and I was happy. Driving back to

Idaho, I had a lot to think about. My desire was still to return to Laramie and pursue a medical degree. Would it change? Maybe. The joy of flying was strong.

Arriving back in Pocatello was a nice Father's Day gift for dad. Now was the time to enjoy the company of my parents and my two sisters. Jeanne would be with us for another two days so I could get used to being with the little one, Michelle. She had become comfortable with the family and even let me hold her now. In the LA train depot, my sister left me holding her so she could go to the bathroom. It wasn't two minutes before she let out a howl heard all over the depot. Everyone looked at me as if I had broken a bone in her little body. Only her momma's return ended the panic.

My father was working the day shift at the railroad, so my time during the day was mostly with my mother. She had a very good understanding of what it was like to have her 22 year old son in the household so much during the day. She had a lot of questions to ask me about my life. I think both mom and dad were wondering if the serious bug with a girl had bitten me. I guess I was doing a fair job of convincing them, in spite of my dating a young friend of my younger sister.

The 4th of July came, and we had a great time with the celebration in Pocatello. They had a big fireworks display. It reminded me of bombing the airstrip at Peleliu with bursting flak. I guess I must have looked concerned as they ask me a lot of questions at that time. I did have time to play some golf with my younger sister. It helped pass the time. Also, Dad was an avid fly fisherman. We had spent a lot of time with him trying to teach me the art of setting the hook, and how to catch one rainbow, let alone the two he could land with one cast. I was a real rookie! We had a magnificent three-day trip to his "Shangri-La" in Yellowstone National Park! Scotch too!

My parents had made a lot of friends living in Idaho, and they were all asking us to dinner, and asking me over and over, "What was it like at Peleliu?" It was hard not to tell them what a "hell on earth" it was.

On the ninth of July, I had to prepare to leave on the tenth. I know my parents were still concerned as they had seen the Corsairs at El Toro and realized I would still be flying a lot, but not in combat. I told them as best I could what a choice assignment Navy VRF-3 was going to be. Flying all over the USA and receiving travel pay too. Once I became a lead pilot (qualifying to lead others on a flight) it would be choice! This was the "scuttle-butt" at least.

10 July 1945

Departing for a two plus day drive to Terminal Island, San Pedro, California was exciting to me, but not for my parents. The pulled up the strong faces, kissed me and said, "Good luck and do not lose your air speed!" This was my favorite way to say "goodbye." San Pedro was just south of Long Beach, California and was dropped in among a lot of oil wells. There, I found it to be really interesting driving over the two wheel casing bridge fastened by cables from abutment to abutment! It was not very safe unless you had a designated driver was at the wheel. "Faint Heart, Never Won Fair Lady!" We learned to manage it!

Now it was time to concentrate on life away from combat and all that Peleliu had presented to us.

Chapter 16   Life At Navy VRF-3

11 July 1945

Leaving Pocatello was a little tough. Driving down to Salt Lake City, I decided to take it easy and enjoy the three or four more days of leave time I had before check in at Terminal Island. I decided to spend the night in Las Vegas. A day was enough after spending most of it in and out of the different gambling parlors. I guess being alone in Vegas is not so great anymore. I arrived in the LA area on the 13th and took my time getting into San Pedro.

First stop was to report in at the check in office where I checked in with the Officer of the Day people who made certain they had my orders correct. Next stop was the paymaster to close out my travel pay and to obtain additional gasoline chits as gasoline was still rationed. Then I went over to the BOQ (bachelor officers quarters) where I received a big surprise. I was given the keys to the best quarters I had seen in some time. Each officer shared a two-bedroom suite, with shared bath and shower. Each room had a fine easy chair, a fine desk with chair, and there was a big window overlooking the parking spot reserved for your car close to the doorway. Our mess hall was just a few yards away under a covered walkway. Meals were on a chit system and drinks were less than a quarter. The most expensive drink on the menu was a French '75 at 35 cents, and beer was very cheap. Had I gone to heaven?

It was customary to make a courtesy call on the commanding officer's desk. I learned that a few other VMF-114 pilots had also arrived for duty at VRF-3. Virgets, Mosca, and Reed to name some of them. The next morning, seven of us chose to make the call. After reporting in, the executive officer, a man in his early forty's, explained the commander's absence. The first thing he said to us was, "Gentlemen, I'm afraid I have bad news for you!" Damn, I thought we must have been reassigned to an operating squadron, probably on a carrier. But his next words were, "You are the first combat pilots that have been assigned here. You probably will be

144

here for the duration!" Man, what a relief! I could have jumped over his desk and kissed him.

VRF-3 was one of Navy's three Ferry squadrons, whose job it was to reposition all types of Navy-Marine aircraft to operational Air Stations for use in training and the war effort. Sometimes a group of pilots flew on MATS to pick up planes to move to other stations. The return to home base could be with another plane we picked up, either on MATS or commercial air. We never knew what type of plane we would be assigned to fly from Point A to Point B.

The next day the operations officer gave us a briefing on what we could expect of our duty schedule moving forward. We learned that we would draw per diem pay (or travel pay) for any time away from Terminal Island. We were informed that a typical month would involve two weeks of flights where we would not have to RON elsewhere and the remaining two weeks would be flying from A to B to C etc., any place in the USA and Canada. That certainly did not make us mad. This duty would be super! Well deserved and appreciated by all!

On my first duty day, the 18th July, I would have 0.6 hours instrument check ride with Navy LT Dunqan in the front seat of an SNJ, #27498, and another 2.0 hours with unusual positions, (under the hood) to insure I was current with instrument flying. Both checks went smoothly!

On 19 July, Virgets and I enjoyed two different flights touring the local countryside in an SNJ, #90734, for over an hour each enjoying the mountains and scenery of Southern California. Tough duty, someone has to do it!

On the 20th another 1.6 and 2.1 hours orientation flights in an F6F-5, #93821, plus another check ride in an SNJ, #90738, with Navy Lt. Silva.

We then had four days off to get re-acquainted with the area. On the 24th I flew a TBM, #85661, which was a Torpedo Bomber for

2 hour introduction flight. This plane is a great ferry plane as it has a big tunnel opened by a door on the bottom right side of the aircraft. The big easy chair is sitting high on the front end. No way for a collision on this one and there is a clear, easy sight line for carrier landings. This was another chance to view the amazing landscape of Southern California. On the 26th, I had almost three hours to familiarize myself to the area from San Diego up to Los Angeles and to locate the various airports for future reference.

The 29th was the beginning of my ferrying jobs. I and 17 other pilots climbed aboard an R4D-1, #03138, for a short flight to North Island to pick up and ferry a TBM3E, #91177, to 29 Palms, California. Marines based there were experiencing the heat of the desert. WOW! It is well above 100 degrees in the summer. I was very happy to have LT's Wicht and White waiting to escort myself and four other pilots back to San Pedro. The next morning on the 30th of July I flew as co-pilot with Navy LT Erikson for 1.8 hours familiarization in flying the JRB. It is always great to learn another airplane. I'm looking forward to another month with VRF-3.

August 1945

I passed 2 August, flying a JRB, #44561, with Navy LT Sorenson and myself as co-pilot on a short flight to Burbank, California's Lockheed Aircraft Headquarters. We were there to pick up a PB-2, #37426, a twin engine, low slung bomber, for a 3 hour flight to Red Bluff, California with Navy LT Jones in the left seat, and myself in the right seat. This was my first opportunity to co-pilot a large twin-engine plane. While at Lockheed we took lunch at their plant's restaurant. During lunch the famous Major Richard Bong, now a test pilot for the new P-80 jet named "Shooting Star", entered the room and sat at a table near to us. I had seen Bong and his P-38 fighter pilots on a stop off the New Guinea Coast on our way to Peleliu. We chatted for a minute or two and then we headed out to our plane. Actually this was my "learn on the job" introduction to the procedures involved in performing co-pilot duties. I knew I had to do it but I was never comfortable not having control of the stick. Jones was patient, but as I learned on our first landing, a bit stubborn! I spent most of the time to Red Bluff,

California memorizing pre-flight procedures, takeoff and landing speeds, flaps and power settings.

As we approached the airport location, I noticed a tabletop type of runway in that prior to the beginning of the runway there was a high bank that extended for several feet, the runway and then there was a steep drop of off several feet at the other end of the runway. It was a short runway and this indicated that we take absolute notice of the speed of our rollout at the end of the landing. As we approached the fence at the end of the runway I knew we were hot and I was pressing my feet on the brake pedals already. I informed Jones of my speed concern, his answer was, "Hell, this truck will stop on a dime and won't nose over!" As we approached the end of the runway, we both were burning rubber with the pressure we both had applied on the brakes. Sliding to a stop we were so close to the end of the runway that the front view out of the windscreen was blue sky. We had to call a tow truck to turn us around. Now you know why flying co-pilot was never my first choice! All's well, that ends well!

We refueled and took off for the next flight, 2.6 hours to Yakima, Washington. RON was in Yakima. No BOQ was available so we each got a motel room. We both were ready for a good nights sleep as the beautiful flight in the morning was up Puget Sound into the wonderland at Whidbey Island Naval Air Station, Washington.

What a beautiful morning greeted us the morning of the 3rd of August. We took off, set the autopilot switches, and proceeded to enjoy the super scenery full of rivers, lakes and tall forests, on a trip that would have been expensive to the usual tourist. Whidbey Island was surrounded by gorgeous views. Unfortunately, I was not going to be able to enjoy the delights of the Island on this trip. In later years my wife, Connie, and I spent four days and nights at the BOQ facility enjoying the beauty I had missed on my ferry trip. All too soon I was hustled off to a little flying boat bouncing in the water that was moored to a landing. It was a JRF-2, #32959, pilot unknown, and plane's nickname was Widgeon! The take off was a thrill a second. Finally we were airborne and I noticed that the cabin had leaked like a sieve during takeoff! Fortunately, I was seated in the right seat and dry. After a short one half hour flight we were landing on the river at NAS Sand Point, just northeast of Seattle, Washington. For the first time I used my orders, and my priority card, for a Pacific Coast Airline flight back to Long Beach and a car to Terminal Island. I returned to the BOQ on the 5th of August. I picked up the newspaper on the 7th and read of the tragic death of Major Richard Bong, the famous Army Air Corps Jet Test Pilot, at Lockheed Headquarters, Burbank, who had been killed when his "Shooting Star" had an engine failure right after takeoff on the 6th. This was just three days after we had met him in Burbank, on our trip to Whidbey Island NAS.

Three days off and on the 7th of August I was once again on a R4D-1, #03138 (I'm well acquainted now with this plane), with Navy pilots LT's Burton and Brand, along with 15 other parachute bagged pilots for a 1.5 hours flight to Brown Field, south of San Diego. We were flying to pick up a TBM-3E, #85808, Torpedo Bomber for a 1.4 hours flight to Ventura, California. Awaiting us there were my good friends, LT's Burton and Brand. By now I was calling them the "gold dust twins." 12 of the other pilots and I (I do not know where the other four went) then returned to Terminal Island.

On the 8th I played "Ring around the Rosie!" with five flights. First on a JRB, #44561, with Navy LT Bergy, myself and five other pilots, on a .5-hour flight from to Van Nuys, California. Then I boarded a PV-2, #37226, Lockheed Twin engine with Navy LT Witters as pilot and myself as co-pilot for a .6-hour flight back to MCAS El Toro, California. Thirty minutes later, LT Bergy piloted in a JRB, #44561, with myself and five other pilots, we flew from El Toro to Van Nuys in .8 hours. A cold drink later we were off again with LT Witters piloting and myself as co-pilot in a PV-2, #37192, from Van Nuys back to MCAS El Toro. The final flight of the day was in a JRB, #44561, with good 'ole LT Bergy as pilot and myself, plus 5 others departing from El Toro to San Pedro in .6 hours. This was an unusual goofy day at VRF-3! I became dizzy reading it in my logbook!

Two necessary days off later on August 10th the rumors were hot and heavy about the surrender of the Japanese! I checked in that morning at flight headquarters and learned I was to fly co-pilot on a PBY5A, the big amphibious flying boat that I had observed doing such fabulous rescue jobs in the Southwest Pacific Theater. It was the first time I had flown a plane with a flight engineer operating the power. Three hours of flight time was planned to NAS Alameda. The two pilots were seated next to each other and the flight engineer was above, directly in between the pilots, and handling the power throttles attached to the ceiling in front of him. As I have mentioned, this was unusual to me! The nose gunner was directly in front of the two pilots below.

I had a wonderful view of the scenic Pacific's coastline, mountains to east, and a panorama of the densely populated country below. As we descended into the NAS Alameda's airfield I could see all the ships, every different type imaginable, plus all of the bridges and automobile traffic hustling to and from San Francisco! This is the plane that has a constant speed no matter what action is dictated. It was a great one-time experience!

I reported to the operations officer and signed the paperwork to an F6F-3, #41180, to be flown to Hollister, California. For some unknown reason, I RON'd in Hollister, and early the next morning picked up a plane, but I have no memory of the Bureau number, for the trip back to San Pedro.

Now the day San Francisco erupted! August 14th would be similar to the shock we received from December 7th, 1941, the president called that day a day that would "live in infamy", and it was a day that would remain in our memories forever. So would this day, August 14, 1945.

I took on in an R4D-1, #12403, with my friends Navy LT's Bergy and Carter in command for a flight lasting .6 hours that would transport 18 pilots and me to Lockheed's company headquarters in Burbank, California. There, Navy LT Blessing and myself as co-pilot would fly 1.6 hours to Madera, California. From there we boarded a PV-2, #37407, for the 1 hour back to NAS Alameda.

149

In spite of all the rumors that were flying the announcement of Japan's surrender had not yet hit the wires.

Landing at NAS Alameda, I started looking for an F6F-5, #42274, which was to be fueled, and then dispatched. I had already filed my flight plan for Los Alamitos, California. By now I was concerned about VRF-3's rule requiring that we land at our destination prior to sunset. This ETA (estimated time of arrival) before sunset rule was, in my opinion a stupid rule. About this time, I looked over in the direction towards San Francisco and suddenly all sorts of fireworks exploded, smoke filled the air, and planes started flying under the bridges. Obviously the Japanese surrender had been announced, and as I was running late, it was just as obvious that my plans for a hot date that night in Redondo Beach, California were about to become dubious at best!

I called the tower for takeoff approval, initiated my flight plan, and asked for permission for immediate takeoff. The tower kept calling for F6F, #274, "Where are you?" By that time, I had taxied into place and was ready to roar down the runway, everything was in a state of confusion. I started to roll and my F6F was functioning great. I had no trouble taking off and getting to 2,000 ft. altitude by the end of the runway! I made a climbing turn to the left; the throttle was "bent over the firewall!" at full horsepower! I rapidly was at a speed of about 350 knots! Normally it was about a two hour flight to Terminal Island, San Pedro, California.

I did not know the exact time of sunset in California, but I did know I did not have time to arrive at NAS Los Alamitos, get a ride to Terminal Island, and then make it to Redondo Beach at a decent time. Plan B was being formulated in my mind!

In one hour after taking off I was estimating that I would be close to the required ETA to land at Terminal Island. I decided I had about maybe 20 minutes leeway before they would be closing the field. Normally, you call San Pedro radio when you are about ten minute from touchdown. I began requesting that when I was for sure about twenty minutes away! The tower must have been thinking I was goofy!

Finally, dusk was approaching, and sure enough "F6F 274, the field is closed. Vector to NAS Los Alamitos." That did it; I knew my goose was cooked, UNLESS I DECLARED AN EMERGENCY, ROUGH ENGINE ACTING UP, TURN ON THE RUNWAY LIGHTS! Odds were they would "Roger!" that, which they did, and I greased F6F-5 onto the runway, knowing that I would immediately be told, "F6F, on shut down immediately report to the Officer of the Day's Office!" They did, and I agreed. I walked into his office, helmet and goggles in hand, saluted and who was seated at the desk but Commander Buddy Rogers, a well-known movie and radio star! He stared at me, and smiling asks, "Son, what the hell was going on up there?" I reviewed the happenings of the afternoon to him, making certain I emphasized the happenings at Alameda and mentioned my "hot-date" waiting for me up the beach at Redondo!" Being a down to earth and understanding Naval Officer, he wished me well with "get the hell moving, but don't speed as there are a jillion cops on duty!" I hurried over to my BOQ room, showered, shaved, dressed, and carefully motored up to Redondo Beach, which was as I stated one helluva good party!

I'm going to digress and tell a story from 1985. Several years ago my dear friend, almost adopted son, Gary Cowan, had several big connections in the golfing world. As such he was invited to participate in the King of Morocco's pro-am golf tournament in Rabat, Morocco. 25 well-known professional golfers and 75 amateurs would compete. He included me and three friends on the guest list for what was the trip of a lifetime for an 8 handicap golfer such as me. My dear Marine buddy, Phil Samson, and one other friend shared this trip of a lifetime. We spent several days as a guest of the King, which I can recommend highly as the only way to travel! About three years later, one of the many well-healed amateurs from Palm Springs that we had met invited the amateurs to his posh golf club in Palm Springs for a "memory lane" three-day golf and banquet nights' party. One evening, after a great meal and enough scotch and water cocktails, I happened to notice Mr. Buddy Rogers and the well known host from the television show Password, Allen Ludden, were enjoying a drink at the bar. Remembering what had happened the night we learned of the

Japanese surrender, I bet my friends $10.00 each that I would go up and ask Commander Rogers if he remembered that night. They accepted, and I asked Buddy the question. He immediately said, "Hell yes, I sure do. Why do you ask?" "Do you also remember the young Marine Corps pilot who reported to you that night?" I replied. Rogers laughed and said "Did you make the party on time?" He then came over to our table and ordered a round of drinks for us. Mary Pickford, America's sweetheart, his famous deceased wife, would have been proud of him! I pocketed my $30!

18 August 1945

LT Nick Virgets, I and 16 other VRF-3 pilots boarded R4D-1, #03138. This would be our third flight on this bird, with Navy LT's Miller and Row piloting and co-piloting, for a 2.5 flight from San Pedro to NAS Alameda. The same thirteen pilots and parachutes after another flight that day of 3.7 hours would RON in Yakima, Washington. The morning of the 19th this same group took a short flight of .7 hours to NAS Pasco, Washington. There we cut loose eight pilots and continued with a 1.6 hours flight on to NAS Astoria, Oregon. This was on the Pacific coast and was a nice place to be based.

Nick and I had supper and libations at the BOQ in Astoria and spent the evening making plans for the next eleven days. We were going to be on the road for a never to be forgotten coast-to-coast airplane ferry trip. Where would we store enough clothing in the F6F-3s we were scheduled to fly? Luckily, we had the time to solve that problem.

First thing the morning of 20 August we checked out two F6F-3's, both painted bright yellow. They had been used as tow-target planes for gunnery runs. Right away we started thinking about some interesting things we could do with these two action "producers!" We filed our flight plan, got the weather reports for my favorite airport, Red Bluff, California and San Pedro. In August in this part of USA generally has great weather. After 1.4 hours to Red Bluff and then 1 hour to Terminal Island, we still had plenty of daylight to fix the space for clothing on the F6Fs. On the

21st, we flew a short 2 hours to Coolidge, Arizona. This was an Army Air Corps field with a number of Navy enlisted mechanics and fuel squads to handle itinerate Navy planes. It was also the place previously mentioned as a fine place to RON. We could get steak & eggs for 50 cents. There were also some Austrian prisoners of war here who were interesting fellows to talk to for sure.

The 22nd of August was a special day for cowboy clothing stores in EL Paso, Texas. I phoned my Aunt Arlene and told her about when she could see two yellow fighter aircraft at legal low altitude buzzing her area of the hills west of El Paso. After using a little more than normal throttle settings, we had more than enough time to find housing, and plan for her to pick us up for some sight seeing and shopping for cowboy gear for Nick. We also made a visit to a famous restaurant she had recommended for a meal, the Florida Bar and Grill, over the border in Juarez, Mexico. We had a great visit with my aunt. Nick purchased a good-looking set of cowboy boots, cowboy shirt, belt, and Levis pants. He was ready to come out of chute number #2 on the bucking bull, WHIZZER! All in all, it was a fun packed ferry stop. The "FCLO's" (Navy flight control liaison officers) at each ferry stop were in for a laugh!

On 23 August we had an early breakfast, filed flight plans, and received weather reports for El Paso to Ft. Worth (Virget's home town). Two "rhinestone" cowboys, flying yellow F6F-3's! After 2.6 hours flying time we taxied into the RON spot designated for visiting "cowboy's", folded the wings to please all the onlookers, and hopped out of our planes to visit with Nick's parents. We were certain the visitors in the area were wondering what the heck was going on. We told them we were on our way for a special air show! No one, not even the FCLOs had a question.

It was our eighth day on the coast-coast flight, another short day of flying, and we were having a ball. Peleliu was not on our mind, but it certainly was not forgotten. We were just making up for lost time. For some reason, our time in Ft. Worth was short, and we said good-bye to Virget's family and filed for a 1 hour flight to Shreveport, Louisiana. We had taken off a little late; it was a cloudy day, and the sun was just starting to set. Nick landed first, and I was just turning off my downwind leg and approaching the runway when suddenly a small yellow aircraft turned in front of me, cutting me off of my approach. Had I been in a Corsair instead of the F6F I would have undoubtedly crashed. Man it was close as I hit full throttle, pulled back on the control stick and waited to hear a crash. Somehow I missed the Cub aircraft and also the field tower as I gained altitude and speed to prevent stalling out. Now that it was over I was really mad at the pilot of the Cub. After landing and getting out of the cockpit, I noticed the small aircraft close to me. I signaled him to stop so I could pull him out of the plane and tell him what I thought. It was a 16 year old kid who was a helluva lot more scared and upset then me. I finally calmed down and talked to him. Again, all's well that end's well!

We checked into the Washington-Youree Hotel. I remember it well, as later in the next month, my dad who always sent my cashed checks to me, had written on the backs of two $20.00 cancelled checks, "Hmm" he wrote, "musta' been a helluva good night"! Little did he know!

On the 24th we took off from Shreveport; the engine was barely warm after one hour, and we were slowing down on our purposely-long approach to Jackson, Mississippi. The famous Deep
South city, near to the "Yazoo River!" The city motto is "the city with a soul." One thing about this trip, we really got to observe the beauty and history of America. We RON'd here and had a beautiful hotel and southern dinner. I have always had a feeling for the Deep South.

On the 25th, we are getting close to our final destination. 2.4 hours away over the tree laden, curling rivers — the countryside is so beautiful! Two hours later we are approaching the huge military bastion of NAS Norfolk, Virginia. This complete trip has given me a wonderful appreciation of what we have been fighting for the past few years.

The airport is on the ocean, and huge ships dot the view. A very busy place and we have to circle and clear for landing. We grease both yellow birds onto the runway. We changed our mind about the attire we had on for this destination because of the overwhelming amount of brass (high ranking officers) here. The "three stars" probably would not approve of any "cowboy" attire! We chickened out!

We checked into a beautiful BOQ. Unfortunately, the available rooms for lower ranking officers were full. Wearing our flight suits, and looking a little exhausted, the room clerk took pity on us, checked the availability of the admiral rank rooms, and issued us keys to a two bedroom suite that was to die for! It was hard to believe. We showered, shaved, put on our best uniforms, and took the elevator to a gorgeous dinner hall. Boy, how about living well above our rank! We found out they had a supply of single malt scotch that we could not dent, a scarcity on the west coast, but we tried. The next morning, I did not have a "hangover", but I was above average thirsty!

All of our champagne living disappeared as we awakened the morning of 26 August. The real world was back upon us. When we checked with flight check in, we learned we both had "Turkeys" (military nicknames for TBM-3's) to transport clear to San Diego. Good and bad.

Slower speed, but great for storing all our gear! Mine was #53906. It was brand new and in shining condition. Nick had the same luck with his assignment. After I finished my pre-fight and go around check, I climbed into the high-perched cockpit. As I was finishing my takeoff checklist, I noticed the brand new sparkle of the "easy-chair in the cockpit", I looked for the canteen bottle that was supposed to be stored next to my arm and it was missing from its storage place. I immediately hollered to the mechanic and asked where the missing flask was! He answered, "What's the matter, SIR, are you thirsty?" I answered in the affirmative, and he replied, "C'mon with me!" I climbed down, not being in any hurry, and accompanied him over to a large tank filled with ice. Inside I discovered bottles of Pittsburg Duquesne beer. I took one and downed the welcoming liquid, probably a little too fast, and climbed back up into the cockpit. My partner Virgets satisfied his thirst also. I thanked the young mechanic and prepared for take off. We finished the necessary flight procedures, cleared for take off and were on our way for the three hour flight to Atlanta.

We got to cruising altitude, got into a not too uncomfortable side-by-side position, and started to cruise. I had noticed a manual in the pocket on the side of my seat on the automatic pilot system, reachable in cockpit. I thought to myself, "Well, I might as well be comfortable on this three hour flight." I flipped the switch to turn the system on, looked up at my gyrocompass, and decided to set it on the proper heading to Atlanta. I flipped the button to cage the gyro, and HOLY MACKEREL, IMMEDIATELY THE PLANE FLIPPED OVER ON ITS BACK! I broke all records stabilizing the plane, turned the system off and decided I had better open the manual and read some of it. Yes, I had committed a cardinal sin! I read in huge red letters, DO NOT ENGAGE YOUR GYRO BEFORE SETTING THE AUTO PILOT! In addition, it turns out the beer was lousy, and it had made me sick. When we got to Atlanta, it was a Sunday afternoon, and there was a large crowd watching our arrival from an observation area on the roof. When I taxied into position and got out on the wing of the plane, I started to belch and made a mess on the wing. Nice going JARHEAD!

I quickly went over to the first aid for an Alka-Seltzer and started to feel better. Virgets gave me the business, but I was ok. We refueled, checked our flight plan and weather, then proceeded on for a 3 hour flight to Shreveport where we spent another quiet night at the Washington-Youree hotel.

On the 27th of August we had an easy 1.2 hour flight to Ft. Worth, said a quick hello and good-by to the Virgets, then departed on a 3 hour hustle to El Paso, then a 1.8 hour hop to Coolidge, Arizona. Dang, the FCLO wanted us to hurry on to San Diego. We could not figure why his hurry. Maybe he heard about our cowboy escapade! 2 hours later we finished our round-trip, coast to coast adventure of seventeen flight hours, nine days, and about 3200 miles. Interesting, love the ferry squadron!!!

Almost home in a R4D- 3, #03138. We know this bird; Navy LT's Bergy and Sorenson, who we know as well, are in the cockpit. In 45 minutes, we are home to Terminal Island where we enjoy two days in August off before starting another cross-country adventure on the last day of August!

I had not realized that the long trip had played heavily on me, as I slept about ten hours on the night of the 27th of August. Feeling great and well rested and having checked the flight assignments the night before, I joined Navy LT's Carter and Deatheridge plus eight other pilots with parachute bags and, for me, a well-packed assortment of clothing to be packed in a F6F-5N (night fighter version). My orders were to pickup the F6F-5N, #71027, in NAS Santa Barbara on the morning of the 30th, take it back to San Pedro, check the loading of the plane, and then start on another ferry flight that would end in Norfolk, Virginia. On the 31st of August, the last day of the month, I took off for a 2 hours journey to Coolidge, Arizona.

Evidently the FCLO at Terminal Island wanted me to be well fed and happy, starting the long trip after a good night at the Navy ferry stop in Coolidge. He must have enjoyed steak & eggs there once, along with the magnificent pastries the Austrian POWs prepared there.

September 1945

On the 1st September, a F6F-5N, #71027, would be my transportation on a 1.7 hour flight over the desert to El Paso, Texas. This would be a three-day, five stop quick flight, flying alone to Norfolk. Sometimes you get a little bored. Having flown this path, over nothing but water tanks and windmills, feeding the range cattle on the way, one needs a little excitement. The answer to this was to "press the pedal to the metal" and put the plane down almost on the ground (in Marine lingo this is called "flat-heading!"). The thing you had to look for was windmills and electrical poles and wires; also ranchers and retired fighter pilots!

One of the things I remembered was that when we first got back to the states, no matter where we flew, over land, water, lakes, or ponds, we still wore our May-West life preserver float vests. We were still in the habit of thinking, "safer over water then land facing Jap ack-ack fire!"

My second flight on the 1st was the flight from El Paso to Ft. Worth. Since the end of WWII, the Navy was repositioning a lot of planes. I fear they were also saving money as peacetime brings that about. Once again I refueled in Ft. Worth, went thru the necessary procedures with the flight and weather offices, and had a short one hour flight to Shreveport, Louisiana. Upon approaching the field, I recalled the near miss I had there on my first trip into that field. My mental image of being inverted over the turn, the river below and barely missing the tower! This time it was routine. I was welcomed back for another fun evening at the Washington-Youree Hotel. Only one twenty-dollar check was cashed there this time! I did have a day off while in Shreveport. My little black book served me well as I called the young lady who invited me on a picnic during the last trip to town was successful this time.

The morning of the 3rd, the weather report showed a front moving into the area in late afternoon, so I filed a for an early flight plan and took off in time to beat it to Atlanta three hours later where I refueled and was able to make it again, another three hours to NAS Norfolk by late afternoon. My logbook is vacant until the 12th of September. So was my little black book, so I must have returned to Terminal Island by commercial air. I do remember my overnight at the BOQ in Norfolk was not in the admiral's quarters this time!

By this time in September, the conversion to peacetime was in my mind. In spite of enjoying every moment in VRF-3, my future was going to be elsewhere. I loved serving in the USMCR, but realized my duty was going to be returning to the University of Wyoming.

There was still time to enjoy my current assignment. A R4D-1, #12403, was still doing "taxi-service" from base to base in Southern California. Navy LT's Carter and Deatheridge were doing the taxi driving, loading up Lt. Daniel and eighteen other

158

pilots and depositing them elsewhere over Southern California. This time it was a mere thirty minutes from San Pedro to Santa Ana for myself and three others, to ferry four TD2C-1's to the big asphalt circular mat at NAS North Island near San Diego. The Navy had not yet marked off regular runways.

This particular job was what the four of us had been waiting to do! These were little target drone airplanes, built for artillery anti-aircraft practice by the Marines and other services. They were radio controlled, but had a very small cockpit and a three wheeled tricycle landing gear, which when used with pushing the control stick forward in cockpit, you could turn this into a racing vehicle up to fifty plus mph. The four of us had discussed and planned this operation. Ground control men with their red batons were to directing us to parking spots as we were taxing two by two. The first two planes started their race gaining speed, the handlers waving frantically realized what we were doing and then picked up the game. They were enjoying it as we were speeding towards the parking spots. Before it was too dangerous, we slowed down and the fun came to a close. They were anxious to see the little planes up close. Luckily they went along with our fun.

Our R4D with LT's Carter and Deatheridge waited for us to board, minus one pilot for the short ride back to San Pedro. Things were slowing down as three days off was on the board. On the 15th of September I was in a R4D-1, #12403, again with Navy LT's Brand and Burton, the "Gold Dust Twins," in the cockpit for a 2.4 hour ride to NAS Alameda where I was to ferry F6F-5, #93373, back to San Pedro. This was a 1.6 hours fast shot to Terminal Island.

The 17th of September it was a F6F-5, #94271, from San Pedro to North Island in .8 hour. This time, again the same, R4D-1 and same twosome, Navy LT's Deatheridge and Carter and myself and 13 other pilots flying to San Pedro. I must admit it seemed strange.

The 18th VRF-3 is rearranging planes all over the West Coast. I doubt if they will bring planes to the coastal area to store. I'm getting to know Navy LT's Carter and Deatheridge well, using them every day as taxi drivers for me. One hour to Van Nuys,

California to pick up and take an F6F-5P down to San Diego, North Island. I must have hitchhiked a ride back to San Pedro.

Two days off to keep the Studebaker President warmed up! On the days off activity in the beach towns was very pleasant. There was a lot to do and see.

On the 21st, I was on a R4D-1, #03138, with Navy LT's Cox and Scully, myself and 17 pilots for .5 hours to Van Nuys. I do not know where the other 17 pilots went but I flew a F6F-5P from Van Nuys to San Diego, North Island. I then had a TBM-1C to fly 0.8 hours back up the coast to San Pedro. It really wasn't as boring as it may seem. I never tired of flying along the beaches.

I met Captain Wally Weber in the O-Club at Terminal Island. He was one of my hero's from day one in VMF-114. He had shone up looking for a ride to Oklahoma, his home state. I had checked the future scheduling for me and had seen a flight in a TBM-1C, # 73338, for me to fly to Oklahoma, his home state. This was a one in a million coincidence and I was thrilled to have the opportunity to spend time with a guy I really admired and a close friend.

Wally was a slow talking "Okie" from Muskogee, Oklahoma. He had a great sense of humor, was a good golfer, and a dear friend until he passed away in 2010. I looked forward to a fine time. On the 22nd of Wally and I had breakfast, went down to the flight line, and took care of all the flight preparations. After filing the flight plan, obtaining weather reports, and doing preflight inspections of the bird we were flying. The TBM was a three-man plane, the pilot, rear gunner, and torpedo man in the big tunnel, centerline below, which was quite roomy unloaded. We picked up a couple of pillows, a blanket, and loaded Wally in the tunnel. We could communicate along our flight, even tune in entertainment between stops. The first stop was Navy flight service at the airport in Coolidge, Arizona. Two hours air time from Terminal Island. I remembered that the big football game of that year was the University of Oklahoma versus Pittsburg University. Wally was an alumnus of Oklahoma. We landed at Coolidge, refueled; coffee'd up, stretched our legs, and looked forward to another two hours to

El Paso. Wally's view outside was through a couple of side windows.

We saddled up and took off for El Paso. Our flight plan took us down to Tucson, Arizona, then on east. The Tucson area was a high desert, surrounded by four mountain ranges. Tucson was a city of about 55,000, with a large Army Air Force Base, Davis-Monthan. Mount Lemon, a resort type area that topped at about eleven thousand feet of elevation. It was a very prominent checkpoint along our route. The Oklahoma-Pitt football game was a very high scoring contest! Wally and I were both very much tuned into the contest, which later ended in a 45-44 game! Normally we would have turned east a few miles past Mt. Lemon. Evidently, I was very much wrapped up in the broadcast and I neglected to make our turn. A little later I started to wonder. I had remembered passing a large smoke stack that I knew was a mine near Douglas, Arizona. We were at least thirty minutes pass our turn east and were heading over the border into Mexico. Definitely on course to El Paso, that was not good as we were going to Oklahoma!

I immediately took out my map, and looked up the frequency of the Army Air Corps training base in Douglas, Arizona. I called Wally and said to him, "Guess what captain?" Before I could say anything else he answered "So what Lt! I am busy listening to a football game!" I started calling the Douglas Air Base to ask, "Do you see a NAVY, not MARINE torpedo plane overhead?" The answer was, "What's the matter, you lost?" Quickly I answered "Not any more! Thanks OUT." This time I was still ok as I generally stated my ETA (estimated time of arrival) on the late end! This allotted enough time for me to correct in the event of becoming lost. We RON'd in El Paso.

23 September 1945

Weber and I got up for breakfast and a short planning session on how we could get him from Clinton to Oklahoma City, Oklahoma. I was going to fly him there but the FCLO nixed that thought. Anyway, I flew a 2.6 hours flight to the Navy Ferry Unit in

161

Clinton, Oklahoma where I bid adieu to my friend from VMF-114, a great pilot and my mentor. We remained close until his passing in 2010.

I felt certain the good days of VRF-3 were becoming short as we lost our status position on commercial airlines. There were several pilots waiting to get out of Clinton. Finally, we got a space on MATS (military aviation transportation) in the old but reputable C-45 (Gooney bird). The take off was followed by a steep left turn. I was seated on the right side and had good observation of the refueling caps on the mid-wing position. I was looking right at one of these caps as it flew up and off of the wing, and fuel flowing out followed this. I do not know how it would have helped me, but I was wishing my parachute were in my seat, rather than in the back of the cabin. The pilot reacted to the emergency immediately, leveling the plane and reducing the flow of fuel from the wing. Fortunately we were on the ground almost immediately, and the emergency trucks were foaming the wing. All ended well, except transportation to the west was non-existent. We finally were bused over to a small commercial airline that finally got me back to Terminal Island, San Pedro on the 24th.

I was elated on 27th of September when VRF-3 again put me on a PBY5A, #46667, to co-pilot a 3.6 hours flight from San Pedro to NAS Alameda. That was another experience that I enjoyed immensely. I never got to be in the left seat command, but the experience helped my own ego! I immediately picked up a TBM-1, #06083, for a 2 hours flight back to Terminal Island, San Pedro. The end of September 1945 my logbook showed 901.3 hours.

PBY-5A

October 1945

The fat lady was singing now; the VRF-3 party was almost over! On 2 October there were two flights. First, another race in a small target drone, TD2C-1— well, not this time; then a one hour hop from San Pedro to North Island, San Diego. This time I decided to be "Hot Rod Sam!" I had always wanted to fly with a baseball cap on and costly green Ray-Ban sunglasses, instead of helmet and goggles. Radio conversation with the North Island Tower was not possible; instead they used a green signal lamp. On my last approach for landing I looked at the tower for the lamp, and in order to get a better look, I leaned out of the cockpit, forgetting the wind stream and bingo, expensive sunglasses were broken on the tar-mack. JAR HEAD ONCE MORE! I had a Second flight on the same day in an F6F-3, #42694. This was a .6-hour buzz trip to Los Alamitos, California. The logbook has no record of how I returned to San Pedro.

Once again we were in an R4D-1, #2403, and with Navy LT's Deatheridge and Sorenson. We must have been moving a large number of planes that day as we had myself and 21 other pilots on a flight to Hollister, California.

3 October 1945

My third flight on the 3rd was another F6F-5, #70679, for a 0.6 hour quick trip from Hollister to Madera, California. There was time for lunch, and then I departed for a one-hour flight to San Pedro, California.

The morning of the 4th of May in an FM-2, # 46860, the second series of WWII Grumman Wildcat fighter airplanes. I had not flown one for quite a while. It was great to get back into this fun flyer! It was a short flight to the Thermal Navy refueling station. I had forgotten how seriously hot Thermal could be in May. I opened the cockpit hood, and placed my hand on the rail to climb out of the plane. Neglecting to put my leather flight glove back on my right hand, which resulted in a slight, but painful burn! I will remember not to do this again.

I must have gone AWOL, or disappeared, as my next entry for the same airplane was on the 4th. This was for a one-hour flight to Coolidge, Arizona. I know I enjoyed the RON in Coolidge, but not for seven days! On May 11th my log has me flying from Coolidge, Arizona to El Paso, Texas. 1.6 hours logged. That must have been a mistake, as I remember vividly that on the 12th of May we, this was a lead flight, RON'd in El Paso and had a great supper at the Florida Restaurant and Bar.

12 October 1945

I had three other VRF-3 ferry pilots with me on this, my last flight in VRF-3! We had filed a flight plan from Midland, Texas to Clinton, Oklahoma. The weather was overcast with about 500 feet clearance at Midland. We drank coffee, had a bun, and waited for the weather to lift. Finally, you could see the weather starting to clear a little. They cleared us to take off with the forecast of only a few hundred feet of overcast remaining. I led the take off, telling my number two pilot to hold for me to radio the rest, to follow each other to break out of the overcast one by one. We would then circle, and join up for the rest of the flight. We preceded number two, followed by number three, breaking into the clear. As we circled above the overcast, waiting for number four to break out, suddenly a huge group of white-feathered large birds were skimming along the top of the overcast. Four was already about to break into the clear and I knew he was going to fly thru this bunch of birds. There was nothing I had time to tell him before he collided with the mess. His plane, as he cleared the overcast, was covered with feathers and bits of white birds. I did not have any idea of how long it would be before he would have a white-hot engine. We checked him closely and amazingly he was ok. How lucky we were for him not to have an emergency.

It was smooth sailing into Clinton, Oklahoma. The area at the Clinton airfield was beginning to fill up. At the end of WWII the US had hundreds, if not several thousand, planes and pilots that needed to be phased out of active duty. As I landed there, I realized that I was not far from the time I would need to make some difficult decisions regarding my future. No need to worry about it now.

I checked in with the FCLO at Clinton, said goodbye to one of my favorite planes, the FM-2 Wildcat fighter. Looked for transportation back to San Pedro.

I was lucky to be able to find a "Gooney Bird" (C-45 Douglas twin-engine) flight back to El Paso where the VRF-3 Navy Ferry unit would be able to issue me a commercial flight back to the West Coast. I was able to get space on American Airlines from El Paso via Phoenix to San Pedro. Having stayed overnight and been able to shower, shave, and dress in my Marine Green uniform; I would be able to enjoy the flight west.

It was a hot bumpy flight; almost empty of passengers out of El Paso. American Airlines was noted for their cute and friendly female stewardesses, and that day on board was a delightful young lady. When she served me, noticing very few passengers on board, she asked, "Do you play the card game - Gin?" I was not about to say no! So as not to bother others we took seats in the back and started to play Gin. My jacket was a bit warm, but I wanted the young lady to appreciate my gold wings, combat ribbons, etc. It really got bumpy as we flew on! For some reason, I needed the "burp" bag, much to my embarrassment! I was not a too impressive combat fighter pilot now! She took pity on me, and before the plane landed gave me her phone number and address in Ft. Worth. Unfortunately, I still have the little black book, but never had the chance to use it! One ferry stop too late!

By the time I returned to Terminal Island, the tremendous job of transferring all the pilots of VRF-3 to new assignments, civilian life and Marine, Navy, Army Air Corps Reserve assignments was just beginning! No one now knew where or when they were going! We were still drawing pay, but had nothing much to do.

As sad as it was, it was now time for me to put my cherished Naval Aviator's Logbook back in its felt bag and careful store it away.

AIRCRAFT FLOWN USN-USMC (1942-1945)

150 HP Luscombe "all-metal" low level trainer

N2S Stearman – Yellow Peril

SNV BT-13 Vultee " Vibrator"

166

SNJ "Texan" Advanced Fighter Trainer

F4F Grumman Wildcat

F4U Corsair FG2

F6F-Grumman "Hellcat"

C-46 Curtis Commando

TBM Torpedo Bomber

JRF Grumman "Goose"

PV-2 Lodestar Multi-Purpose

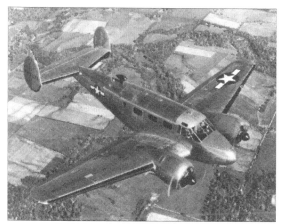

JRB Beechcraft Multi-Purpose

TD2C-1 Culver PQ-14 Target Drone

PBY Consolidated Catalina "Dumbo"

WYOMING NATIONAL GUARD AIRCRAFT (1957-1971)

Cessna 182 (1957-1971)

DeHavilland "Beaver (1957-'71)

CIVILIAN AIRCRAFT (1971-1984)

Piper Lance, Cozumel Mexico

171

Cessna 310, Cabo San Lucas Mexico

Beechcraft "Musketeer," Tucson, AZ

Pitts Special Acrobatic

Chapter 17   Transfer To The Marine Reserves

20 October 1945

Things at VRF-3 were very confusing now. Everyone was checking all the requirements to go on terminal leave prior to changing to reserve status, or to go to an active duty assignment. Also, I was trying to determine the amount of leave time, travel time to your home destination that I would be allowed, etc.

Most of the pilots were checking the information board or their duty box each morning and then heading for the beach or any other place they had neglected to visit. One thing seemed certain and that was flying in VRF-3 was completed. The pilots from VMF-114 were either waiting for a new duty station or requesting terminal leave and a reserve assignment. I had decided to take an assignment to the reserve unit and a date that terminal leave would expire.

After spinning my wheels, I finally learned that I could start my checkout on 1 November 1945, and my Terminal Leave date would be 17 December 1945. I took care of my goodbyes with the VMF-114 pilots. Several of them would apply for regular USMC status.

I took care of all the necessary business, checking in any government owned item I had and was allowed to keep the heavy duty sheepskin lined jackets, pants and boots. These were great items for the winter seasons of Wyoming. My final stop was the paymaster's desk. They figured up the travel pay and leave pay I would be due. The amount of money I had coming surprised me as it seemed to be too much! The only reason I asked was I didn't want to have to pay any excess dollars back to the government! It seems that I had forgotten I had a contract with the US Navy and USMC that included a bonus of $500 per year or $1,500 plus travel and leave pay handed to me from the paymaster! I had joined the Officer's Club on an active basis and they were closing down their operation as well. I was also carrying cash returned to me by the

Officer's Club so when I finally left the paymaster's office I was one very happy Naval pilot! I immediately found a bank to exchange the cash for a certified check.

Fortunately, I met a Navy pilot whose home was Ft. Collins, Colorado, and he was looking for transportation. I had made arrangements to meet my mother in Salt Lake City, Utah, and I was happy to have a partner at least that far. He turned out to be a good travel partner!

When my travel partner and I said goodbye to active duty and departed we were not in any rush to drive too far each day and decided to drive as far as Las Vegas, Nevada. The plan was to have dinner in one of the nice restaurants, do a little gambling and RON there. We were going to depart the next morning and was a good thought, but best-laid plans are often destined to change. I had previously planned with my mom that I would keep her abreast of our trip's progress so she could meet me in Salt Lake when we got there.

Well, we made it to Vegas in good time, decided to have a drink and supper and then go on the next morning. I hit a dollar jackpot … that and the fact that we somehow met two young ladies from LA changed our plans. This was going to be a party, and it was going to last a bit longer. The next day was spent at the pool, and we decided to leave the following day. I called mom and changed our itinerary, but no, I did not tell her we had experienced car trouble. She knew immediately why our plans had changed. I could never fool her, so why try?

Finally, we proceeded on our way to Salt Lake City. We were driving, shortly after dusk, just past a small town in southern Utah. We heard on the radio that there had been a shooting, a couple of people killed. We no sooner heard the announcement on the radio when a patrol car with lights flashing pulled us over. Immediately after I had stopped the whole front seat area was flooded with strong beams of light by two patrolmen, one on each side of the car. I rolled the driver side window down, and a large pistol was jammed into my shoulder. I was questioned intensely, and started to reach for identification when the jamming of the pistol became stronger, I was ordered to keep my hands on the steering wheel. This situation WAS GETTING SERIOUS. Finally it toned down somewhat, and we were able to produce our travel orders and ID cards. A patrolman told us the info they had was TWO YOUNG MEN IN THEIR TWENTIES, DRIVING A RED CAR WITH IDAHO LICENSE PLATES were seen speeding towards Salt Lake City. We were happy to receive a small apology, their good luck on our way north and to have a wild stop over. It was miles before we were able to relax!

Winter freeze in Pocatello Union Pacific Railroad Yards!

After a wonderful homecoming and the transitional emotions of having such a different homelike lifestyle, I realized that, for the short time, I would be living in my parent's apartment, and I needed to get a job. Fortunately, my father knew many individuals that would help me line up some interviews. I had made up my mind to enter the University of Wyoming as soon as the second semester started, after the Christmas vacation. This decision naturally limited the job choices.

The quickest opportunity was from the Union Pacific Railroad Company. Lieutenant Colonel Singer, who was recently returned from his active duty assignment with the US Army Corps of Engineers, had accepted the job of surveying the railroad tracks and locations in the Pocatello Railroad Yards. I was hired on as his survey assistant with the important job title of CHAINMAN and GOFER! The hours were good. The drawback was winter was in full fledge and it was cold as hell! I sucked up my determination and weathered the cold!

Now, things were going very smoothly, until the mailman delivered a letter with the return address of M. Anderson. My mother looked at the envelope, as a mother should, until her curiosity got the better of her and opened it. She had always been the most understanding of mothers, well above average, but she had forgotten that her son, age 22, had been flying airplanes in combat, and had tossed the thought of "what if" out the window.

He was still very rational, above average in maturity, responsibility, maturity, and determined not to add responsibility for unnecessarily stupid decisions. Well, the letter held a few references to moonlight evenings on the beach, etc. It took several minutes of serious conversation with mom and the strongest reassurance that her son was not about to marry some 'floozy" or young lady looking for "Marine fighter pilot" notoriety! She calmed down and told me "your dad was very worried after reading the letter!" You should talk to him!

I learned the difference between working in the rail yards of "naught-naught plus nine" (surveying) and "slow-rolls and gunnery runs in Corsairs!" My later military experience was as commanding officer of a reserve U.S. Army Corps of Engineers Combat Engineer Battalion!

Time, job, the Christmas season, and sleeping on a pullout couch passed quickly and before I knew it I was packing for the trip to Laramie, Wyoming to become a student again.

I phoned the Student Union's office, asked for the manager, and soon was talking to Edna Tichac. I inquired as to applying for a job, telling her that I was a returning veteran and that I had worked in the student union fountain room, neglecting to mention my salary then was only 14 cents per hour. What followed when I arrived was something else!

My next move was to find housing. I phoned the men's residence hall, talked to the manager, and made a request for the same room, third floor, east wing overlooking the football field and Hell's Half Acre gym! The lady said she would do her best, but due to the number of men returning to school, it would have to be a room shared with two other students. Well, we will see upon arrival. I had already applied for and had been accepted for classes beginning in early January. Things were taking shape.

My drive to Laramie was about six hours of wondering and thinking about what the campus would be like now. My main thought was getting going on a Pre-Med course that would be the ticket to acceptance into medical school someplace.

Registration day had always been a Chinese Fire Drill in my experience, but this year seemed to be a "cinch!" A few years of maturity maybe! My final class schedule was Quantitative Chemistry, Physics, and Qualitative Anatomy. All of these classes also had laboratories once a week. The University gave me a year's worth of credit for my military experience. This would make it possible for me to graduate in May of 1948.

I found that I was able to make decent grades while going to class, playing college baseball, working in the student union fountain room at least three hours a day and also having one helluva good time!

Speaking of the student union fountain, my meeting with Mrs. Tichac progressed per the following. I outlined to her the fact that I was now much more mature, having flown many combat missions and having spent the amount of time I had as a Marine in combat. I felt I would be qualified for the position of student manager, placed in charge of the students hired to work in the fountain. She smiled knowingly, and replied, "Yes, Bud, I feel you are qualified to work here, but presently I can offer you the same job you previously had at 12 cents an hour! Please consider this and let me know! BOY, TALK ABOUT BEING PUT IN MY PLACE! I left her office startled, perhaps a tad upset; perhaps, maybe I had my chain pulled. Let me test her! Determined to prove my work habits and ability, I accepted her challenge. Maybe I could show her my ability to entertain customers with being able to stack a double ice cream cone successfully behind my back. More later on this!

My room request was approved at the Men's Residence Hall at an exorbitant cost of $3.00 a week. The room had one single bed and a metal two-deck bed. My two roommates were late shows, so I possessed the single bed as the ranking officer. The space available in the two closets had to be divided between the three of us. One desk, two chairs, a lamp and a window in the middle of the exterior wall, not bad! It served the three of us, Larry Tobin, Joe Donlin, the "Donlin torpedo" and me. Two plus years, we had lived together with never a "harsh word between us"! Believe it or not! Tobin flew Corsairs during WWII as a Naval Aviator and later became a medical doctor. Donlin was a combat veteran in Italy! He passed away at a young age after years as a successful Wyoming sheep rancher.

My two "roomies" were devout Catholics, so Lent was like going to church for 40 straight days! They forced Protestant me to accompany them down to the church every morning at 6:30 AM! Fortunately, the Catholic and Episcopal churches were separated by one block! On the way back to the campus one morning, I asked the question "What is the difference to the Lord, me going to one and you to the other church?" The answer was very simple. "We will ride to heaven in a Cadillac and you in a Studebaker." Problem solved.

My supervising USMC Reserve Unit was the 13th Naval District, headquartered in Chicago, Illinois. There was a mammoth paper confusion that existed due to the number of assignments of returning veterans, and we were not in constant communication. My entire career might have been different, were this not the case!

I was in close contact with the Marine Corps detachment in Denver. The recruitment of student athletes who might be interested in the Officer Candidate Platoon Program, which was available to them upon graduation, was an assignment given to me. I provided several candidates to the Denver unit, all of them from the Athletic Department at Wyoming.

Ron Drost, one of my baseball recruits, had an outstanding career as a USMC officer that included time in combat in Vietnam. Three times we drove together to Denver for a physical examination, and each time the doctor examined his heart his blood pressure disqualified him. It turned out this was all due to his excitement of being at the Denver unit. Finally, we tricked him by calling him into the training room, without any prior notice. The Athletic Department physician surprised him with the blood pressure cuff and he passed with flying colors. He had multiple combat tours in

Nam, and also several awards while there. He also is a Purple Heart recipient due to his exposure to Agent Orange. He still attends baseball reunions with us every two years.

In spite of being busy and active in student body affairs, I found my grade point to be much better than one might think! The two and one half years to graduation went by quickly.

The student body voted me the honor of the "Brotherhood Award" for male students. My senior year I was elected Student Body President and Captain of the Baseball Team. I graduated in May, the first Daniel to complete the first phase of my college education.

My senior year did have one "bump –in –the road" however! My close friend, Larry Tobin and I both requested recommendations from a doctor in Casper, Wyoming to the St. Louis University Medical School. He received his acceptance letter in February, and I waited patiently for mine. Instead, in early March, I received a telegram telling me that my acceptance name had been rejected because they had never received my final grade status report. Once again, my life took a big bump! I had no idea of what I would do after graduation. For some reason, the thought of returning to the USMC did not enter my mind. Also, absent was the thought to try for the next year's class at St. Louis, or to return to Wyoming for a master's degree.

Life went on. In rapid order I signed a contract with the Saint Louis Cardinal Professional Baseball Organization, spent two years at Cody, Wyoming High School as the head basketball Coach and assistant football coach and introduced a baseball program. The future Wyoming US Senator, Alan Simpson, was captain of my first year's basketball team. In 1950, I returned to the University of Wyoming as Head Baseball Coach and Athletic Business Manager. I remained at the University coaching baseball, and keeping active in the Wyoming National Guard.

Chapter 18   Life At The Army National Guard

April 1957

At the end of WWII, the USMC allowed the active reserve component each year to receive points for maintaining their eligibility credit for retirement. In 1957, the USMCR notified me that if I did not obtain a specified number of points on active duty they would transfer me to inactive status and that would eliminate me for qualifying for retirement at a later date. I quickly wrote the 13th District Naval Unit requesting retirement from the USMCR. I would then accept a captain's commission in the US Army Corps of Engineers Army National Guard unit in Laramie, Wyoming. This took me right back to the days working for the Union Pacific Railroad in Pocatello and my crew chief's association with the Corps of Engineers.

The decision to leave the USMCR was a tough decision, as I firmly believed "ONCE A MARINE ALWAYS A MARINE." I STILL DO. I wondered what all of my Marine Corps buddies would think. One thing I made up my mind to do was never wear my army uniform without my gold Naval Aviator wings.

The state headquarters of the Wyoming Army National Guard was in Cheyenne, Wyoming. Several of my friends were active in the Guard so my entrance into the Guard was quick and comfortable. I had to attend several active duty engineer schools for promotions and retirement points. In addition to these summer time engineer courses, during the year I had a certain number of correspondence hours to complete. My boss in the Athletic Department, Glenn "Red" Jacoby, was a retired reserve lieutenant colonel, so my summer contracts allowed me to spend three months on active duty to complete these Corps of Engineer schools. The Guard enabled me to ensure a retirement pension at age 62. The Guard also required monthly drills at the Laramie headquarters on one weekend and two weeks of active duty visits to "CAMP MOO!" Guernsey, Wyoming in the summer. This was the base on the outskirts of a historic little community on the old OREGON

TRAIL of the 1860's. This trail wound from Kansas to the west coast, and obvious deep ruts from the pioneer wagons were visible in several areas of land. There were also large collections of rattlesnakes, especially during the hot summer days.

The "Camp Moo" living quarters of my career were quite different from most state facilities! Buildings for living quarters at the time were almost non-existent. One building housed the staff officers, ranks of major and up. The remainder of the troops, enlisted, warrant officers and officers, lived in tents. This was true for all troops when in the field for training. The hills and open land of the area were ideal for artillery live fire and all sorts of engineer training. Being a chemistry major in college qualified Captain Daniel to command a water purification unit for training in the field, making potable and purified water from ponds and other types of available water sources. I will always remember the day when one of the officers from the office of the Inspector General commented, as he observed my unit at work on a pond where several cattle were urinating, "I will be damned. Look at this. The captain is making drinking water out of cow piss!"

In November of 1958, my father passed away and about three months later, in January 1959, my mother also died. Their loss, so near to each other, hit the family very hard.

In early 1959, I was selected to go to Hawaii and Japan to conduct Baseball Clinics for the FAR EAST AIR FORCE COMMAND.

The dean of American League Umpires, Ed Rommel, and National League Umpire, John Rice, together with Dick Siebert, Head Coach at the University of Minnesota and I were assigned to go on this eight week trip. I was excited and looking forward to this trip as the professor of military science (PMS) of the University of Wyoming's Army ROTC unit was just back from Japan and had many contacts. We were in Hawaii for about two weeks and then on to Japan for about six weeks. This was indeed a highpoint in baseball to date for me. We traveled as VIP's with a designation of two-star general's rank. I found out what the difference was between the "Two Bars" captain's rank and the "Two Stars" general's rank and that is RHIP (rank has it's privilege is absolutely true). Nightlife with Siebert and Rice was unreal! DOMO AREGOTO!

Prior to my departure for Japan, Colonel Outsen, PMS, University of Wyoming ROTC set up visits to some of the high officials in the Japanese government. It was the most interesting part of my trip. In order to make these courtesy calls I had to have an interpreter and I was assigned a Mr. Sekei. I met with Vice-Minister Imai, Japan Defense Agency Tokyo, Mr. Takeuchi, Central Chairman, Procurement, and General Hayashi, Chairman, Joint Chiefs of Staff, Japan Defense. Each of the offices was very elaborate, with a Geisha Girl "Jop-Jop" serving tea and goodies as we conversed. Very posh! Mr. Imai was the ex-Chief of Police for Tokyo. He looked much like a "bull-dog." He looked to be a very tough character.

Mr. Takeuchi invited me for a weekend party in the southern islands of Japan. I had to decline due to the lack of time. The U.S. officers at MAAG-Japan told me I had missed what was normally a real "wild party!" Ah – such is life.

General Hayashi was a young man. He had been a lieutenant colonel at the war's end and quickly rose to "Five-Star Rank." He was an avid baseball fan and imitated "The Stan Musial" batting stance and swing very authentically! On the way down in the elevator I practiced some of my Japanese phrases on Mr. Sekei. When I ask him how authentic I sounded, he said "Not bad, but just like a Japanese dock-worker!" Meeting the above named Japanese high-ranking men in government positions was a big honor. Sekei told me they all spoke clear English, but until you visited them eight times they would have an interpreter!

Time passed quickly as each day had assigned duties. Seibert and I had been assigned presentations for the clinic portion of our trip. Air Force Far East Command brought the Special Services officers assigned to various units into Tokyo for a week of special baseball clinic-teaching presentations. These clinics were held at Johnson Air Force Base, located over an hour's drive from the Sanno Hotel.

This interfered with Siebert's sleep schedule. Having spent several years in Professional Baseball, most of it at the Major League level, he was used to night games (and night social activity). The two of us were able to set up a schedule of alternating the pick up time of our chauffer (furnished by the military) each day. I would have the 6 AM one day, going back to the hotel at noon, when Seibert would arrive for the afternoon schedule, to be picked up at 5 PM. It would alternate each day. Some how it did not work every single day! We adjusted to the mix up!

Our favorite nightclub was the MARANUCHI CLUB. "Seib" wore a big World Series ring and at the club, enjoyed exhibiting it to the female Japanese baseball enthusiasts. We found the Japanese loved baseball. Seibert would flash the ring with comments like "me big home run hitter, Babe Root!" We nick named him "Pinocchio!" Umpire Rice and I razzed him constantly. Seibert then told the young Japanese ladies that I was Mickey Rooney. That brought giggles and "Rooney-san, you dance, laugh and sing!" The entertainment went well into the night.

Army Colonels sponsored fine dinners and top-notch liquid refreshments. We found they were in great condition for this type of fun as the Far East Command brought the group of men in on a Friday evening, and turned them loose for the weekend. This resulted in a group of sleepy individuals at the clinics on Monday morning. I had the first session at 8:00 AM on a Monday. After my introduction, one sleepy, droopy-eyed lieutenant slowly fell off his chair! I promptly said, "gentlemen, it is time for coffee!"

The Air Force Officers treated us very well. Their suggestions were our commands. A two star general was looking for a squash-game opponent. It happened I was the only contestant available. We played two fast games and retired to the locker room for a shower. As I sat down to change shoes, my throat started to swell closed, and I was about to pass out! An ambulance promptly arrived and quickly took me to the infirmary for antihistamine. It was instant recovery!

Returning to the mainland, away from the glamour and fun of the trip to Hawaii and Japan, I found myself assigned to look after young 2nd lieutenants with classified documents, at the Special Combat Officer's Intelligence School in Fort Sheridan, Illinois. As the ranking captain, I was their class commander from July 20th – August 3rd, 1958.

For promotion to major and to assist my transition from USMC fighter pilot to engineer officer, I attended military schooling, the Engineer Officer Basic Course at Fort Belvoir, Virginia from 15 June to 24 August 1959. Living close to the engineer school, I was able to take the family and draw housing allotments for this time. As an "old" Captain I was again designated class commander. During the course I supervised the combat engineers in the job of assembling Bailey Bridges over rivers in contests for speed and accuracy. Summers in Virginia are hot and humid. As the class commander, one extremely hot afternoon, I was given the assignment of setting up one section of bridging for time and correctness. My company was composed of young, eager 2nd Lieutenants, striving to set a record in competition. At 1300 hours (1:00 PM) we assembled. Telling my troops, "It is 100 degrees and the Officer's Club bar opens at 1600 hours. If we set a record we will be sipping ice-cold brews at 1600 hours." Guess who won! My company did!

My family was able to travel with me if the school was more than two weeks. Our apartment was close to the swimming pool at the O-Club. Our three sons spent each afternoon there diving for pennies. Passing officers were amazed at the amount of time they could stay under water. They finally decided that being from 7200 feet altitude in Laramie, Wyoming enabled them to have a larger lung capacity than the average child!

I remember that my first assignment in the Guard as a captain was the S-2 slot (Intelligence Officer), which was an important job on the battalion staff during any war game training activity.

In July of 1961, I attended the Disaster Recovery Course, again at Fort Belvoir, Virginia, and, again, with my family in tow. We were driving home from this stint at Belvoir, when after dark, having just crossed the Colorado state line when the Denver radio announced, "three reserve units from the mountain area have been called to active duty!" The 1022nd Combat Engineer Battalion will report to Fort Lewis, Washington on October 1st, 1961! "OH, MY GOD I THOUGHT" as I pulled the car over to listen to what they were saying.

My thoughts returned to early 1950s when I received USMC warning telegram that I would be activated for the Korean conflict. I sweated this out for thirty days until I finally received the news that I was on standby as they currently had enough fighter pilots in the rank of major. This time it was real and I would go to Fort Lewis.

We had recently built a really nice three-bedroom house with a party room and indoor-outdoor BBQ facilities. Worse yet, my military pay would not completely equal my current income. What a financial mess this might be. OUCH!

The radio was correct and I left Laramie to report to Fort Lewis on 1 October 1961. Along with three young lieutenants we loaded one of their cars and started driving to Ft. Lewis, which is located just outside of Tacoma, Washington. I would be assigned BOQ housing until my family could be assigned housing, hopefully within about thirty days. Once they arrived we would settle in and the boys would attend second semester at a base school.

The trip west driving to Tacoma took four days. Traveling with three young lieutenants was a hoot! I realized my age. We arrived and reported to the proper office. A "salty" older Master Sergeant looked at my DD-214, which showed my date of rank was 1 January 1945, 16 years ago. He grinned and said, "Begging the captain's pardon, whose mess kit did you poop in?"

We were assigned to a WWII style barracks. It was a wooden building with big cracks in the window frames and doors. We found out that these were well-ventilated quarters as the Washington winter weather arrived. Weather in the area was cloudy, raining, cool to colder, sun-up was dark due to the overcast, and the evenings got dark early. The US Army had activated and recalled the FIRST DIVISION, the BIG RED ONE, a famous WWII division that numbered several thousand men. The large numbers of the recall to active duty had overwhelmed this big military post. Fort Lewis was a huge facility. The 1022nd Combat Engineer Battalion was one of six combat engineer battalions located on the North side of the post. These were all wooden buildings, leftovers from WWII, and in need of serious repairs. The battalion headquarters was divided into the command group (commanding and executive officers and the senior enlisted member of the battalion) and the staff offices: S-1 (personnel), S2 (intelligence), S3 (operations), and the S4 (logistics). My staff was composed of Captain Daniel, one master sergeant, and 4 to 5 additional enlisted men.

Wyoming volunteers filled the entire unit and were from all sections of Wyoming. We had many ranch representatives who were "gung-ho" workers, excellent men dedicated to doing a great job. Getting the unit organized and use to full time military customs took time and command effort.

My first task was formulating the model for one of the important component parts of the war games to held in a couple of months in Yakima, Washington. In most war games the good guys (US Forces) would be pitted against a bad guy opposing force (OPFOR) and, similar to baseball, there were umpires that acted as control elements. The size of the operation was large, so too was the CONTROL element, constituted of men from the different participating engineer battalions.

I was detached from the 1022nd and put in charge of creating the format of and rules for the games. This was a large task. My staff was composed of five master sergeants from the participating battalions. Senior Master Sergeant Black was very competent and possessed the perfect personality to lead the four additional men under his supervision.

The officer commanding the unit was a short, overweight and thoroughly incompetent lieutenant colonel, who unfortunately had been captured his first day in real combat in WWII and was a prisoner of war (POW) for a period of time in Germany. I think this experience had destroyed his ability for common sense. My unit had been hustling for weeks and completing the umpire's manuscript successfully with only minor changes to be made. I suggested to the lieutenant colonel that in view of the great job these men did, we should give them some time off in the afternoon as free time to go golfing etc. He went into orbit and blew a fuse telling me "if you can't find something for those men to do, pointing to the waste baskets, tear up the paper into bits, and scatter the bits around the office for them to pick up!" Now it was my turn, I gave him my best intimidating stare, turned to my men, and said, come on with me, we need some fresh air! The colonel could not handle it!

My civilian pals in the American Baseball Coaches Association, or ABCA, had been working on a super assignment for me. Having no funds, they had approached the US Army's Chief of Staff, who happened to be a personal friend of Ohio State's Baseball Coach, to approve my travel to Tokyo, Japan, to meet with the Chairman of the Japanese Olympic Committee (his office was inside the Emperor's Grounds in Tokyo!). The mission of the trip was to gain the addition of baseball to be included in the 1964 Olympic games. Before I entered the colonel's office to secure his permission to accept this duty, I had carefully placed the general's signed orders allowing my trip where he would see them. He was speechless and I laughed all the way to Tokyo! I was to fly to Japan Space Available, or Space-A! Save me space!

So 1962 would be my second trip to Japan. Different from my first in that the Air Force had very little to do with it, mainly transportation arranged by the US Air Force's Military Aircraft Transportation System (MATS). Contacting space availability at Ft. Lewis, I had no problem catching a flight to Travis Air Force Base, CA. Many flights come and go every hour to the Far East. Fortunately I had Top Secret Clearance and was assigned as Courier for TOP SECRET material, being sent to military bases in

Japan. This flight was to be on Flying Tiger Airlines flying contract for military assignments.

My trip to Japan was to be on a brand new transport plane, split tail type (loading cargo from the back area) four engines and brand-new. It had been picked up recently at Lockheed Aircraft Company in Burbank, California. Part of the design was developed in Ontario, Canada and combined with Lockheed. I was the first passenger to board, up the ladder into the front section of the fuselage. There were airline seats and four sleeping bunks, located just aft of the pilots and radio/navigator areas. It wasn't long before a very attractive Flying Tiger's stewardess climbed aboard and took a seat near me.

Soon the plane was loaded, the pilots appeared, and finally a US Navy chief boarded. He was assigned to accompany me as a courier. He was armed with a .45 caliber pistol and handed one to me. Two pilots entered their seats and our flight to Cold Bay, Alaska was underway.

We were cruising along. I was in the pilot's area asking questions about this new model plane. Our point of no return (navigating measurement regarding fuel) had just been passed. Suddenly, a loud crack (similar to a pistol shot) shattered the glass in the front windscreen. It reminded me of the problematic rear windows in automobile station wagons that shattered mysteriously.

Front cockpit windows in this plane were seven layers of high-grade glass material. The copilot was busy thumbing through the plane manual and talking to Montreal, Canada where plane parts were manufactured. The command pilot turned to me and said, "Pardner, if I were you I would get my body back to one of those bunks and go to sleep. Just hope this window does not implode." If that happens we are in deep trouble!" I obeyed his recommendation and had a sound sleep. Fortunately the implosion did not happen and we landed in Cold Bay, which was aptly named, as it was a very barren landscape. Upon landing the crew gave me two options. One, unload the classified material and wait a day or two for another flight. Two, wait until we determine if those seven layers will remain in place until we land at "Tachi" Air Force Base Japan. I chose to take their decision when the crew said we could proceed to Japan. Mechanics, pilots, and crewmembers climbed all over the cockpit wind screen and came to the conclusion we could make it to Japan.

Weather en route was overcast, instrument flying, so I once again took advantage of the bunk, located in the front portion of the cabin. When I awakened we were a short time from our destination. I again wandered up to flight central and asked "What's our touchdown at Tachi?" Answer, "Oh, about an hour!" I glanced at the large fuel indicator and estimated remaining fuel would be a close situation. He recognized my questionable look, answering, "Flying Tiger Pilots do this all the time!" I made up my mind going home I was taking US NAVY FLIGHTS!

As the crew tried to operate the new method of unloading cargo by swinging the tail open it became stuck. The good-looking stewardess deplaned; the pilot and co-pilot said goodbye and the Navy Chief and I waited to claim and disperse our classified material. Welcome to Tokyo. After a long wait, I was able to confirm my reservation at the SANNO Field Grade Officer's Hotel in Tokyo. I thanked the chief, shook hands and bade him "nice hunting!"

My host on this trip would be a man who has accumulated great wealth in manufacturing several hi-tech items. I phoned the contact number, arranging a meeting for lunch tomorrow. So far, so good. One of the largest, best college baseball teams was to play at 2:00 PM Tokyo time. This would be a treat for me as the day prior 65,000 rabid baseball fans filled Meji Stadium. My host apologized saying today's crowd would be only 30,000. College Baseball in Japan! Crowds here made the game seem like a football crowd back home with cheerleaders on the stadium floor with certain pre-planned words in their cheers. Also, pitchers threw pitches until they could throw no more. No 100-pitch count, no three or four days rest between starts. Game time was scheduled for 2:00 PM. Each team had a very short warm up time. Umpires met at home plate, line-up cards were exchanged, teams bowed to each other, and the game was on. Loud cheers followed each pitch. The game is very much like one at home. The crowds were different!!!

I finally received an appointment with the Chairman of the Japanese Olympics Committee for the 1964 Olympic games. His offices were in a building on the grounds of the Japanese Emperor's Palace, and that was as close as I was allowed to see anything of Emperor Hiroito.

I presented my request for his consideration and help in obtaining baseball as a demonstration sport in the 1964 games. He was the usual very polite and considerate of Japanese gentleman. He was completely confused by the alphabet letters of all of the concerned organizations involved in my presentation. (ABCA, American College Baseball Association; NCAA, National Collegiate Athletic Association and all of its different divisions, Divisions I, II, III, etc.). I had gone to lengths attempting to obtain his understanding of the alphabet soup! It was a two-hour meeting and I was gratified by his interest and attention to our request. As it turned out it was a successful presentation as baseball was included as a demonstration sport in the games. Family sickness prevented me from accepting a baseball coaching position in the 1964 Olympics Baseball Demonstration games. WHAT A BUMMER FOR ME!

My sponsor did arrange for me to spend an evening with an elderly gentleman in his eighties who hosted me at one of the elegant college club restaurants. This gentleman was considered to be the father of Collegiate Baseball in Japan. Our evening was most interesting with an elegant meal. We exchanged small gifts. My gift to him was a tie clasp of a baseball player attached to a bar with NCAA engraved on it. His gift to me was a large, heavy bronze plaque representing Japan's College Baseball Hall of Fame.

It was, altogether too soon, time for me to return to the USA. I was able to catch a contract military flight to McCord Army Air Corps Base in Tacoma, a few miles from Ft. Lewis. It was much faster than the Flying Tiger's flight to Tokyo!

190

When I checked back into the headquarters of the 1022nd Engineers my fellow guardsmen brought me up to date on what had happened in my absence. I was immediately attached to a battalion Nuclear/Chemical group that was conducting training for a small, 2 kiloton, "nuke," a bridge demolition device that each recalled engineer outfit had in their "TO&E" (Table of Organization & Equipment). Trailer vehicles were transferring them from location to location with armed guards and MP Units (Military Police) as front and back escort protection. Somehow records investigators found that I had a chemistry major from college hence my new assignment.

General Zerath's (Two Star Division Commander) go-fers found out that I was also a College Baseball Coach in civilian life and this discovery led to another interesting "fork in my road." It turned out that the Big Red 1 Division from Wisconsin had also recalled 25 professional baseball players from AAA Minor League and Major League organizations into active duty. Special Services Officers realized the wealth of entertainment opportunities for the troops now existed.

This group had some famous players, such as shortstop Tony Kubek of the NY Yankees, George Thomas from the Boston Red Sox and Jim McElhany from the Chicago Cubs. Twelve other players had played over five years on Major League Baseball clubs! Special Services quickly formed a baseball team and scheduled their first series in the San Francisco area with college teams to include the University of California, Berkley and three others in the vicinity. The All-Star Fort Lewis Rangers promptly beat UC-Berkley by scores like 18-0, 16-4 etc. When this happened Senator Engle, a University of California alumni, wondered what in hell these soldiers were doing playing baseball instead of devoting their time to traditional Army training at Fort Lewis.

It did not take long for the leadership at Fort Lewis to realize there was a need for a professional manager or college coach to handle this situation. I was again attached to a different unit. I was TWO-BAR, Captain Daniel, and OIC (officer in charge) of the Fort

Lewis Rangers! For me, this was a heavenly assignment. I was thrilled and honored to continue to serve my country managing several Major League baseball stars! Seriously, this turned out to be a fine situation and created hours of entertainment for soldiers and civilians. We scheduled games from Portland to Seattle and in between, playing colleges, professional teams, teams from other bases and even Federal and state prisons. The fact that baseball fans had the opportunity to see well-known Major League baseball stars in person was very popular.

The major "bump in the road" in the summer long program was when I exercised my military and collegiate baseball contacts and we tentatively set up a schedule collegiate games using MATS travel. The team was excited UNTIL the California Senator contacted the General again. My office telephone rang and the general's staff officer in flowery terms asked, "What in hell is going on down there. The general has cancelled the baseball program and no one, not even the man above is going to change the general's mind!" Crash went the phone line!

When this recall first started and the famous Tony Kubek appeared on scene, press, radio, and the general's staff got in line offering several favors that Kubek might use. When the cancellation occurred, Tony became very upset. He came to my office, picked up the phone and asked for the general's office. I could hear the conversation. The general's secretary took Kubeck's call, recognized the name and asked "Are you in the Army? Rank? Etc." She then reminded Specialist Fourth Class Kubek that he does not call a two star general's office with requests! Somebody got to the general evidently, as that same staff officer called my quarters at 6:30 AM the next morning to tell me the program had been reinstated with certain limitations. My answer to him was "gee, the good lord acts in generous ways, does he not?" The colonel came BACK TO EARTH, and to baseball practice that afternoon and seemed to be a very nice guy!

The summer passed quickly. Seattle's 1962 World Fair was in full operation and offered family entertainment the three boys loved. They also had a great time with the baseball players and become closer than the average kid ever enjoys! The Fort Lewis Rangers finished their season with a won-loss record of 33-1. The players presented me with an engraved trophy!

In August of 1962, the Cuban Missile Crisis cooled down, and the 1022nd Engineer Battalion was returned to civilian status. My family and I returned to Laramie and the University of Wyoming. I was promoted to Major and given the position of Battalion Commander.

Colonel Jack Conger, the former Operation Officer of VMF-114 during the Peleliu battle was now commanding officer of the USMC reserve unit based at Buckley Field, Denver, Colorado. He was looking for "cross country time" to get his necessary flight time required by Marine Aviation. The Wyoming Cowboys football team was scheduled to play in the Sun Bowl in Albuquerque, New Mexico. Our coaches were looking for a way to go scout possible opponents in the game. Conger was able to build up flight time and furnished a trip to Abilene, Texas in a twin-engine Beechcraft. Coach Daniel was the Marine qualified co-pilot for the necessary scouting trip. I had not seen "Congo" for some time, so we had much to discuss as we flew towards Abilene! A twin-engine Beech had a 25-gallon fuel tank in the nose of the fuselage. Three football coaches, two of whom were in the military reserves, were seated in the aft (back) section. We were in the pilot's seats in the forward cockpit; very busy catching up on old memories! Suddenly the two engines became very quite as they emptied the small fuel tank. I turned and laughed when I saw the look on the football coaches faces. It was only seconds before the emergency fuel pressure switch corrected the problem. It provided laughs and conversation on the entire trip.

We RON'D in El Paso, TX and enjoyed supper across the border in a magnificent nightclub in Juarez, Mexico. The Kingston Trio, the famous singing group was performing their hit songs and the five of us were adding our melodious, alcohol-laden voices to their entertainment. We quietly clammed up as very strong looking ushers requested that we do so! To say the least, the complete trip was a success and the Cowboys won the Bowl Game.

Colonel Conger continued to be a Wyoming Cowboy fan, as he furnished flight time to pick-up football game films, delivered to Denver for developing and back to Laramie on Sunday. He also later provided me transportation for scheduling my spring baseball schedule in Arizona and Southern California.

In January of 1963, the American Baseball Coaches Association elected me president of the Association. This was a tremendous honor voted to me by my peers in the organization.

1945 was the year it was formed and it has grown to over 6500 member coaches. This total covers all collegiate, high school, amateur programs, plus many international organizations. During this growth period only 225 plus coaches have been voted into their Hall of Fame, an honor I received in 1993.

My initial job as president of the ABCA was to obtain a speaker for the annual Hall of Fame dinner, the main event at the annual convention, to be held in New York City at the New Yorker Hotel. I immediately thought of US Senator Milward Simpson, my biggest fan and supporter. He was in his first term from the State of Wyoming. I immediately phoned his office. Luckily I was able to talk to him right away. He suggested I fly into Washington, DC and meet with him for breakfast to discuss this request. The Wyoming Air Guard had flights scheduled to Washington frequently, so it was simple for me to schedule a "Space-A" trip. The trip turned out to be a great success as we met for breakfast, discussed the special events, dress for the occasion, and any other facts he needed. I met with him again during my three-day stay in DC. Milward was a tremendously talented after dinner speaker. I knew he would "wow" the audience and be the star of the evening!

I met Senator Simpson as he entered the hotel. He had arrived by train, after a busy day in DC. After he had dressed, we made our way to the door of the banquet. Simpson was nattily attired in a tuxedo, making him so well dressed that Lee Eilbrecht, our Executive Director, mistakenly took him for the Maître d'. He quite rudely looked at the senator and said loudly, "I instructed you to close this damn bar at 6:30!" The crowd went completely quiet!

Lee was trying to limit the cost of the bar for the Association. I had barely time to provide a scotch for the Senator. He handled the situation fine! I made certain Simpson was talking to other guests, and hurriedly went up to the dais and switched the name cards, so Lee and the Senator were sitting side by side! When the crowd was seated, and the program about to start, we almost had to carry Eilbrecht off. The look on his face was unbelievable!

Senator Simpson, the professional speaker, said in his opening remarks the following! "Guests, Coaches, and baseball fans, I am honored to be your speaker at this wonderful affair. I enjoy big affairs such as this. I'm a tremendous athletic supporter! But, I find that this banquet happens to be ONE TOUGH PLACE TO GET A DRINK!" It brought the house down!

April 1963, the Wyoming Baseball Cowboys dedicated their new pride and joy, Cowboy Field and Stadium. It was constructed in a joint venture between the City of Laramie and the University of Wyoming Athletic Department. It was a beautiful stadium setting, lined with a lighting system and stately green trees. Four Pony and Little League fields were adjacent to the north of Cowboy Field and together they received national attention as one of the finest complexes for youth baseball in the country. This all grew out of a copy of the Detroit Tiger's spring training facility in Florida. It was designed by myself, Athletic Director "Red" Jacoby, and University President, Doctor "Duke" Humphries, all of whom believed in the values of a strong athletic program.

In the summer of 1963 the NCAA selected me to be the commissioner of a new collegiate summer baseball league called the Basin League. It was comprised of six cities in Nebraska and South Dakota, with its headquarters in Rapid City, South Dakota. This was an old semi-pro baseball league with a solid reputation, but it had to operate under NCAA amateur rules and regulations. It was to be regulated by community business owners, offering summer employment for outstanding underclassmen from colleges and universities in the USA. My responsibilities were to make certain each team's roster of amateur baseball players lived by the rules. I enjoyed this assignment for three seasons, traveling to each of the five cities, operating out of the headquarters in Rapid City. My Guard schedule those summers was such that I could complete my military requirements and still manage the Basin League.

During the 60's Cowboy Baseball participated in the following US Military sponsored tournaments during our spring break travels to Arizona, Southern California and Hawaii. These tournaments were made possible by room and board facilities furnished by the Air Force, Army, Marine Corps, and in cooperation with MATS (Military Air Traffic Services). These tournaments included the following locations and universities.

Riverside California National Tournament

UCLA
University California
Riverside
Brigham Young University

Yale University
University of Mississippi
University of Washington
University of Wyoming

Armed Forces Tournament at Hickam Air Force Base, Honolulu, Hawaii

Hawaii University
Army Baseball Team
Brigham Young University

US Navy Submarine-Pacific Team
University of Wyoming
USAF Team

USMC Invitational at USMC Recruit Depot, San Diego, California

University of Wyoming
San Jose State University
Pacific University

USMC Recruit Baseball Team

Later in my career the following courses helped me to stay on active duty and reach my promotion goals. Every opportunity was interesting and rewarding.

Combat Intelligence Course, 30 July - 12 August 1967, Camp McCoy, Wisconsin

Senior Officer Preventative Maintenance School, 15-30 January 1969, Fort Knox, Kentucky

In December of 1969, I married a fascinating Italian beauty I had met on a "blind date" during a Wyoming baseball trip to Arizona. Today, after 44 years, and "never a harsh word", Connie Landi Daniel and I are still very happy, living in Tucson, Arizona.

Wyoming National Guard Ball 1969

It was not easy to obtain promotion to lieutenant colonel, as I had to complete over five hundred hours of correspondence courses. In January 1970, after completing the correspondence courses, I received a diploma from the Engineer Officer Advanced Course at

Fort Belvoir, Virginia indicating that I had satisfactorily completed that course. I was then promoted to lieutenant colonel in January 1970. During all those years I was able to combine my coaching career and the Guard, enabling military travel for both Guard and baseball events.

On 4 May 1970, amid all the anti Viet Nam protests that were occurring nation wide, the Kent State College affair occurred. Rioting broke out on their campus, a National Guard Unit was activated, issued live ammunition, and in the confusion four students were shot to death. This inflamed college and university students' nation wide. On the Wyoming campus at Prexy's Pasture, rioting students with loud speakers setting bonfires increased the tension of the crowds. Numbers of enraged young people rapidly were on the edge of destroying property and getting out of control.

I was the Wyoming National Guard Officer responsible for civilian mob control in the Southeast section of Wyoming. The governor of Wyoming surveyed the problem that was developing and activated the 1022nd Combat Engineer unit in Laramie to handle the situation at Prexy's Pasture. I activated the men, called them to form at our headquarters building, and wait for additional orders. There I put them "at ease" and very strongly commanded them not to load their weapons! Brigadier General Stimson (a Laramie resident) and I proceeded to an area behind several trees, keeping in touch with the troops at HQ's, and observed the rioting students and others! We were doing everything in our power not to make the same mistake that Kent State had. I finally decided the bonfire had burned down some, and with a loud speaker ordered the crowd to calm down. By this time we had ordered a small number of troops, with unloaded weapons to positions on the edges of the crowd. Several hours later, the mobs dispersed and the problem was over.

My career in the Wyoming National Guard was gradually moving towards the time that I would be forced to retire. Regulations were that unless you were an O-6 (full colonel wearing eagles) after 30 years of commissioned time, retirement was compulsory. On

September 9, 1971 I officially retired and received a plaque from the National Guard Bureau, and a Certificate of Service for 29 years in the United States Military, which read **"15 years USMCR and 14 years ARNG."**

The transfer from the Marine Corps to the Guard turned out to be the right thing to do for my family and my career. The Guard gave me the opportunity to not only continue flying, but to expand my experiences in leading the men of the engineer battalion. The recall to active duty was difficult financially, but it reinforced my love and respect for the military and the sacrifices made to protect our country.

Just prior to my military retirement, I made a major decision to retire from the University of Wyoming as baseball coach to seek other career opportunities. So, the 1971 spring season was my last and it ended with a double header with BYU, called because of snow on May 26th. As for my sons, Tim was married and attending UW, on his way to a career in the Army Corps of Engineers. Tom was majoring in Recreation at UW, and Mark joined us in our new adventure to Tucson, Arizona.

Wyoming Army National Guard

S2 Officer, 1022nd Engineer Battalion, Ft. Lewis, Washington

Chapter 19 Death Dealer To Engineer To Cowboy And Now A Wildcat

The 70's Plus

It was a hot, searing, dusty day in July with monsoon rain clouds forming in the skies as we pulled into Tucson, Arizona, unloaded our rental truck and unhitched Baby Red. We had pulled Connie's Triumph convertible that had been buried in a snow bank in Laramie, Wyoming since December of 1969. **The '70's were just around the corner.**

July 1971 was the time to change my University of Wyoming life and accept the opportunity to move to Tucson, Arizona. Leaving after all of the years and the memories of my life at Wyoming made this a tough decision, but one that turned out to be the right one. I would also be leaving the comradery and the personal and professional motivation of the Guard behind. Military retirement regulations required retirement after 29 years commissioned service. I needed new challenges to keep me from stagnating at the end of a successful career at Wyoming.

I had accepted a new position at the University of Arizona. The job title was Executive Director of the University of Arizona Athletic Scholarship Program. In reality it was the formation and development of the organization of companies, alumni groups and individuals who were interested in donating money to support Athletics. In mid-July I moved into my new office, met my new secretary, Andrea, who became an important right hand to my projects. We decided to throw some balls in the air and see where they landed. We proceeded to call this new club, the WILDCAT CLUB, and went to work. It became an immediate success as the Tucson community was athletically and financially the "Goose that laid the Golden Egg!" The success lasted eight years under my direction. Then panic and political idiocy took over! I was moved to supervising student teaching for physical education. That enabled me to be on the golf course by 2 PM! My golf handicap slowly went down!

Eventually I spent fourteen interesting, sometimes wonderfully pleasing, and other times frightfully aggravating, years at the University of Arizona. I learned that in life the upper strata of a University can be tough to understand. I have to say that, in the end, it was a worthwhile adventure!

After I retired from the University of Arizona I received several opportunities for employment, including one from Alphagraphics, Inc. Their offer was one I could not turn down. They even offered Connie a position she reluctantly accepted. Both offers contained financial opportunities with future increases. My title was Director of International Master License Development, and Connie was the Coordinator of International Conferences and Conventions. Several sales trips to Great Britain, Australia, Europe, and Canada were made. We also worked with the development of Hong Kong and formed a co-op of 16 small countries in Europe. After initiating the development of licensing in Russia, and after two and one-half years employment, we retired from Alphagraphics Inc. It was a great tour for the both of us. I also had found that my golf game was suffering from not enough play!

Tucson is a very strong military community, and the home of Davis-Monthan Air Force Base. Several thousand Air Force officers and enlisted personnel are stationed along with hundreds of military aircraft operating daily. It is also home to the US 12th

Air Force Headquarters. My retired status allowed me to keep abreast of many educational opportunities and base services.

I had maintained my commercial pilot license and took some refresher flights in a Cessna 310 for FAA multi-engine flying. Connie and I took private plane trip with Janet and Jack Slocombe to Cozumel, Mexico and another to Cabo San Lucas, Mexico with one of our best Wildcat Club members, Ernie and Elaine Metz. Sadly, a few months after our trip, they were killed during a landing approach to one of Arizona's resort areas, when he developed vertigo, and they crashed. This was a tragic loss of two dear friends. This happened in the Cessna 310 in which we had taken the flight to Mexico.

One plane I flew on several occasions was a Beechcraft 4 seat low wing plane. Beechcraft Aircraft Company had implemented a program of starting civilian flight clubs. My night flying instructor, a retired Air Force colonel, and I had flown this plane on occasions. I had also used it myself on several local flights to Phoenix for Wildcat Club meetings. Another aviation tragedy occurred when my instructor was demonstrating this plane to two other retired Air Force Colonels in New Mexico. On takeoff it exploded and killed all three! This caused me to stop and re-evaluate my safety program for any future civilian flights.

One interesting flight occurred when a Wildcat Club buddy asked me to help him drop a friend's ashes from the air over the Catalina Mountains. It went very well until we realized the Border Patrol might observe the operation and think we were dropping drugs, a somewhat common occurrence in southern Arizona. Fortunately that did not happen!

During the early 70's, I became active in Tucson's Chamber of Commerce Military Affairs Committee. One very interesting opportunity was when DMAFB (Davis Monthan Air Force Base) furnished transportation on Military Air to Nellis Air Force Base to observe operations of the "RED FLAG" training exercises, several miles north of Las Vegas. This was a fantastic opportunity for a former Marine fighter pilot as we acted as official observers on a very large TV screen in a hanger at Nellis. Jet Fighter aircraft representing enemy forces and US Air Force fighters in combat were reflected in images on the screen as they located, attacked and shot at one another. It was a terrific show of aerial combat. Our group was the guests of the Air Force, and we were housed at one of the casinos on the strip. We returned to Tucson the next day.

Another opportunity that my wife Connie and I enjoyed was as guests of the US Navy and the US Naval Academy on a four-day trip to Annapolis Maryland. This trip was made in cooperation with the Academy recruiting program coordinated by reserve Navy Captain Don Strand. Selected educators from Tucson schools and community members were invited on the trip. Observing the various cadet activities, dining hall meals and their routines was very interesting. Hundreds of cadets entered the mess hall by academic class and rank, with first year cadets under very strict rules. Two days of observing educated us to the program that produces top class young officers. These cadets were readying themselves for the experiences they will have in the near future with the fleet.

In 1984, we had the opportunity to visit the Champlin Fighter Museum in Mesa, Arizona. It is the home of the American Fighter Aces Association and museum. In scanning the many plaques and stories of America's warriors, we noticed the absence of our leader, "Cowboy" Stout, who had been overlooked and should have been recognized along with Colonel Jack Conger and Colonel Don Fisher of VMF-114. All of these Marine pilots had shot down at least five enemy aircraft, qualifying them as "ACES." I met with the curator and received the necessary information and procedure to make certain our leader, Cowboy, was added to this prestigious museum.

As retirees, we also had the opportunity to travel stateside and abroad, and, if space was available, stay in Visiting Officer's Quarters on military installations. We always took time to visit the base museums and static displays of aircraft. Over the years, we stayed at sixty-one bases in twenty-five states and Italy and New

Zealand. Most often we were assigned a private BOQ room according to my retired rank of lieutenant colonel. But every once in awhile, lady luck and an understanding Airman at check in, would upgrade us to a colonel's suite or general officer's quarters. Some memorable bases and experiences follow:

Our very first attempt at "Space A" resulted in a stay at Brook AFB, San Antonio, Texas. There we had a spacious very well appointed two-bedroom apartment. The dining table was set with china and crystal as only fit for a general. Surely this was a mistake and Connie was so nervous that instead of ordering dinner to be delivered from the O-Club, she sent me out for pizza so no one would realize we were there.

At Ft. Jackson, Columbia, South Carolina we stayed three nights in a three bedroom cottage on the lake. This time we were getting used to upgrades—relaxed and enjoyed the experience, even parking in a general's parking slot near the cottage.

At Whidbey Island NAS, Washington our quarters overlooked the flight line. At midnight the roar of jets taking off awakened us. Could there be a national emergency occurring? Eventually, I figured out it was a night flight training exercise doing Touch and Go landings.

Kessler AFB, Michigan, found us in a small BOQ room sharing a bath and overlooking the parade grounds. Our wake-up call at 6 AM reveille was the newly enlisted detachment marching and loudly singing cadence reminding us what the military is all about.

At Kings Bay Naval Submarine Base, Georgia, we were invited to participate in a Welcome Home parade and party for a nuclear sub returning from a 6 months cruise. The tears of joy when families reunited made us so proud to be Americans and to be a part of this emotional experience.

A trip with an unplanned stay at Ft. Bliss, El Paso, Texas resulted in a post Christmas holiday party. A huge snowstorm centered over El Paso, closing the interstate both east and west bound. We limped into the base and fortunately got quarters in a lovely old guesthouse. We immediately headed to the PX food court and liquor store to stock up for the evening before they closed the base and sent non-essential personnel home. Other guests did the same, and so we had a community cocktail party under the Christmas tree in a beautifully decorated room and shared "life in the military stories" with our new friends.

The cottages of Bellows AF Station, Hawaii were nestled on a beautiful beach on the northwest coast of Oahu. My Marine buddy and wife from Peleliu days, Phil and Loree Samson joined us for a week of golf and sunset happy hours. We spent a special night dancing to music of the 40's at the former O-club on the side of Diamond Head with a spectacular view of the Pacific.

Ft. Leonard Wood, MO (fondly know as Fort Lost in the Woods) found us once again upgraded. Of course, that could have been because we were there for son Tim's "Change of Command" Ceremony. He was assuming the position of the garrison commander, and we were awed at the pageantry, the speeches, the parade and the respect shown for a military tradition carved in time.

In 1985, we made a trip to France to visit son Tim and family. As a major in the U.S. Army Corps of Engineers, he was attached to the US Embassy and was the TRADOC liaison officer to the French Military Academy at Sainte Cyr-Coëtquidan and at the French Military Engineer School in Angers, France. We then toured by automobile for three months, wandering through the French countryside, Germany, Italy, Spain and Belgium. We drove 14,000 kilometers and had the trip of a lifetime. Forever in our memory was a trip to Normandy touring the battlegrounds of WWII! In 1984, President Reagan attended ceremonies there commemorating the 40th Anniversary of D Day. Tim had been very busy representing the U.S. Embassy at several celebrations in cities and villages along the "Route of Liberation." The museum curator at Saint Mere Eglise, at my son's request, arranged a personal tour for us, which cemented those pictures and memories in our minds. We personally made our multi country tour without travel agency advice. We would drive until mid-afternoon, locate the center of the town, find an outdoor café, order wine and cheese and then find a small "auberge" (a local inn) and made plans for the next morning. We found the natives in the outskirt villages were kind and very interesting, and willing to discuss WWII history. Tim spoke excellent French, which helped to make the tour of the chateaux country of France complete.

Italy was a challenge as you always had to watch your wallet, but the Italian boat songsters in Capri fell in love with "Concetta." We managed to part with some Lira. (Italian money) We were fortunate to find two BOQ's, (Bachelor Officer's Quarters) in Italy at Vicenza, and at Camp Darby, near Pisa. Our last stop before heading home was to visit NY friends Mella and Jerry Wawack in Brussels. Unbelievably, our stop in a Club for a goodbye drink found us sharing a table with a couple of Wyoming Cowboys. This is truly a small world.

We decided we had never tried to obtain a "Space A" flight in the 50 states. After a drive to Fort Ord, California where we stayed with Tim and family, Hawaii beckoned. So we searched the schedule at Travis AFB for available flights, heard about a New Hampshire National Guard four engine Turbo Prop C-130 leaving Mather Field, California. It had space the next morning. Connie and I spent the night and went to the airport early for our flight. She spotted the four props and did not have a smile. When I explained it was a jet turbo plane perfectly capable of flying to Hawaii, she decided that would work. After loading aboard the aircraft, we found we were the only couple in the cabin for the trip. Canvas benches turned out to be comfortable as we could stretch out for the eleven hours flight to Ewa, Hawaii. Toilet facilities startled her as they consisted of a bucket and canvas curtain for privacy. Not a United Airline luxury liner!

After seven days on the beach on Kauai we returned to Honolulu and went to the Space A desk at Hickam Field to search for a flight back to the mainland. We would have to spend the night in the lounge and take our chances for morning. It was Friday night and "Happy Hour" was starting at the Officer's Club. Having checked

207

with the Marine Corps desk, and stored our luggage, Connie was discussing our status with Marine Staff Sgt J. H. Bridges, a Protocol Marine Liaison. He learned I had served in the Corps as a Corsair fighter pilot at Peleliu, and asked if we desired to go to the Officer's Club. He would provide transportation there and back. What a gracious offer we readily accepted. A Marine vehicle appeared driven by a very attractive blonde Marine enlisted driver, she saluted, provided typical Marine classic service, offered to pick us up when we requested our return. This young Marine made me feel like I was a two-star general with her courtesy, professionalism and Marine training!

When we returned to the Protocol Desk, Staff Sgt Bridges asked if we would like to go Space A to Australia or New Zealand. There were two four-engine Cargo 141 Star Lifters scheduled to refuel and depart for either destination and we could have our choice. WOW…lucky we always pack our passports…just in case. Their return schedule would allow us to return to Hawaii in a week. We readily accepted the opportunity and decided on New Zealand since we had already visited Australia. After takeoff we were climbing to departure altitude when Connie became uncomfortable because we only had $90.00 in cash for the long trip and only summer clothing and it was winter "down under." I comforted her with the fact that we had credit cards, so relax and enjoy! Our flight was quite interesting as the crew was very cordial inviting me up into the cockpit to observe all of the navigational systems. The female pilot in the left seat was an Air Force Academy graduate and invited Connie to spend time in the cockpit as well. This was an event for her that made the flight memorable.

Upon arrival in Christchurch, New Zealand the "Kiwi" in charge of Special Services supporting the Navy's operations in the Antarctic welcomed us. They assisted us in obtaining quarters at the naval base the first night, let us borrow some winter clothing and even helped us rent a car for our travels to Queensland on the South Island. Highlights there were cruises on Lake Wakitapu to a sheep shearing station and a day in the Fiords on Milford Sound. The week was a wonderful tour of all sights and experiencing profound appreciation for the people of New Zealand.

There was a Veteran's Club (American Legion type) a short way from our hotel. The bartender there greeted us warmly. I noticed a large painting of a Corsair on the wall. He told us of the New Zealand Corsair pilots who meet there daily for a "pint"! The US Navy had given the New Zealand Air Force several Corsairs while I was stationed at Espiritu Santos. My assignment at that time was checking six "Kiwi" pilots out in their new planes. We barely missed seeing those pilots as they had just departed the club.

All too soon it was time for us to check on our C-141 crew returning to Hawaii. We made certain to meet them at the O Club after they had landed, offering them a round of drinks, while we made certain of space on the departure next morning. Upon our arrival at the departure desk, the airman greeted my wife with news that on the passenger list for the flight to Hawaii was a mental patient being escorted by two AP's (Air Police). This might preclude her being on the flight due to the location of valuable instruments near the rear cabin rest room. The patient would have to use the restroom with the door open. Quickly, with a good response, was Connie's remark, "Airman, I have seen every situation imaginable in my several years of hospital volunteer work." This negated any refusal for Space A. We were able to enjoy our return stateside! Military ID cards rewarded us again!

In the late 70's Pima County gave a large tract of land to a fledging association that would grow to be called the Pima Air and Space Museum (PASM). I attended several of the early organizational meetings and worked with a retired US Marine Gunny Sergeant, a manager of a local motel, in attempting to procure a Corsair for the museum. In the interim the Corsair was put on display at the Tucson Inn. He mounted it on a pedestal, positioned as if it was diving into the swimming pool. Prior to bringing the plane to the Pima Air Museum, the Marine Sergeant successfully talked a Marine general into sending four Marines from Yuma to the Tucson Inn to refurbish the Corsair. They did a wonderful job making certain it would remain in good condition. They also spent the evenings eating and living "the life of Reilly!" at his motel. The plane eventually wound its way to Hanger 4 where today it is a prized museum display with wings down in a flight position next to the Air Corps' P-51 fighter. Many discussions occur daily as to which plane was the best of WWII. This has not been settled yet. It depends on which experienced pilot wins the argument that day, Marine or Air Force. The Marines generally come out on top!

Fast forward to Cinco de Mayo 1998 when on that May 5th we celebrated my 75th birthday in Hanger 4 under the wings of the Corsair. Over 75 guests, many of the family from out of town, enjoyed cocktails, BBQ, dancing and participating in the traditional cake cutting ceremony using a US Marine sword. Décor was Marine maroon and gold with Marine flags and model planes as centerpieces. After a close up inspection, my golfing pals accused me of telling falsehoods, saying I would have been too small to be able to get into the cockpit of the large fighter Corsair!

Bud and Ralph Lagoni/75th Birthday Party at PASM

Starting in June of 1998, I began volunteering as a docent in Hanger 4. I have logged over 3,000 hours next to my favorite jewel, the Marine F4U, Corsair telling war stories of blood and thunder to visitors at the now amazing Pima Air and Space Museum. We have nearly 300 planes on static display in the four new large hangers and on the expansive grounds. The museum is currently the outstanding tourist sight in Tucson.

On Saturday mornings, the Volunteers at PASM schedule presentations by those who might have a story of historical interest. I had the opportunity in 2003 and 2006 to make PowerPoint presentations recalling my story of flying the Marine F4U in Southwest Pacific combat, and the Battle of Peleliu during WWII. In 2007 at the Annual Volunteer Appreciation Dinner I received the Arizona Aerospace Foundation Commendable Service Award.

In 2004 a group from Sierra Middle School invited several WWII veterans to be interviewed by 6th graders as they planned on publishing the biographies in a book for sale to the citizens of Tucson. The title of the book is "THEY OPENED THEIR HEARTS. TUCSON ELDERS TELL WWII STORIES TO TUCSON YOUTH." The number and quality of stories from WWII that the veterans shared with the students was gratifying.

I agreed to participate in the project and was invited to the school to be interviewed by one young boy and five young girls. Each had prepared questions to present to the veteran. A video operator would record the entire question and answer session, and also record any pictures or items of interest. The students and I gathered for the interview and made introductions. The young students were well prepared, relaxed and amazed me with excellent and quite mature questions. One question that emotionally affected me was "What was your reaction when you faced your parents upon return from your combat tour, realizing what they had gone through during your absence?" I had to pause before I answered. It was a wonderful experience, one that I shall always appreciate. Students had the opportunity to comment on their interview experience. Quoting one young lady, "Mr. Daniel was very nice, he had baby blue eyes!" The group had a special viewing, and presentation of the book, with several celebrities from city and state government introducing each veteran's story. The book sales were brisk.

Beginning in 2004, a young history teacher at Empire High School, Jeremy Gypton, and each school year gave me the honor of meeting with his 11th and 12th grade students. We would work together and present a PowerPoint presentation to his history classes. Our subject would cover the "The Battle of Peleliu WWII," introducing the students to the war in the Pacific. We covered the facts that Peleliu was a small island at the south end of the Palau Island chain, located in the Southwest Pacific Ocean, some 600 miles east of the Philippine Islands. The USMC's First Infantry Division led the invasion on September 15th, 1945. Operation "STALEMATE" was supposed to be over in three to four days. Faulty intelligence misinformed the invading USMC infantry, resulting in one of the most costly and lengthy (72 days) battles of the Pacific War. Casualties for US Marines were over 6,700, and more than 10,000 Japanese were killed.

Each class of 25 students watched the combat video footage of aerial bombardment of Napalm Bombs (265 gallons of jellied gasoline dropped from 150 feet by the VMF-114 Corsairs) on the caves of Bloody Nose Ridge, Peleliu. Students were amazed when they realized aerial combat was occurring at a distance equal to the entrance of the high school and the main road west to their housing community. Following forty five minutes of discussion, another twenty minute question and answer period was allowed, and most of the students were able to remain after the presentation to ask more questions. Students impressed me with the quality of the questions asked. It was an inspiring study of their maturity, interest and search for knowledge. This continued from 2004 through 2010 when Gypton sadly changed jobs. Empire High School in Vail, Arizona is one of the unique high schools in the Tucson area. They have no schoolbooks, but each student is provided with a laptop computer.

A Belgian Air Force exchange officer, Stephane Casteleyn who lived across the street from us was on a three-year exchange program teaching foreign pilots how to fly the F-16 fighter aircraft. This is currently one of the USAF top planes in their inventory. We became friends and enjoyed his wife and twin children born during his tour. One morning, he casually inquired if I would be interested flying the F-16 Simulator at the Arizona Jet Fighter Program at the Arizona National Guard. My answer immediately was YES, YES. He instructed me to meet him at 0800 at the National Guard airport hangers located at the Tucson airport. He would escort my wife and me on a wonderful tour, explaining new equipment and its purpose. Boy was I excited as he helped me into the pilot's seat of the simulator. He showed me a quick introduction to the cockpit, and to all of the current controls, dials and information on the front panel.

He then departed for the instructor's panel, and I made my first take off in this powerful jet fighter. The elevator control stick, normally located between your legs was a pistol-like handle that you tenderly held in your right hand. All of the flight control movements were automatically handled for you. The up and down flight adjustments were based on degree angles. Example– Approaches to landing were obtained by holding seven degrees on the screen in the "heads up" instrumentation visible in the middle of the forward windscreen. I was also able to break the speed of sound in vertical flight. Almost everything came to me naturally even though I had not been in the cockpit of a fighter for several years. The most important difference I experienced in the simulator was the lack of "G" forces (gravity pulls). It was also a very quiet experience, as you didn't hear the roar of the after-burners, or the powerful twin engines.

After several minutes of thrilling maneuvers, figure eights, slow rolls and fundamental aerobatic maneuvers, I decided to do some touch and go landings. I put the plane in a seven degree let down and as all pilots brag about, "I greased this baby onto the deck." After another landing, it was time to bring this experience to a close. I approached the runway that I saw on the scenic area screen, and began my approach. My instructors' voice told me in my headphones that I was headed for the taxiway, and that would be ok! I immediately thought to myself "NOT ME JACK!" I immediately did a quick hard left-right turn on the ailerons, (TURN CONTROLS) and bounced onto the runway. Stephane told me later "That last landing was interesting. I had never done a carrier approach before!" That is an example of the saying" that every landing you can walk away from is a good one!"

My logbook shows: Date- 1/28/09   Type –F-16 #03514   Duration 1.5 hours   Pilot- LTC Daniel   F-16 Simulator at AZ National Guard Operations Flight Desk – Connie Daniel – Instructor "STEF," Belgian Air Force, assigned to AZ National Guard

I received a phone call from a dear friend, Sammy Jay Alaya, one of the few living relatives of the Cowboy Stout family. Her daughter, Cassidy wanted to interview me over the telephone. She was putting together a project for her sixth grade class in Cheyenne, Wyoming. Her great uncle was Cowboy Stout, the commanding officer of VMF-114. She wanted to develop her version on CD, of "Cowboy's War" as a tribute to the memory of her great uncle. The basis of this history would be told through letters Cowboy sent home to his mother and dad. This young lady finalized a thirty-minute story on a DVD, including her interview with his wingman Lt. Bud Daniel, that is an emotional, wonderful tribute to the famous Marine fighter pilot. Stout was killed in action on March 4th, 1945 on a low level Napalm mission over Koror Harbor in the Palau Island Chain. His combat medals included the Navy Cross, Purple Heart, 3-Air Medals, and the Navy Unit Citation and combat area ribbons. Several pictures add to the story that is the emotional expression of her love to an uncle she wishes she had known. The book, Semper Fi In The Sky, the story of the Cactus Air Force at Guadalcanal, also recounts Cowboy's service to his country.

The crowning event in my many opportunities to maintain a close association with the Corps happened in 2007 at the 232nd USMC Birthday Ball. The combined USMC Reserve units in Phoenix and Tucson had this event scheduled at the JW Marriott Resort Hotel in Tucson. The USMC Major, in charge of the celebration, happened to mention to his uncle Pat Thorpe, one of my former baseball players that he was looking for a speaker for the event. My Irish admirer casually told him, "Heck, just call my coach, he is a heck of a talker!

I received a call inviting me to be the main speaker at the event. I was honored with the opportunity and accepted. Having outgrown any appropriate Marine uniform, I rented a tuxedo, pinned on my gold wings, medals and ribbons in the correct order and started to work on my speech.

My largest problem was figuring out how to co-mingle my love for the USMC, and explain how and why I had completed my military career in the US Army Corps of Engineers! I diligently compared my Marine experience as mostly my family of brothers and pilots in combat. I referred to VMF-114 and the esprit' de corps that grew among our Skipper, Cowboy Stout, and fellow Marines as a family.

USMC 232nd Birthday Ball, 2007

The USMC Ball was scheduled for November 10th. Ten days prior to that date, I suddenly had a set back with my normally slightly gravely voice box. I immediately called for a meeting with Dr. Emami, my ear-nose and throat specialist. I was having a serious problem. He examined me, noted that my left vocal cord was paralyzed and recommended a surgical implant procedure that would push that cord over to enable the other one work. He checked his schedule and immediately scheduled the surgery. With the help of a speech therapist, by the time I had to deliver the speech my voice was strong. I'm probably the only USMC Officer who volunteered to have his throat cut to perform at a historic Marine annual function!

I arrived for the gala event that was rapidly filling the ballroom with young and middle aged, handsome Marines in their famous

Dress Blue Uniforms. Most were escorting beautiful ladies, dressed in stunning evening gowns. A Marine Honor Guard escorted the special guests, presented the March on the Colors, led the singing of the National Anthem and the Marine Corps Hymn and respectfully stood at attention for the reading of historical messages from the Commandant. This covered forty minutes of the beginning rituals. As Guest of Honor, I had to march and stand at Marine attention. My wife and son Tim, who had flown in from Missouri, fully expected me to fall on my bottom at any minute. My walker saved me!

It was time for my speech. Fortunately the sound system was excellent, and I had no trouble gaining the large crowd's attention. The hit of my speech was when I quoted Army Colonel Hackworth and his poem referring to the characteristics of dogs bred to reflect qualities of the Army, Air Force, Navy and Marines.

Quoting Hackworth:

"Army: St. Bernard, big and heavy, sloppy, bit clumsy, powerful, has stamina, built for long haul.

Navy: Golden Retriever, good-natured, hair a bit too long, wander around, but they love water.

Air Force: French Poodle, pretty, pampered, country club of forces, always travels first class.

Marines, they come in two breeds, ROTTWEILLER and DOBERMANS!
--- Some are Big and Mean
--- Some are Skinny and Mean
--- They are Aggressive on the Attack
--- Tenacious on Defense
--- Have really Short Hair and ALWAYS GO FOR THE THROAT!"

I had worked hard on my speech and fortunately it was well received, even a standing applause at the end! I do not know if they were very appreciative of my words or just happy that the speech was over so the dinner and dancing could begin.

After dinner, four Marines rolled out a large cake decorated with a Globe and Anchor for the traditional cake cutting ceremony! As the oldest Marine in attendance (84 years of age), I was served the first piece of cake. I then handed the youngest Marine (18 years old) the second piece. The dinner-dance swayed on with young Marines in dress blue, sometimes jitterbugging, or closely clinging and enjoying as young men and women do. It continued until midnight.

I must say I was thrilled to have had the opportunity to express my respect and admiration for the Marine Corps and every Marine in attendance that night. It blossomed out from my feelings and tone of my speech.

The years have flown by, but the memories linger. My career opportunities, our retirement experiences and the knowledge that family, comrades and friends continue to bring me joy help me watch the fires dwindle down and the embers glow.

Chapter 20   VMF-114 History And Squadron Reunions

Squadron History 1943-1963 (Excerpts from Wikipedia)

"VMF-114 All Weather Fighter Squadron was formed at MCAS El Toro on 11 July 1943. In August of '43 they departed for Ewa, Hawaii. They trained there until December '43, and then moved to Midway Island, home of the "Gooney Birds." In February '44 they departed for Espiritu Santos, then to Green Island for six weeks of strikes against Japanese garrisons that had bypassed the Bismarck Isles. This was a costly combat tour.

On 26 September 1944 they landed to support the First Marine Division in the battle of Peleliu. Ngesebus Island was bombed and strafed in support of 3rd Battalion, Fifth Marines. This was eight months of hell. The 1st Marine Division had invaded Peleliu on 15 September for what General Rupertus told the troops would be a "cakewalk" lasting no more than three to four days. 76 days later the island was declared secured. The landing on Ngesebus and VMF-114's support of the 3rd Battalion 5th Marines has previously been described in detail. The terrain on the island was unsuitable for anything but the costliest and most difficult advances, made possible by VMF-114's strafing and bombing. The squadron left Peleliu on 1 June 1945.

VMF-114 escaped the post war drawdowns at MCAS Cherry Point and on February 1946 was designated Marine Fighter Squadron 114 equipped with Night Fighter F4Us. They later transitioned to the F2H (Banshee). On 7 June 1953 they deployed to the Mediterranean as part of Carrier Wing CVA40.

On 1 May 1957 the *Death Dealers* became VMF-114 AW (all weather) and transitioned into the F9F Cougar and then the F4D SkyRay. From 13 Feb '59 to 1 Sept '59, they were on the Carrier Air Wing-1 aboard the USS Franklin D. Roosevelt, CVA-1. A normal deployment followed to Roosevelt Roads, Puerto Rico until January '61 when they transferred to NAF (Naval Air Field)

Atsugi, Japan. VMF-114 was deactivated on 1 July 1963. The squadron received the NAVY UNIT COMMENDATION FOR SERVICE in the Battle of Peleliu, 15 September '44–31 January '45."

Many of the pilots remained in the Marine Corps assigned to other squadrons either on active duty or transferring to the USMCR. Of the original squadron only Jack Conger, Bob Peebles, Roy Reed and Don Fischer stayed in VMF-114 after the war.

Squadron Reunions   1964-2007

The following letter was forwarded to several Marine fighter pilots who had not seen each other since June of 1945. It was the start of many memorable reunions. (COPY OF LETTER)

July 15, 1964

FOO-WANG
VMF—114

COMING UP   TUMULTOUS   TWENTIETH REUNION

1944 ----------------------------1964

PLACE: WASHINGTON, D. C.
DATE: OCTOBER 29 & OCTOBER 30, 1964

GREATEST PEACE TIME GATHERING
IN THE HISTORY OF THE CORPS!

YOUR COMMITTEE, SELF-APPOINTED, SELF-PERPETUATING AND SELF PAID, SUGGESTS TOO MUCH WATER HAS GONE OVER THE DAM.

This was the first of a series of VMF-114 reunions that would start again in 1980 and continue annually until 2007! Pilots who lived in the Washington DC area attended the first reunion. It was formed in a hurry. It did not have a chance to be as well attended as the next ones. Wink Balzer, Colonel Robert Peebles, and Intelligence

219

Officer, "Menopause" Marshall were the perpetrators of the initial reunion.

1980 Tucson, Arizona

Early in 1980,"EF" Frank Sullivan from Brainard, Minnesota, called me and said he had formulated a good mailing list and if I was interested, "WE" could host a VMF-114 Squadron reunion. This was in the end the original Colonel Lindbergh "WE" saying, as he did not intimate that it was to be in Tucson and the majority of organization and preparation would be by Connie and Danny! Tucson was an ideal location for a get together in May. Thanks to the imagination and perseverance of "EF", the reunion was a roaring success. Out of the known thirty remaining pilots, fifteen pilots and eleven wives attended the gala event. Sven Svare from Canada and Sam Porter from Mexico arrived to cheers. Dick Rash, in his late fifties, who had recently been flying F-4's in the Marine Reserves, rode his motorcycle from San Diego to Tucson.

Each day cocktails were served on the patio of the Granada Royal Suites Hotel, and 114 did it proud, furthering all traditions from the little cook's tent on Peleliu that was converted into the Officer's Club! "Fox" Weber was the first to arrive. By 5:00 PM all had gathered and it is difficult to describe the emotional feelings of the men who had not been together for thirty-five years. This was fast turning into a "Friday Happy Hour" at a stateside MCAS! We finally adjourned at 7:30 PM to a private room at my friends Greek Restaurant for a great meal. "Big Spender" Sven Svare graciously insisted on hosting a dinner for all the pilots and their wives.

Saturday, after breakfast on the patio, we departed for a round of golf for those who forgot their real handicap. Non-golfers drove the beer carts or visited the Pima Air Museum and the Davis Monthan "bone yard" with its collection of vintage planes, while the gals went shopping. Later that afternoon Pete Hansen proudly opened his two volumes of pictures taken on his return to Peleliu in 1979. My how the placed had changed much to the awe of the pilots.

Saturday evening, Connie and I proudly honored the gang at our townhouse for cocktails. We then moved to a local steakhouse for a great meal. Nick Virgets was the last pilot to arrive, banging on our rear gate, just in time for a drink. Old buddy Ralph Lagoni of VMF-122 and wife Jean joined us telling even more tales of "thunder in the Pacific." Sunday morning brought back memories of "mornings on "R&R" in Sydney!" Never did a cold beer taste better. Connie, after her first exposure to VMF-114 reunions uttered, "Gosh, by now I would have thought these guy's would have slowed down a little!" We took a vote, and the next reunion would be in Dallas, Texas in April 1981. We all were saddened by news of "Wink'" Balzer's early passing after a heart attack in Needham, Massachusetts.

1981 Dallas, Texas

Nick and Bobbie Virgets hosted VMF-114 in Dallas with a little help from his firm, COORS BEER. They put on a never to be forgotten B-B-Q at the Dallas brewery. The golfers enjoyed the Texas courses and Bobbie arranged for a spa day for the ladies. Jack Conger, who missed Tucson, arrived with flaps down, ready to party. It was great to see the "All American Boy" our famous ACE with the first 10 Japanese planes shot down in the Cactus Air Force's battle of Guadalcanal! Sixteen pilots were in attendance, and it seemed that the squadron memories became brighter and the recounting of them fuller. Once again, emotion took hold and no one was ready to leave until our next one was planned.

1982 Jasper Park, Alberta, Canada

Our suave and personable Bob Svare was a perfect host for the next reunion and a wonderful visit awaited us. Living in Tucson, Arizona, we chose the flight to Calgary, Alberta Canada. We had been in touch with Herb and Betty Mosca, who were driving, and arranged to meet them. It was a joyous reunion with a great couple. After touring Calgary, we drove to Banff, which was a beautiful drive, and visited the Fairmont Banff Springs Hotel. Then we traveled on to Jasper Park, with a stop to enjoy lunch at the Chateaux Lake Louise.

We arrived late afternoon and gasped as we viewed the wonderful lodge that Bob Svare had reserved for our group. Fourteen pilots and twelve wives had a choice of lodging in cabins or great rooms overlooking Canada's number one golfing facility. The group, after checking into our lodging, met for a run down of scheduled activities: golf, touring Lake Louise, riding the rapids.

Our host passed out shining white cowboy hat to all of his guests. "Menopause" Marshall, our popular Harvard University Squadron Intelligence Officer and his lovely wife, chose to ride the rapids! This event was the surprise of the reunion. Both in their late 70's,

she was a real gamer! This gathering was one of the best of our many reunions. Golfers played a great number of holes in spite of the goose droppings on their greens. The beauty of the surroundings and Svare's ability and personal control of every reunion activity sent VMF-114 home with great memories of a fantastic party. He passed away in 1988 much too soon!

1983 Shangri-La, Oklahoma

Wally "The Fox" Weber and his lovely wife Jean hosted the fourth reunion, which was rapidly turning out to be an annual affair, at a golf resort in the Tulsa area. Already it was evident that our members were so happy that a vote taken at the cocktail party held on the final evening of the reunion was sure to be one hundred to zip in favor of the following year. Only the location was in doubt until the last round of drinks. Wally was a perfect "OKIE" from

Muskogee, Oklahoma. His quiet demeanor and easy laugh personality made his presentation of the reunion functions a certain success. Golf, shopping and longs walks along the beautiful lake preceded the emotional and amusing stories told during cocktails. Our final evening we attended a dinner dance at the resort. Nineteen pilots were there to attest to each and every story told and once again 114 went home ready for the next one!

1984 Springfield, Missouri

Bill "Nose" Cantrell and wife Bobbie were the next candidates to handle an exceptionally perfect VMF-114 Reunion. I doubt if Springfield will ever recover from those four days. Bill was the perfect politician. He was soft spoken and quietly maneuvered you into his corner. His first move was to talk the local newspaper into printing a front page in large headlines warning the population of Springfield to beware of the onslaught of several wild pilots of VMF-114. Huge headlines on the front page of this special edition of the Springfield newspaper announced that President Reagan had re-activated USMC Fighter Squadron VMF-114 for duty in Springfield, Missouri.

He even coerced one of his political friends, Missouri US Senator Kit Bond, to be interviewed on a local 5 PM TV newscast warning of the coming fighter pilot invasion. At the dinner dance on the last evening, Bill presented a special film collection of aviation operations from USMC films that portrayed VMF-114 Corsair operations in the SW Pacific. This special film also had some additional footage interviewing pilots, including "Nose", recounting their war experiences.

One of Cantrell's personal friends, Bill Johnmeyer, a successful former Navy fighter pilot owned two planes. One was the Primary Flight Trainer we all had flown in training, the bi-wing "Yellow Peril!" The second was the beautiful bi-wing aerobatic "Pitts Special!" Naturally if possible, all of the squadron pilots salivated for an opportunity to fly either of beautiful airplanes. "Nose" called attention, and offered: "Behold, as your voluntary Commander, I am offering all the wives to participate in the following contest. *A 2OO WORD WRITTEN ESSAY STATING THE REASON WHY SHE MARRIED THE MOST WONDERFULL FIGHTER PILOT IN THE WORLD!"* The two winners would flip for the opportunity to select his choice of planes!

We all waited with bated breath for the announcement. The winners: Lt. Sven Svare, will have the opportunity to pilot *"THE YELLOW PERIL!"* A rousing cheer erupted. "Now, for the great challenge *"Lt. DANNY DANIEL WINS THE PITTS SPECIAL!"*

When the phone rang the next morning telling me to be ready in ten minutes to go to the airport and fly the Pitts Special I jumped a few feet in the air, and it felt like I did not return to solid ground for a few weeks! I had not flown any aerobatic maneuvers for several years. I would be flying in the front seat of this little power box with ailerons sections on each of four wings, (top and bottom of each wing portion) which helped to increase and speed up each aerobatic maneuver!

In the rear cockpit would be the owner, Bill Johnmeyer. He had recently won the National Championship Aerobatics in his new Pitts Special! I had a real pro directing me.

He turned the plane over to me to try any maneuver I wanted. Boy was I thrilled. Immediately, slow rolls were my first try. It was a cinch; over and over this small performer was perfect. Then a loop was tried successfully, followed by the Immelman, a one/half roll at the top of the loop. Some lazy eights followed, and then time to recover my sanity.

224

The flight consumed more than a full hour; it was time to go home. I thanked my newfound friend many times, received his

Bob Svare ready to fly the Yellow Peril

congratulations, and felt like *King of the World*! A memory I will cherish forever.

I have recovered the worn, partially faded, full-page section of the *Springfield Leader and Press*, Saturday, May 19, 1984. The morning headlines read:

VMF-114 was born July 1, 1943, MCAS El Toro, CA!
VMF-114 BACK TO ACTIVE DUTY!
Reagan Reactivates WWII Secret Weapon-Invincible in WWII!
VMF-114 Gets New Chance!

Here are some quotes from this fabulous copy:

"Sunrise to sunset, their Corsairs filled the southern California skies. After dark they filled the bars of Laguna Beach. Their work in both areas was exemplary and many of these brave pilots bear scars to this day to prove it!"

"VMF-114 re-writes book on close air support!

In an effort to help the ground Marine Troops of the 1st Marine Division, the white –nosed Corsairs of Major Cowboy Stout's Death Dealers flew the shortest bombing hop in history on Sept. 29th, 1944. 2200 yards from takeoff to target was the distance as VMF-114 pilots dropped 1,000 pound bombs on Jap soldiers dug into inner parts of bath tub shaped Bloody Nose Ridge."

"The same pilots covered an amphibious landing of the 3rd BN Fifth Marines on the island of Ngesebus, a scant half-mile north of

Peleliu. The Corsairs flying literally inches over the riflemen's heads, repressing the Japs counter fire so that the 5th Marines suffered no casualties. VMF-114 was not so lucky. Lt. Rex Gilchrest, after landing, fell off his plane and suffered a sprained ankle!"

"Later on, while waiting for their next assignment on Emirau Island, 114 pilots had the opportunity of watching the famous, cigar smoking ACE, JOE FOSS, training his young pilots. It was like watching the Rockettes, when Joe lit a cigar, 39 young 2nd Lt's fired up! When Joe crossed his left knee, 39 sets of lieutenants left knees were perfectly choreographed! Little did these young heroes know that Joe would have shot their asses off if they had come between him and a Jap Zero! "

Reunions had become a foundation of peacetime VMF-114, even as only twelve pilots were able to travel to Missouri. They continued to be fantastic. And "Nose" Cantrell's as a host was almost monumental!

1985 Hawaii Calls!

Les and Lala Strandman had longed anxiously to host the gala in Hawaii. Connie and I were traveling in Europe on a 3 month self guided tour and had to miss this one. We received the report on another winner hosted by this great couple on the shores of this beautiful state.

1986 Hot Springs, Arkansas

Don Franke and Darlene hosted a fine party deep in the river country, in one of the great retirement communities. Darlene was our only woman Marine who served as a Communication Specialist during the war. Duke and Maggie Gilchrest were also residents and they contributed to the fun and energy of the reunion. We were able to have all of the dinners and parties on the banks of a river adjacent to the community center. A songfest to remember during cocktails was led by Major General Norm Gourley, USMC, a friend of Don's and special guest. The hit of the night:

USMC Birthday Toast

Here's to:

THE WONDERFUL LOVE OF A BEAUTIFUL MAID
THE LOVE OF A STAUNCH TRUE MAN
THE LOVE OF A BABY, UNAFRAID
HAVE EXISTED SINCE TIME BEGAN

BUT THE GREATEST OF LOVES,
THE QUINTESSENCE OF LOVES
EVEN GREATER THAN THAT OF A MOTHER
IS THE TENDER, PASSIONATE, INFINITE LOVE
OF ONE DRUNKEN MARINE FOR ANOTHER

Major General Norm Gurley, USMC, Retired

The "whoopin and hollerin" of the 16 pilots went on for a good ten minutes punctuated by Semper Fi! His booming voice led the group singing wartime songs with almost questionable lyrics! The punch lines to his lyrics were to Marine Corps cadence and really humorous. Gourley had been a member of Joe Foss's squadron, VMF-115, during our stay in Emirau on our way to Peleliu.

1987 Colorado Springs, Colorado

"Timmo" Sullivan and the "Italian Princess Rene", reserved rooms at the "posh" five star Broadmoor Resort, below the beautiful Rocky Mountains. Views were breathtaking! To the west was Pikes Peak, to the north the Garden of the Gods, looking east a fifty mile unrestricted view from the front range of the Rockies to the wheat fields of Kansas!

227

This was the opportunity, perhaps in a lifetime, to enjoy visits with nineteen VMF-114 pilots and wives at bargain rates! Two of the top rated golf courses, gorgeous grounds to roam, and dinners in the finest restaurants! Rene hosted a lovely luncheon for the ladies. Roy Reed introduced us to his new bride, Shirley, who was the youngest wife of the squadron, toppling Connie's reign after all these years. It was another reunion to be remembered! Two of our pilots passed away this year, Nick "Ice Cream" Virgets and Duke "Legal-Eagle" Gilchrist.

1988 Bemidji, Minnesota

In 1988 we were off to the "timber and lakes" land of the Midwest. Wally, "Fox" Weber and his wife Phyllis hosted us in a completely different setting for a reunion. It was a family style get together in a large log house. The main reception area served as our hospitality suite, perfect for story telling and wild remembering. The sixteen pilots gathered were getting

Zip Zabel, Sam Porter and "Fox" Weber

pretty good at this. Piano music and local groups singing popular music accompanied meals. Two popular pilots, Dick Rash and Sven Svare made their final takeoff this year.

1989 San Diego, California

Pete and Betty Hansen, along with Herb and Betty Mosca moved us into another famous ocean resort, the luxurious Hotel Del Coronado built in 1888. This classic beachfront hotel, its red turrets accentuating Victorian splendor, combined with a beautiful azure sky at sunset over the Pacific Ocean. We enjoyed our setting in pure relaxation, and nostalgically watched the young guns in A-6's doing "touch and goes" at North Island NAS. Dinner at the Coronado Naval Amphibious Base was a big hit.

Some of our pilots, had nostalgic memories of spending their last few days enjoying the beach and splendor of the 'Del Coronado, before shipping out to the Pacific in WWII. Bill Cantrell, now a widower, brought his fiancé, Mary Alice…and surprised us by inviting the seventeen pilots and spouses to his wedding. And as only "Nose" could do, announced place and time: tomorrow on the patio of the "Del" with champagne and cake to follow. One more emotional memory to store in 114's logbook. Larry Marshall made his last flight this year.

Pete and Betty Hansen enjoy a quiet moment

My wife Connie and I had the pleasure of spending time with our dear Arizona Country Club friends, Ed and Jody Gutknecht, as they had a beautiful beach front apartment on the 'Del Coronado grounds. Eddie became an "associate" member of VMF-114, as he had been flying the B-25 in Europe in WWII.

1990 Beaufort, South Carolina

Don and Betty Fisher lavishly swamped us with Southern hospitality, as we entered their beautiful river and boat dock home close to Beaufort, South Carolina. A very large banner, in Marine Corps colors with WELCOME VMF-114, greeted us as we approached their domicile! Franklin and Mary Lou Pippen joined the festivities. He has served with 114 in '46 and '47 at Cherry Point.

A catered party with handsomely dressed waiters and waitresses offered us the best in cocktails, and a Southern delicacy, "Frogmore Stew", was served in the South's best traditions. It was a magnificent experience. We departed in complete amazement at the entire evening. Former fighter pilots certainly knew not only how to fly, but also how to throw a party!

We stayed at the Bay Street Inn, an antebellum Southern mansion, turned bread and breakfast, which had been featured in the movie, Prince of Tides, starring Barbara Streisand. Beaufort is the setting where Pat Conroy told the story of his Marine aviator father in a novel, "The Great Santini." A must read for all Marines.

Colonel Fisher had been a member of the famous BAA-BAA Blacksheep Squadron commanded
by the warrior "Pappy" Boyington. At one time, he flew "Pappy's" wing position. He was an ACE, having shot down six Jap planes during the Solomon's campaign. Don had been a Group Commander at Beaufort MCAS at one time in his career and he

230

was able to make a lot of things happen during our tour there. One of the best was the opportunity to sit in the cockpit of the Marines best fighter aircraft at the time, the F-15. This was an ideal opportunity for the Corsair drivers of 114! Our guests at this reunion were Lee and Frank Corbo from New York. Frank was in awe of the opportunity to tour the base, the squadron areas and the F-15. His quote of the day "I may have been only Corporal Corbo, USMC, back in the 40s, but I sure felt like a general today."

Larry Herzog passed away this year without ever experiencing a reunion.

1991 San Antonio, Texas

Bob Peebles and Addie

San Antonio is the home of the Alamo (1836), the River Walk and tourist spots galore! Our hotel, the historic Menger, of Teddy Roosevelt's Rough Riders fame, was a museum experience at every turn.

Bob Peebles and his *irrepressible Addie* made certain we had interesting and great fun! Once again, our hosts had planned a reunion we would remember! The river curled around the entire area, boats floated as taxis, stopping at restaurants, music surrounded you and Mexican Mariachi's sang as you sipped margaritas. The guys and a female golfer or two, had a great course to play. One had to be careful of red anthills. If you brushed on one, you never forgot their stings!

A fine meal and many short speeches always highlighted the last evening. Cheers always met Mosca's annual push for having the next reunion at *Slippery Rock*

"U." But alas, the nomination did not win in the final vote. If one red neck pilot got up and made a serious pitch for skipping a year, or any far fetched idea to NOT have a reunion next year, he was 'booed down" by loud voices. Of course, after another round of drinks, a quick vote would find another couple to volunteer for the next year.

Sadly, we learned of Sam Porters death this year. The ranks are thinning.

1992 Lake Lawn, Wisconsin

Master salesman, "ZIP" Zabel had pushed for a reunion in the beautiful lake country, and he and wife Marion finally won the vote for this fine resort area west of Milwaukee.

Zabel, now home from his work related travels in Mexico and South America, had proudly chosen the reunion spot of beautiful Lake Lawn. Golf, shopping, enjoying our lodge suites and telling war stories were the order of the day. Zip appeared the first night attired in a brand new leather flight jacket, the US Navy issue to every MARINE PILOT. It was complete with the Gold Wings on the left front, and the "Death Dealer Patch" squadron logo on the back. It was dreamed up a long time before by the one and only Joe Wallace, VMF-114's "Joe College!" Zabel's family had ordered this for him prior to the reunion. Every 114 pilot in attendance was jealous! Most of us had worn out our initial issue by the Corps.

1993 Tucson, Arizona, VMF-114's 50th Anniversary

Connie and Danny Daniel had inherited the honor of planning a very important, milestone reunion! We jumped into the challenge of trying to come up with a very special few days for a "barnburner" party.

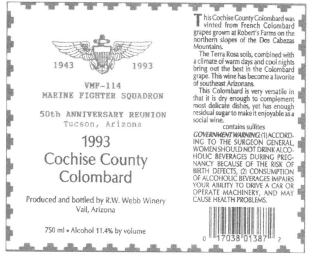

1943   1993

VMF-114
MARINE FIGHTER SQUADRON

50th ANNIVERSARY REUNION
Tucson, Arizona

1993
Cochise County
Colombard

Produced and bottled by R.W. Webb Winery
Vail, Arizona

750 ml • Alcohol 11.4% by volume

This Cochise County Colombard was vinted from French Colombard grapes grown at Robert's Farms on the northern slopes of the Dos Cabezas Mountains.

The Terra Rosa soils, combined with a climate of warm days and cool nights bring out the best in the Colombard grape. This wine has become a favorite of southeast Arizonans.

This Colombard is very versatile in that it is dry enough to complement most delicate dishes, yet has enough residual sugar to make it enjoyable as a social wine.

contains sulfites

GOVERNMENT WARNING: (1) ACCORD-ING TO THE SURGEON GENERAL, WOMEN SHOULD NOT DRINK ALCO-HOLIC BEVERAGES DURING PREG-NANCY BECAUSE OF THE RISK OF BIRTH DEFECTS, (2) CONSUMPTION OF ALCOHOLIC BEVERAGES IMPAIRS YOUR ABILITY TO DRIVE A CAR OR OPERATE MACHINERY, AND MAY CAUSE HEALTH PROBLEMS.

Our first step was the place! Our good friend and former Marine sergeant, was the business executive of the Radisson Hotels, Inc., Tucson. He also had been an umpire for the Wyoming versus Arizona baseball games in the 1950s. Connie had worked with him in high school programs in Tucson. We knew Gil very well, and hoped we would be able to sell the anniversary concept we had in mind.

The hotel facilities were perfect for our plans. Four stories built in a u-shape – with balconies overlooking a beautiful courtyard in the middle. We made up exaggerated plans to present to Party Manager Gil Carillo. First, we wanted the US Marine Corps Band to open the evening's festivities. We would contact the Marine Aviation unit in Yuma, Arizona to fly *four F-15 jet fighters* over the hotel in formation. The Reserve Marine Corps Unit commanded by Gunny Sergeant Jones, the most well dressed "gung-ho" Marine Sergeant in the Corps, would lead a 21-gun salute and the presentation of colors. In addition, a rousing edition of the Marine Corps Hymn would play. By now, needless to say, Gil was standing on his desk with his mouth open! We were able to line up all but the Marine Corps Band and the four F-15 fighter aircraft. The hotel residents were briefed for the gun salute and plans were finalized.

Our bar in the Ready-Room featured a poster-sized print of a nude painting from the Weber- Daniel Peleliu O-Club in 1944. Pete Hansen painted "our Lady of the O' Club" which the squadron retains. A private label of Arizona's best wine commemorating the 50th Anniversary was given to each couple in attendance.

Pete Hansen/Our Lady of the Peleliu 'O Club

We then got serious and lined up our favorite musical groups for the evenings dancing. The hotel had two different dinner/dance venues. We had a Mexican fiesta in the courtyard featuring a country western band, with lots of singing and dancing. Connie had asked them for only background music - but after a few margaritas, all spirits were very high. The grand finale…a "Rockette" line kicking to New York, New York!

Before our final dinner, we assembled in the courtyard to participate in the Presentation of the Colors and the Gun Salute to honor all those Marines in attendance and those that went before. "EF" Sullivan offered prayer for our country and for those that made the ultimate sacrifice. Pete Hansen read "Lest We Forget" naming our departed pilots. With the Marine Corps Hymn playing we marched to a private dining room, where a DJ was playing the sweet sounds of the big band era.

VMF-114 Squadron's Reunions continued to roll on and all too soon the vote was taken to next gather in Hawaii!

1994 Honolulu, Hawaii

Once again Les and Lala Strandman answered the call to host another memorable reunion featuring Hawaiian tropical
Hula dancers, Hawaiian tropical luaus, flaming tiki torches, ocean breezes and white caps breaking in the background. The Mai Tais

under the Banyan trees on the beach were a favorite memory easy to renew for all.

All of 114's pilots had spent previous time in or going through the islands on their way to other assignments.
The luxurious Hale Koa hotel had thankfully replaced Fort DeRussey, the original military stopover for many of 114's pilots. This was a beautiful place, but not the old Hawaii feeling. Hawaii was and is a wonderful place to visit and all of 114's membership appreciated the Strandman's hospitality. This year "Slim" Kilbourne and John Bernhardt took their final flight.

1995 Bradenton, Florida

The palm trees of Florida greeted the 114 group as Roy Reed called the roll. Roy greeted each pilot with several pins of every aviation type. The most memorable was a very nice blue F4U Corsair. I still have that Corsair pinned on my Pima County Air Museum white cap. This reunion was remarkable, as Roy had located a number of enlisted men from the squadron and eight of them answered the call. It made us all aware once again that the enlisted mechanics were the reason we believed in ourselves that we would fly safely and return in one piece. In addition, of interest was that my sister Arlene and her husband Jack, who was with the first Marine assault on Peleliu, were guests and they showed a video of NBC's Dateline, *"Peleliu, The Forgotten War."* This year marked the loss of two of 114's most personable pilots, Dave Neiswanger and Don Fisher.

1996 Santa Anna, California

This was 'old home" week for the VMF-114 squadron. Originating here in 1943, most of the pilots were very familiar with Laguna Beach bars and restaurants, and also the close by towns of Corona del Mar and Newport Beach. The squadron's "Handyman" Bill Elzey and his always-ready female golfer, the lovely Doris, a former Navy WAVE, were in charge of planning a homecoming party here.

They entertained exceptionally in their beautiful home in Santa Anna. The highlight of the stay was a tour of the now closed MCAS El Toro. It had changed a great deal from the time some of us were based there. It had been Elzey's last tour on active duty.

The old saying "some things never change" was never truer than at the O-Club (Officer's Club) MCAS El Toro. Many a night spent there wound up with signed chits that had been forgotten in a scotch fog, later surfaced on your monthly bill. Some were signed with a note on them, make it a "Double in a dirty glass!" You never knew when a Hollywood Celebrity would show up to participate in the activities...from Bing Crosby to Marilyn Monroe!

1997 Branson, Missouri

Bill "Nose" and Mary Alice Cantrell were the head honchos at the second Missouri get together. It was the same excellent, above average reunion including films from USMC Combat Carrier Operations of some later squadrons flying, landing and sometimes missing the carrier deck. We had a lot to critique watching those films. Branson is recognized for its many stage productions with famous comedians and stars from yesteryears. You'll find a theater on every block with continuous entertainment.

Bill Sonnenberg, a 114 pilot who said, and believed, that it was the same Jap gunner who had actually shot him down twice! He had two successive pick-ups by Navy Dumbo crews (air sea rescue flying boats). He used a parachute to jump from a flaming Corsair after one, and a successful (in that he lived) water landing after the second. Our squadron doctor administered 12 small bottles of Kentucky Bourbon to Bill after the second pick up. He was feeling no pain upon his arrival back to Peleliu. His "lucky card" ran out as he passed away in 1997.

1998 San Francisco, California

The Marines' Memorial Club and Hotel is located in the heart of downtown San Francisco, at the corner of Sutter and Mason Street, near Union Square. The building has several stories of nice rooms and on top there are large, beautiful memorial rooms full of important Marine history. Our final night's dinner was held in the historic Commander's Room, which was decorated for high-ranking military personnel. It was a beautiful meal and we experienced distinctively perfect military dining. Fourteen pilots and wives enjoyed the impressive surroundings with Pete Hansen and Barbara hosting the reunion.

Danny Daniel, Jack Conger, and Pete Hansen recall old times

One restaurant was situated on a high floor that had panoramic views of the Frisco skyline. The Memorial is just steps from the theater district, and close to the famous cable car stops. Rides down to the famous wharf district made the traditional stop at the popular Buena Vista Café, which features their legendary Irish coffee.

This year reduced the lineup of VMF-114 pilots as Frank Pippen and former Commanding Officer Bob Tucker passed away.

1999 Denver, Colorado

The famous Brown Palace in Mile High Denver beckoned our "legal eagle" Tim and Rene Sullivan to host this reunion. Both were well educated on fine wine and the way to entertain!
Emotionally, each get together brought on feelings of a year passing and the realization that this wonderful feeling of "A BAND OF BROTHERS" was growing stronger! The squadron made good use of the "swinging door" entrance to the cocktail lounge where the well dressed waiters were handsomely led by their supervisor, who seemed dressed similar to a US Navy captain! Joe Wallace and Jack Conger were surprise members in attendance. It was a wonderful reunion in the high country!

Once again Herb Mosca pleaded for consideration of "Slippery Rock-U" for the next reunion. Much to his surprise he did receive a unanimous vote but for a minor change. Beautiful Ashville, North Carolina was the location selected. Bob D'Arcy slipped the bonds of earth this year.

2000 Ashville, North Carolina

Herb and Betty Mosca hosted our return to the Deep South, where we stayed at the historic Grove Park Inn. The Inn's list of guest's dates back to the Civil War and included eight US Presidents. The site was initially known during the Civil War as Fortified Hills. It was built of granite stones with walls five foot thick of granite boulders. During WWII it was used as an internment center for AXIS diplomats. The US Navy used the Inn as a rest and rehabilitation center for returning sailors. In 1944-45 the US Army used it as restoration center.

It was a beautiful area deep in the Blue Ridge Mountains. The Moscas' held our evening meals and Happy Hours in the historic rooms of this old southern Civil War era hotel. The motion for Slippery Rock as the next year's reunion site was laid to rest, as Herb opened the final evening's happy hour's discussion. The lumber area of Minnesota was the winner. The group mourned the loss of the popular "Timo" Sullivan and Zip Zabel."

2001 Bemidji, Minnesota

Wally and Phyllis Weber would host the reunion in "EF" Sullivan's lumber and lakes country. Sullivan had unfortunately suffered the loss of his right leg below the thigh in a hunting accident shortly after his return from WWII and it was difficult for him to do all the organizing. The Rutgers's Lodge was comfortable and we had the run of the public areas and restaurants. Once again Wally entertained with his Muskogee"Okie" wit and drawl! Time, health and age, was gradually reducing our membership. The humor, close feeling for each other still filled our hearts, as we mourned the loss of our "Handy Man" Bill Elzey during this past year.

2002 Honolulu, Hawaii

Some things refuse to change. The last meeting in Minnesota did not lesson the determination to continue to the last two living 114 pilots. The strength of the Marine bond carried on with a vote to return to Hawaii. Les and Lala Strandman are becoming veteran party hosts!

The Hale Koa was again the 114's residence for an unusual happening. Early one morning the sirens in Oahu blared loud and clear. The hotel staff announced loudly that the Western Pacific had experienced a huge earthquake under the water and tsunami waves were approaching Oahu.

Panic hit most of the residents, but not two of our party wise Marine wives. Darlene Francke and Connie Daniel calmly called room services, ordered enough ice to fill and cool down our bathtub and filled it with enough beer and wine necessary to handle this calamity! We happened to have the room assignments that would not have to be evacuated. It so happened that the golfers were on the other side of the island and were not notified to evacuate. Thank you Golf God! The warning was finally lifted so no evacuation was necessary. It was, however an interesting event.

Hula Dancers, flame eaters, and Polynesian foods were prepared on the beach. All had a great time. VMF-114 pilots dedicated the party to the memory of the super organizer "EF" Sullivan who passed away this year.

2003 Las Vegas, Nevada

The gaming tables, nightclubs, famous entertainers, and the magic of the Las Vegas strip were all ready for the invasion of VMF-114's annual reunion. Pete Hansen volunteered to host the reunion. He was no stranger to the film, TV and entertainment world. He jumped out of the Corsair cockpit after the war into the difficult ladder climb of an acting career. Working very hard, his star began to shine. He worked his way through the ranks to a long and successful TV role as the lawyer in General Hospital even winning an Emmy. He was also the star of large company commercials (General Electric). Pete never lost his love of 114, and has always handled the requests of his fans, be it signatures or answering the requests of fan's mother who would just like to say hello to him. This actually happened when we left a Mexican restaurant the final evening of our first reunion in Tucson.

This reunion was the *60TH ANNIVERSARY OF VMF-114.* Our attendance was gradually less but the widows of fallen pilots were still wonderful in their attendance. Pete Drury, our Southern Gentleman from Savanna, Georgia, passed away. He never recovered from losing his buddy "Jiggs" Smith, who was KIA, over the New Britain Islands in 1944.

2004 Colorado Springs, Colorado

Pike's Peak calls, and our "Italian Princess" RENE, the vibrant widow of "TIMMO" Sullivan, graciously volunteered to host the reunion at the famous Broadmoor Hotel. She and her deceased husband had handled our reunions in 1987 and 1999 and everyone was looking forward to a repeat performance.

The pilots, wives, and widows of fallen heroes, enjoyed the elegant room facilities, and elite settings of the restaurants at the Broadmoor. The mountain scenery, gorgeous views from the outstanding golfing facilities, magnified the enjoyment of five star restaurants. Herb Mosca and our ordinance officer, Bernie Boress had joined the list of fallen members of our pilots and ground crew officers. Bernie had an exemplary record retiring as full colonel in the USMC. Herb had retired from a high position in Grumman Aviation in their Far East operations.

The last evening's meeting to decide where we would go in 2005 would follow the usual method of decision-making. It was noticeably more sedate without the excellent persuasion of pride by the Senator of Slippery Rock University, dressed in a beautiful sweater, with a large SRU on his chest. The vote was for Scottsdale, Arizona.

2005 Scottsdale, Arizona

Popular Peter Hansen and friend Barbara again answered the call to host our meeting in the sunshine of Arizona. Pete's daughter, Gretchen, was well versed with the tourist industry of Scottsdale, and she helped to finalize the program.

Golf participation had declined to four men, hooking and slicing the small ball all over the desert. They were still determined, if not too professional!

There was no lack of excellent, fashionable restaurants in the Scottsdale area. This made the evening cocktail hours and meals interesting and enjoyable. It was time for the last evening's decision for 2006. Bob Peebles, the quiet distinguished Marine colonel, conducted his usual quality control. It was a close decision. Our numbers were gradually growing smaller, and travel more problematic. He offered San Antonio and it was voted unanimously.

The fallen hero list took a bad turn in 2005. Boyd McElhany, Roy Reed, and Les Strandman had their last call. The future was not rosy!

2006 San Antonio, Texas

Bob and his companion Billie did a great job of hosting a fine reunion in spite of the state of the remaining pilots general health and travel ability. Strangely enough, the number of widows interested and anxious to attend was vibrant.

The pilot roster, in spite of bad reductions last year, was "hot to trot!" Six pilots answered the muster. The stories were still interesting and exaggerated. Memories were a bit cloudy, but the fire in the belly was still alive.

Without going into detail, it was a good and worthwhile reunion. The meeting the last night indicated that vote "might be the last call." Tucson was voted in and the Daniel's were ready to fly another flight. Word was received during the year that Joe Wallace mixed his last vodka and orange juice. "Smilin" Jack Conger was gratefully relieved of his suffering as his stoke finally wore him out. For years he recognized his fellow pilots, but was unable to talk. It was a blessing for a real warrior to fly his last.

2007 Tucson, Arizona

What would turn out to be our last "ooh-ra" was shaping up as a good finale! The cooperation of the PASM (Pima Air and Space Museum) gave us a wonderful place to celebrate. Our initial good luck was the ability to rent housing for the group at THE LODGE AT VENTANA! We received beautiful suites, at fantastic rates. Everyone was completely satisfied! Their suites were located in a large U shape. The center was a gorgeous green area looking out at the Catalina Mountain Range. We were able to finalize transportation to and from the Pima Air Space Museum in large SUV's.

Lunch was catered under the F4U Corsair! The pilots were able to tour the museum and enjoy some 300 airplanes in static (on display) formation plus several enclosed in huge hangers.
PASM is currently rated # three in the nation.

Since 1996 at the reunion in Santa Anna, Dr. Pat Scannon has been our guest at the annual VMF 114 gatherings. He is a practicing physician in the San Francisco area. In 1993 he first traveled to Palau as part of a team in search of the armed trawler sunk by then Ensign George W. Bush. While the team succeeded in the mission, Scannon was left searching for more. He discovered that during WWII many planes had gone missing over Palau and most of those MIA mysteries were left unsolved. After more than a decade of searching on and around the islands of Palau, Scannon and his "Bent Prop" team have been responsible for finding and identifying more than two dozen missing WWII aircraft, many with MIA's *(the above information is from the BENTSTAR web site and written materials in "What is the Bent Star Project?")*

A documentary *"Last Flight Home"*, produced by the group, chronicled this quest through the jungles and waters of Palau. It included some very interesting interactions with current residents who led them to many of the dive sites. We viewed the video with other Museum guests and visitors including Lt Col Buddy Smith Commander of the US Marine Bulk Fuel Company A, Tucson Arizona.

VMF-114 cannot thank Dr. Pat Scannon and his team enough for what he has done for us over several years! His Palau group found Cowboy's Corsair in the shallow jungle swamp. His body had been previously returned to Torrington, Wyoming for burial two years after WWII. The group also found the wreckage of Ken Wallace's plane, identified by the Bureau of Aeronautics number (BUNo) on the tail. Pat's group is still going to Palau each March, diving and searching jungles for MIA pilots and their planes.

Pat Scannon
Provided courtesy of Bent Star

Pat once wrote in a letter to the squadron, "The first time I walked the Peleliu runway I knew there was something special about this god-forsaken strip of white coral surrounded by jungle. Honestly, I felt the rolling rumble of huge single engine gull winged monsters roaring by, flight after flight, vibrating beneath my feet. I looked northward and also felt the not-so distant crack- thump of iron bombs exploding behind Bloody Nose Ridge followed ever more slowly by threads of smoke."

"Meeting all of you filled a large vacuum in me, created by that experience something far too few Americans ever get a chanced to feel. You young men, who did not hesitate, fought on and over

Peleliu, protecting as best you could each other and our country. You could not possibly have known how you fit in the big picture, but you had faith in your country and your leaders and, in the process bonded with each other for a lifetime, and longer. You all have something together that I am fortunate enough to even rub up against...a certain and deep pride in having stepped up to the plate and survived – it is ingrained in you. I know because I have been in your presence, both at your reunions and on the north-south runway of Peleliu. Perhaps this pride is so striking to me because it is very difficult to find or even comprehend in my generation. I wish I were a Marine to be able to say Semper Fi to VMF114, but that is a signature to be earned the hard way. But I can and do convey to each of you the spirit and sentiment carried by the words."

Yes, all good things must come to an end. The final meeting was somber and very emotional. Travel problems due to the age, and in some cases travel difficulties were on the minds of most of the pilots. Finally, the decision was voted on and after twenty-eight consecutive years of VMF-114 Squadron reunions, we quietly accepted the fact that in spite of desire, reason won out! 2007 was the final of a dream! At the time only eight known pilots were surviving: COL Bob Peebles, Lt Col Danny "Bud" Daniel, Lt Col Don Francke, Lt Col Bill Cantrell, Captain Peter Hansen, Captain Gay Greenfield, Major Wally Weber and Major Sam Mantel.

Wally Weber lost his last battle in 2009. Bill Cantrell told his last flying story in 2013 and Gay Greenfield left this earth in 2014 ... **and now we are five!**

**Final Reunion: Weber, Hansen, Daniel, Mantel, Cantrell, Peebles
Missing: Francke, Greenfield**

What had this squadron done after they first met in 1943? They weathered combat tours, long over water flights in all types of weather. Suffered tragic combat and operational fatalities! Spent eight months of hell on the island of Peleliu, each with hours of flying low level ack-ack suppression missions, surviving in tents and 100 degree plus heat, and living through more than one typhoon! Fighting and realizing in the end that it was a battle that never should have occurred!

They learned the terrible truth that "old men make decisions that young men die for!" What had they accomplished?

As the years wound on, suddenly in 1980 they realized that the esprit de corps, love and respect for each other, and friendship were stronger than they knew. A desire surfaced to continue this bond. When they first met in 1980, the wives rapidly picked up on this fact.

I'm sure that all of us have put together pictures and bound them in some kind of album. We have picked them up from time to time and reveled in the memories of what we enjoyed. One thing for certain, the pilots of VMF-114 knew how to pick wonderful places and resorts in the class spots of Canada, Hawaii, and the US mainland. Over the years we shared our joyous reunions with our children, grandchildren, brothers, sisters, aunts, uncles and even former in-laws.

And after all these years, we agree with Gunny Sgt Wolf who wrote, "To observe a Marine is inspirational. To be a Marine is exceptional!"

HERE'S TO THE WIVES WHO LISTENED TO WAR STORIES OVER AND OVER! ON OCCASION, ARGUMENTS OF WHERE, HOW, AND WHEN, WERE ALL BLURRED BY GOOD SCOTCH, BOURBON, OR IRISH WHISKEY!

THINK OF IT, TWENTY EIGHT YEARS OF CONTINOUS REUNIONS, EACH DEDICATED TO OUR SKIPPER, COWBOY, AND TO THE CORPS!

What a wonderful memory.

Here's to the fantastic:

"Hose Nose—Bent Wing Bird" ---- F4U Corsair!

SEMPER FI

VMF 114 Reunion - Hawaii

VMF 114 Reunion San Francisco 1998

VMF 114 Reunion
Jasper Park, Canada - 1982

Chapter 21   The Military Brotherhood
Transcends Time: 1942-2014

CAPTAIN RALPH (NONE) LAGONI – (NONE=NO MIDDLE INITIAL) USMC

I met Ralph as we checked into Primary School NAS Pasco, Washington. Little did I know that it would be a lifetime of a very close friendship! We remained close as Naval Cadets until we received our GOLD WINGS, separated for Operational Training, and rejoined each other upon arrival at MCAS EL Toro, California. We separated again before shipping out, and met in at the Battle of Peleliu in combat. Squadron VMF-122 vs. VMF-114! The best reunion was in Chicago, 1954. Ralph, Bill Goodson, "Doc" Jewell, and "Danny" Daniel met for a week end terrorizing the pubs of North "Chi" including one drummer and one famous night club incident and one "gotcha" story too funny to tell!

In civilian life, he graduated from the University Iowa Medical School, practiced medicine in Davenport, Iowa and later joined the Student Heath Center at the University of Arizona. Our families were together, we watched our children grow, and did not part until his death in 2009. Ralph and Jean hosted two VMF-122 reunions in Tucson and joined our VMF-114 events. I dedicated a memorial brick laid side by side with mine in Semper Fidelis Memorial Park overlooking the National Museum of the Marine Corps, Quantico, Virginia. Ralph was a true hero and brother! *Once a Marine, Always a Marine!*

CAPTAIN PHILLIP "FLIP" SAMSON, USMC

Phil was a fellow Aviation Cadet at NAS Pasco, Washington who became a lifelong friend and golfing partner. After winning his GOLD WINGS and commission as a 2nd Lt. in the USMCR, "Flip" wound up in multi-engine planes. He was assigned as Major General "Nuts" Moore's adjutant (military nick-name "gofer") and pilot.

After several months, while VMF-114 was on Peleliu, Samson would come to the island on the General's inspection tour. He would often seek out my tent and in a spotless khaki, neatly pressed uniform, stick his head into my tent and say "Hi there" in his inimitably way. Noticing my appearance in shorts and Boon Dockers, (Marine issue short boots) he would say "oh excuse me, I was looking for Lt. Daniel."

Months later I was on my way stateside, with a stop at Pearl Harbor. As we landed, I looked out the window and noticed a vehicle with TWO STARS on the front bumper. The back door opened and the head of another stuck through the door and stated, *"I'm looking for Lt. Daniel. He is to report to General Moore's headquarters, I'm here to pick him up."* It was Phil, sporting that special smile! He escorted me to the General's Quarters. After a warm welcome, General Moore scheduled a daily meeting with me for the next three days. Each day there was about an hour scheduled for the two of us to discuss Major Cowboy Stout's life and tragic death. On my final day General Moore paid me a wonderful complement, after discussing my future. He offered the opportunity for me to receive a permanent commission in the USMC. I asked if I could give him an answer the last morning of my stay. He answered that he would look forward to my decision. I met Samson and we talked into the midnight hours. After serious discussion and thought, I mentioned to the General that I had only completed one year of college, and in order to move up in any job, I would have to complete my education. As much as I loved the Corps and flying I would have to decline his offer! We shook hands and he wished me well. This was one of my life's most difficult decisions.

After we moved to Tucson we spent seventeen fun years sharing an invitation to the Arizona Country Club's Annual four day golf tournament and nightly dinner parties. He invited me to share his 68th birthday present, two hours in the cockpit of a WACO Biplane, our primary flight school type trainer, on a WWII War Bird Flight! We didn't realize it at the time but it was our great farewell memorial tribute for two *GOLD WING MARINE*

AVIATORS! He passed away in 1991 from complications of diabetes on the surgery table.

Phil and Bud at Arizona Country Club

Phil and Bud Reliving Naval Flight Training

His son, Mark Samson, read my eulogy for Phil:

16 April 1991

To Loree,

A special saunter-a warm smile and a cheerful "Hi There" greeted me from the sands of Pasco, Washington to the sands of Morocco, to the shores of the South Pacific and Hawaii, to the beaches of Cancun, Mexico. This was my dear friend Phillip.

A special friendship was renewed and new ties developed when Connie and I got together with Phil and Loree in 1974. For 17 years we enjoyed a marvelous week of their gracious hospitality, socializing, dancing and golf as the Samson's guests at the Arizona Country Club Member/Guest.

Phil and Loree were responsible for the most inexpensive vacation to Cancun, which then led to a substantial investment in our timeshare condo. We enjoyed 5 wonderful vacations together. I did get even with Phil by conning them into joining us on a trip that was one of his lifelong desires, playing in the King Hassan II Golf Pro-Am Tournament in Morocco. And then there was the follow up "OH MY GOD" trip to Palm Springs.

My communication with Phil seemed to always be in "sync" – be it on the golf course, in the air or at the 5 PM Happy Hours by their pool. I always asked for scotch and water. He always returned with scotch and soda, and I learned to like it.

Our friend, Gary Cowan, put it best in a phone call when he said, "Gee Mary Francis and I did not get to spend near the time with Phil that you and Connie did, but once you spent a little time it felt as if you had always known him. He was a most special kind of person."

I regret that we will never get to read the much discussed book he would write, or to see the Hemingway type photo that was to be on the cover – or to drink the toast to the "Last Cerveza." Here's to you Phil – God, I will always love and cherish the memories of our times together – from the Corps to the time on the links.

Goodbye and SEMPER FI old Buddy!

ELDON GROUT, ARMY AIR CORPS

Eldon grew up on a family farm, on the outskirts of Mankato, Kansas. I first met him when he started dating my older sister, Jeanne. He started his flying career in 1935 while a 16-year-old student in Mankato High School. My first close acquaintance with him was when he approached me wearing his leather flight jacket and long white scarf, and offered me a ride in one of the tandem cockpit, bi-wing planes of the 'thirties. He instantly became my hero, as he was also a star on the high school football team. In 1938 he married my sister and they started their married life in Kansas.

When WWII started he enlisted in the Army Air Corps and having already obtained his CAA Flight Instructors Card, began his wartime service in the CAA (Civil Aeronautics Authority) War Training Service.

He was a born pilot, moving up in the Army Air Corps Flight Program, finally training pilots in the final stages of P-51 Mustang fighter in California. He was awarded the Victory Medal for his service. He loved to tell the interesting stories of incidents that occurred during his days of teaching American, Chinese and South American pilots to fly several different types of planes. During his flying days he flew forty-one civilian aircraft and four military trainers and he met and befriended many of the "old time famous aviators!"

He first soloed in 1935, received his license from a "bush-pilot", Herb Hailings. He received his Commercial License and first flight instructor's rating in 1942. He received CAA and Commercial Instructors Rating at the start of WWII and was issued his CAA Administrator and CAA Examiner appointment in 1946. After WWII he moved to Beloit, Kansas and was a partner in a flying school and airfield until a tragedy happened during a tornado. He and his partner were building a hanger when the winds blew down a wall, killing his partner. He gave up that business, but never gave up flying at every opportunity until health problems cut short his flying. **In his career he was a CAA Examiner, flew charter, ambulance, and crop spraying flights, and logged over 10,000 hours as an instructor**. He never turned down a flight with someone who needed more time in the air.

After the war, Eldon made use of his many talents. In addition to farming and raising cattle in his civilian life, he worked as a meat cutter and dairy farmer. He and Jeanne ran a wheat harvesting business for several years that toured from Texas to Canada during the harvesting season. This operation used several large machines that moved by trucks, loaded with the huge harvesting equipment. Automobiles followed in processions over the highways from town to town.

Later in life, he and my sister moved to Boulder, Co where he delivered mail for a junior college and developed his wonderful talent in woodworking, restoring antiques and furniture. He gallantly fought kidney problems to the end. He passed away still flying through a storm.

JACK ADAMSON AND BILL ADAMSON, US NAVY

Jack and Bill were Seamen assigned to different USMC units during the invasion of Peleliu. Jack was attached as a Wire Communication Specialist, USMC 1st Division. On September 15th 1943 he was on the second wave of LST'S (Landing Ship Tanks) to land on the beaches of Peleliu. He survived after falling out of the LST, and later became lost in the confusion. The MP's (military police) helped him find his unit. In the process, his twin brother, unbeknown to him, was involved in locating radar units on the island. Somehow their paths crossed and they accidently met without either of them knowing the other was on Peleliu. Bill also survived the fury and hell of the battle. Later, Jack was on site at the Bikini Island atomic test-firing project! I didn't meet Jack until he met and married my sister Arlene and we learned of our common military ties on Peleliu.

Jack, in civilian life, earned an electrical engineering degree, worked on several nuclear power plants and other large civilian construction projects. He was involved in the Idaho (ARCO), the first nuclear prototype for the nuclear submarine (SSN-571), which was built as an Experimental Breeder Reactor. It was well known at the time that these plants had large asbestos content. He eventually developed the fatal disease, mesothelioma and after terrible suffering, passed away in 2004.

CORPORAL GENE EGIZIACO, USMC

Gene served as a member of the USMC Special Forces that went ashore 21 July 1944 on a special mission during the invasion to liberate Guam from the Japanese. Eight members went ashore in darkness and liberated a compound of men and boys held prisoner by the Japanese. One young man, Carlos Camacho, eventually became the Governor of Guam. After his discharge from the Marines and missing the military, he re-enlisted in the Army Transportation Services. In 1984, on the 40th Anniversary of the Liberation of Guam, Gene and the other surviving Marines were invited back for the commemoration ceremonies. He was inducted into the New York Veteran's Hall Of Honor and continues to serve as a volunteer Counselor at the Yonkers Vets Services. He is my wife's cousin and resides in Yonkers, New York.

STAFF SGT GIL CARRLLO, USMC

Gil enlisted in 1943 at the age of 18 years. He trained in San Diego Recruit Depot, MCAS Miramar, California and MCAS Cherry Point, South Carolina. He completed his training and served in VMF-512, as an Aviation Ordinance Specialist for the F4U "Whistling Death" Corsair! This was the first squadron to install 3.5 rockets, six under each wing!

Carrillo served attached to the 1st Marine Division in combat at Okinawa and the occupation of Tokyo, Japan. They sailed from Miramar on a troop ship and arrived in Okinawa Harbor in the dead of a very dark night. The young Marines and sailors were nervous and scared at the thought they would be fighting the battle alone. At the first light of dawn there was the US Navy's armada! Next stop – Japan, and a very special moment when he reunited with his older brother, Louie. During the occupation he flew over the nuclear devastation of Hiroshima and Nagasaki! He was assigned security patrol after the surrender and he and some buddies "borrowed" a jeep, drove into Tokyo, and as an act of disgust for Japan (and definitely a breech of Marine conduct), they "peed" in the moat surrounding the Imperial Palace.

Gil played pro baseball in the Cleveland Indians farm system, later was Budget Director for Goodyear tires, became a high school baseball coach, then a principal in the Tucson schools. In his retirement he was the Marketing and Sales Director for the Radisson Hotels and was our "go to" guy helping make VMF-114's 50th Anniversary Reunion a huge success.

CORPORAL FRANK CORBO, USMC

Frank enlisted in the Marines at age 17 in 1946 and served for two years, rising to the rank of corporal and received an Honorable Discharge. He was assigned to the motor pool as a bus driver, but his unit lacked a bus, so he turned drill instructor, in charge of marching troops from the barracks to training sights. The Marines shipped his unit to Nova Scotia for cold weather training, but the weather did not cooperate, as the snow melted. This Marine unit lacked leadership as they had difficulty with water supplies for three days. In spite of some unusual happenings, Frank remained an avid Marine, eager for the next day to arrive!

Corporal Frank Corbo, USMC

CPL Corbo and wife Lee met the members of 114 at the reunion in Beaufort, South Carolina. As luck would have it, his nephew was in the final days of Boot Camp at Parris Island, South Carolina. The day before all Marine "Boots" were to receive their Marine graduation emblem "Globe and Anchor", all trainees were in "lock down" and could not even speak to relatives. "Uncle Bud", being a retired Marine officer and a LTC in the Army Corps of Engineers, had to come to the rescue. I said I would try and see what I could do as CPL Corbo and Lee were both most anxious to at least speak with their young Marine nephew. I phoned, gave my rank, and explained that I was a retired former USMC fighter pilot. I asked if was possible to speak to the sergeant in charge of the Recruit

257

Battalion Marines. Not really expecting approval, I received (in the sharpest USMC polite response) an answer to my request. The Marine Gunny Sergeant informed us to be at Bldg. # 15, Room # 102 at 1400 hours (2:00 PM) to speak for 20 minutes to Marine recruit *RAYMOND CORBO*. I was pleasantly surprised and pleased. Young Corbo appeared, his aunt and uncle had trouble with their tears of joy, and received a pleasant shock in the sharp Marine Corps demeanor of their young man, who had suddenly appeared as the perfect USMC recruiting picture, instead of the 18 year old high school graduate.

Frank was amazed and pleased with all of the military events that occurred during the four-day event. The F-15 cockpit tour, Marines marching and shouting cadence, the "spit and polish" and the military courtesy that was evident everywhere! He enjoyed having the opportunity to meet and talk to the former pilots of 114, most of all socializing with this Marine "Band of Brothers."

Frank passed away in 2013 and was buried with full military honors.

LIEUTENANT COLONEL BUDDY SMITH, USMC

I first met LtCol Smith when I was consulted about the invitation to be Guest of Honor and the speaker at the 232nd Birthday Ball of the USMC, which was being held at the Marriott Star Pass Resort in Tucson on November 10th, 2007. He was also wearing the Gold Wings of a Marine Corps Aviator. This made the initial meeting very cordial and fast moving. He offered to assist me in with any problems I might have in preparing for this honor to speak to over 250 Marines dressed in their wonderful Dress Blue Uniforms. I have gone into detail in Chapter 19 of this fine event.

The following year, 2008, once again I received a special invitation to attend the 233rd USMC Birthday Ball; LtCol Smith was the guest of honor. The outstanding event was the recognition of the Bulk Fuel Co A, 6th ESB's Corps of Marines who had just returned from a years active duty on the HORN OF AFRICA. It was impressive. For the second year in a row, I received the honor of being presented the first cut of cake, as the "oldest Marine in attendance!"

LtCol Buddy Smith, USMC, (Center) at PASM

We received an invitation to LtCol Smith's change of command ceremony to accept the command of VMGR-234 TRANSPORT SQUADRON at the Naval Air Station Joint Reserve Base Fort Worth, Texas. Unfortunately, schedule conflicts prevented our attendance.

COLONEL KENNTH J. WALTERS, USMCR (RETIRED)

Ken and his wife, Carol, are wonderful friends we have recently met. He has been a tremendous help in my researching Corsair history and technical information. In my library, thanks to Ken, are the following books and manuals: Peleliu 1944, The Forgotten Corner of Hell, Last Man Standing, F4U1 Corsair Pilot's Handbook 1942, Brotherhood of Heroes, The Marines at Peleliu, 1944 and the heart wrenching video, Peleliu, 1944-Horror In The Pacific. Most recently I received a copy of Front Burner, Al Qaeda's Attack on the USS Cole, and Connie thoroughly enjoyed her personal copy of The Fighter Pilot's Wife, A Military Family's Story. Ken also honored me with a metal die cast Corsair that had been made for the 100th Anniversary of Naval Aviation 1911-2011. It is a gift I will always treasure.

Colonel Ken Walters, USMC, Retired

Ken's military career in two services, the Air Force and Marine Corps, spanned 5 decades (1957-1999). As an Airman Second Class he served at Ramey Air Force Base as a clerk typist for the 72nd Air Police.

After leaving Ramey, Ken's career initially took him to Hawaii and CINPAC in Honolulu ('84'87) serving in Current Operations (J-3). He had a tour at CNO OP (Chief of Naval OPS), then J-2 Joint Staff. He had a tour at the Pentagon '92-'95 and finally he was assigned at HQ Marine Corps '96-'99. He was mobilized for Desert Shield/Desert Storm, as a Senior Marine Watch Officer for Naval Operational Intelligence Center, Washington, DC from 'Feb-Mar '91. He currently serves our country as an analyst with the Diplomatic Security Service, US Department of State. His accomplishments in an outstanding military career in the Air Force, the Marines and government service are well documented.

LIEUTENANT GENERAL RON CHRISTMAS, USMC (RET.) FORMER PRESIDENT AND FOUNDER MARINE CORPS HERITAGE FOUNDATION

My son, Colonel Tim Daniel, US Army Retired, became acquainted through their spouses who had become friends and shopping fanatics. As a result of this friendship the Daniel's were invited several times to the General's home for dinner. A friendship resulted.

Tim had a desire to invite me to Washington DC to tour the recently opened WWII Memorial. We also shared the desire to visit the new Marine Corps Heritage Museum at the Quantico Marine Base with the Corsair and Peleliu memorabilia and displays. Tim mentioned this possibility to the General and he promptly invited the two of us on a personal tour of this magnificent museum.

We made arrangements to meet the General at the museum's entrance. He greeted us warmly and personally escorted us through the gate and proceeded to give us a three and one/half hour complete explanation of each stage of the museum development. General Christmas was a wounded hero of several of Vietnam's famous battles. A courageous and generous leader of Marines, he is clearly loved by all. He is the founder and President (at the time of our visit) of the Marine Corps Heritage Foundation, Quantico, Virginia. This museum has grown by leaps and bounds. It is a class history of the Corps, with every chapter of Marine battles and events. A Corsair and Wild Cat fighters hang from the ceilings, dugouts and machine gun batteries dot the many rooms. Christmas envisioned and made certain all of them were built! It is a monument to his perseverance and love of the Corps.

After our tour of the Museum building we were able to check a map and determine where the two bricks that I had ordered for my buddy Lagoni and me were located. As we toured the grounds, we were able to locate the beautiful brick trail winding up to the Marine chapel. There the bricks lay side by side with the inscriptions:

CAPT RALPH LAGONI
USMCR VMF-122 PELELIU
DFC – AIR MEDAL TWO GOLD STARS

LTC GLENN R. DANIEL
USMCR VMF-114 PELELIU
DFC - PURPLE HEART
AIR MEDAL TWO GOLD STARS

The following thought was in each man's heart!

TWO MARINE AVIATORS, SIDE BY SIDE, AFTER SO MANY LIFETIME MEMORIES, AND MONTHS OF COMBAT TOGETHER AT PELELIU.

REAR ADMIRAL ALAN SHEPARD, NAVAL AVIATOR, ASTRONAUT

Born 11/28/23 and died 7/21/98 of leukemia, at his home at Pebble Beach, California. His wife died five weeks after Alan in 1998.

A Naval Academy Graduate '44, he received his Gold Wings, '47. NASA selected him as one of seven in the first group of astronauts. He received the Distinguished Service Medal, Distinguished Flying Cross, and Congressional Space Medal of Honor. He logged 8,000 hours flying, with 3700 hours in jets. As a test pilot instructor, he often said, "You know, being a test pilot is not the safest job in the world."

Alan was the first American to travel into space on the Freedom 7 spacecraft. He was the commanding officer of the Apollo 14 mission to the moon and the fifth person to walk on the lunar landscape He also hit two golf balls on the moon using a six iron, stiff gloves and a space shovel! Shepard dropped his hands and said, "I hit that second one miles, and miles, and miles!"

In 1983, King Hassan II of Morocco, sponsored the King Hassan Trophy Golf Tournament, started by his father. This would be the 13th event to be held. Morocco had been friendly to the USA over the years. Billy Casper, the well-known pro golfer, through his company, invited 25 well-known golf professionals plus 75 amateurs from the international golf community to participate in a ten-day trip to this magic land. It was a once in a lifetime combination golf and travel including unbelievable events!

Because my "adopted fourth son," Gary Cowan, was president of Billy Casper's golf company, Connie and I were invited, along with two couples who were life long friends, to this event. This entourage of US golfers met at New York's Kennedy Airport, boarded the King's personal airliner and proceeded to Marrakech, Morocco. All the receptions and dinners were black tie events. One of my golfing partners was our dearest friend Marine Corps buddy Phil Samson who flew in from Portugal where he and his wife, Loree, were vacationing.

Our first night in Marrakech was at the famous La Mamounia Hotel, the host of several world leaders for many meetings after WWII and Churchill's proclaimed favorite in the world.

The next morning, we were escorted to the Marrakech railroad station by several carriages, each carrying two couples, to a private railroad car for the trip to Rabat! The Rabat Hilton would be our home for the remainder of the trip in Morocco. After the welcoming dinner, the lights of the magnificent ballroom were dimmed and parade of waiters carried flaming dishes of baked Alaska into the room. The golf tournament pairing selections were decided at this event.

Phil and I noticed we were sitting next to a table where I recognized the famous astronaut Alan Shepard as one of the amateur golfers! I turned to Phil, and informed him that as soon as it was possible, we were going to approach Admiral Shepard and introduce ourselves to him. He was most gracious as I said to him, "Admiral Shepard, we would like to introduce ourselves, two Naval aviators, wearers of the Gold Wings, that have risen to heights, but not nearly as high as those your have!" This brought a huge smile on his part, as he shook our hands warmly, and chatted with us!

Phil Sampson, Alan Shepard and Bud Daniel

That was the first of two opportunities to get to know the Shepards, as we spent time with them on a tour of Rabat. Connie and I found Louise Shepard to be as warm and friendly in our discussions as was the Admiral.

One special event was an invitation to the American Embassy for a reception. It turned out to be the 208th Birthday of the Marine Corps. We enjoyed our toast to the Marines and a special tip of the glass from Alan to the Naval aviators turned Marines.

One day the golf was rained out and I had just sat down in the bus, leaving an empty seat next to me. As Admiral Shepard came down the aisle he noticed the seat, smiled and sat down. In the ensuing conversation he said, "It is a very sobering feeling to be up in space and realize one's safety factor was determined by the lowest bidder on a government's contract!" He later pulled out a silver flask, looked at me and said "You know my daddy always told me a little scotch prevented a cold on a rainy day. Would you like a wee bit?" I could not say "yes" fast enough! What a wonderful down to earth gentleman.

MAJOR GENERAL DONALD W. SHEPPERD, USAF (RET)
(MISTY -35)

When our fling days are over
When our flying days are past
We hope they'll bury us upside down
So the world can kiss our ass.

The Air Force fighter pilot's toast from <u>Bury Us Upside Down-The Misty Pilots and the Secret Battle for the Ho Chi Minh Trail</u>, authored by Rick Newman and Don Shepperd.

We first met General Shepperd as we were planning the 2008 Reunion for the Ramey Air Force Base Historical Association in Tucson. We had seen him as a military analyst for CNN, read the articles written for our local paper and were awed by his courageous military experiences and career. He is a 1962 graduate of the USAF Academy and found himself 5 years later flying F-100's at Bien Hoa Air Base, Viet Nam, where he flew 247 combat missions in 12 months. He was in a jet-fighter outfit that flew in the covert operation dubbed "Misty", flying at dangerously low levels, searching for enemy traffic on the Ho Chi Minh Trail. After the war his career took him to a number of bases, eventually commanding an F-15 wing at Otis Air National Guard Base in Massachusetts. He finished his active duty career as Deputy Director of the Air National Guard at the Pentagon. In 2006, he co-authored <u>Bury Us Upside Down</u>, the powerful, personal story of the Misty pilots.

He was our featured speaker at the final banquet held at the Pima Air and Space Museum, and it was only fitting that our guest spoke from under the wings of a B-24 and B-25. Ken Combs, USAF, Ramey Association President, wrote in our newsletter, "Gen Sheppard spoke as a military analyst, and speaker and writer on the subject of terrorism. His remarks centered on the theme that war has changed from something the American people could lend 100% support, to the international conflicts we see today, where few in this country can agree whether or not we should even be at war. He predicted that these conflicts will wind down slowly and not end abruptly with victorious parades and celebrations." It was a night of reflection and vigorous discussion for our group. We had copies of the General's book available, which he graciously signed with a personal note to everyone, after asking him or her about their military experience.

COMMANDER GEORGE MATIAS, USN (RET.) GRADUATE OF US NAVAL ACADEMY

George, at one time, during his days as a Naval Academy, had thoughts of graduating into a career in USMC Aviation, but later decided against it. This "salty" Naval aviator, a veteran carrier pilot, has logged 6,000 hours and 950 landings (traps) on five different US Navy carriers. He is my close friend and right hand man, during many hours spent together as docents at the Pima Air and Space Museum (PASM). He helps before I have a chance to ask him! He is also a class actor on any holiday (Rodeo, Halloween, and St. Pat's) as he is always dressed to celebrate the day! He has a memory for facts, songs, atomic and nuclear information that mystifies others working with him as docents! His mind is always in forward gear and he writes the cleverest poems for special occasions. Fantastic! I look forward to days I get to share with him.

After one of my surgeries, while I was not yet awake, he entered the hospital room, introduced himself to Connie and stood guard at "parade rest" at the foot of the bed. "It is what the Navy and Marines do for each other," he told the astonished nurses.

George and wife Jeralyne, a senior badminton champ, travel extensively, and miss very few Naval Academy reunions. They are among the Academy Alumni who attended the recent Navy vs. Notre Dame football game played in Ireland. Their son is a retired naval aviator captain.

COMMAND MASTER SERGEANT TOM CAMPBELL, USAF (RET)

He is a member of the docent volunteers at Pima County Air and Space Museum. I am privileged to work with him every Wednesday! He and George Matais make certain I am able to execute my presentation during the hours we talk and entertain visitors at the museum.

He has filled a most interesting list of amazing assignments serving his country in positions on *AIR FORCE ONE*, roaming all over the world on trips as the leader of security forces on this huge airplane. He served during the presidencies of Nixon and Ford. His presentation of the trips and interesting facts and habits of each man are intriguing and worthwhile facts of history.

He is efficient in his doing whatever is needed in setting up my presentations to visitors. Together with George, they are most humble in their thoughtfulness of the needs and assistance for others. Thanks to Tom, my wife allows me to exhibit the gold Corsair he gave to me on a coffee table in our living room. She says it is too fine to put in any other room! That gold Corsair shines brighter each day!

DANIEL SONS AND GRANDSON

COLONEL TIMOTHY MICHAEL DANIEL, USA RETIRED

Tim retired after 28 years of service in the US Army's Corps of Engineers. He commanded units up to the brigade level, where he commanded the US Army Garrison Command at Fort Leonard Wood, Missouri. His final assignment was as the chief of the commander's planning group, headquarters, US Army Corps of Engineers in Washington DC. He served in the Pentagon where he was responsible for the Army's *Long Range Strategic Planning* program and the Army's participation in the Department of Defense study of the *Revolution in Military Affairs*. He was primarily responsible for the Army's initiation of the *Army After Next* research. He served in Turkey where he was responsible for the massive renovation of five army bases. He served for three years in France as the US Army Training and Doctrine Command's liaison to the engineers of the French Army, the French General Staff and the French Military Academy. He served in Israel for two years managing classified construction during *Desert Storm*. After retiring from the Army he was appointed by the governor of Missouri to a cabinet level position and served for three years as special advisor and then as director of Missouri's homeland security program (Sep 2001-Dec 2004). He was the first appointed homeland security official at the state level in the nation after 9-11. He worked in the private sector as a strategy consultant for Booz Allen Hamilton, consulting with the US Special Operations Command and the US Army Central Command/3rd Army. As a civilian his final position before retiring was as Chief of Strategy and Integration for the US Army Corps of Engineers in Washington DC. While in the Army he attended the Kennedy School at Harvard as a National Security Fellow. In 2013, Tim and Carol recently celebrated their 35th wedding anniversary.

Col Tim and Carol Daniel

SPECIALIST 5TH CLASS THOMAS LINDSEY DANIEL

Tom enlisted in the Army in 1972 and completed basic training at Fort Leonard Wood, Missouri. He went to Fort Polk, Louisiana for advanced training and was eventually assigned to the 196th Infantry Battalion, Fort Davis, Canal Zone, Panama, where he was the company's legal clerk. He played on the post's basketball team, and was selected for the US Southern Command All Stars and toured with the Panamanian Olympic team playing exhibition games. In 1973 we traveled to Panama to spend the Christmas holidays with him. It was awesome to go a Pacific beach and an Atlantic beach on the same trip. The tour of the Canal and the fun of vibrant Panama City made it very special. After his service, he earned a BS Degree in Recreation at the University of Wyoming. Tom worked as a Medical Technician at the Veterans Affairs Hospital and is currently employed at Tucson Medical Center in the Surgical Instrument Preparations Department.

Spec Tom Daniel/Panama

SEAMAN 2nd CLASS MARK ROBERT DANIEL

Mark enlisted in the Navy after high school. We proudly attended his graduation from Boot Camp at San Diego Naval Station. He completed Advanced Submarine Training at the New London Naval Submarine Base in Connecticut and served as a machinist mate in the US Navy Submarine Service at Charleston Naval Weapons Station, South Carolina. He is retired from the construction industry and serves in the American Legion Military Honor Guard in Bullhead City, Arizona.

Seaman Mark Daniel

1ST LIEUTENANT (PROMOTABLE)
THOMAS PATRICK DANIEL

Tom (son of Tim and Carol) recently completed three years of service as an engineer officer in the 82nd Airborne Division, where he served a tour in the combat zone in Iraq. He is currently promotable to captain and is a student at the US Army Engineer School Advanced Course at Fort Leonard Wood, Missouri. Tom graduated from the University of Missouri Business School and earned his commission via Officers Candidate School at Fort Benning, Georgia. Tom and his wife Morgan have two beautiful little girls. Tom is gifted in language skills. His first school was in France where, as a 4 year old he understood French but refused to speak it. He learned Hebrew while living in Israel and excelled in Chinese at MIZZOU. After graduation, still filled with Army wanderlust, he went to Korea for two years on his own, taught English as a second language to Korean children, and learned a bit of Korean as well.

1LT (P) Tom Daniel, 82nd Abn Div

LT COL JERRY COLEMAN, USMC

I could not close this chapter of men who have served their country without commenting on one of the Major League Baseball Hall of Fame members who went to war during WWII and later left the New York Yankee organization to complete another tour of duty flying the Corsair, the Marine Corps fighter, during the Korean War.

He was a 2nd baseman for the New York Yankees and played on four of six winning World Series teams. Coleman left the Yankee organization on 23 October 1942 and enlisted in the US Navy's V-5 Aviation program at the San Francisco Trade Building, California. On 1 April 1944 he was commissioned a 2nd Lt in the USMCR. He was assigned to VMSB-341 at Green Island, north of Bougainville. He flew 57 missions in the Solomon Islands campaign and the battle of the Philippines. He returned to MCAS El Toro at WWII's end, stayed in the Marine Reserves and rejoined the Yankee organization.

In 1950, he was on the American League All-Star Team and was the World Series MVP choice. With the outbreak of the Korean Conflict, Coleman once again was called to active duty and joined a USMCR squadron and was sent to Korea. This time he joined the pilots flying the F4U Corsair. This was the plane that was so effective with ground support of the Marine Infantry battling their way out of the Chosen Reservoir. Seventeen days of terribly cold weather as Marine Infantry marched and fought their way out of the trap, supported by *"the bent-wing birds, F4U Corsairs, dropping bombs and strafing the Chinese troops."* Coleman logged another 63 combat missions!

From Coleman's interviews with Todd Anton, <u>When Baseball Went to War</u> and <u>No Greater Love, Life Stories From the Men Who Saved Baseball</u>.

"You know people die in war. It's not pleasant. Sometimes they are your friends. Your emotions change, your spirit...well, dies a little!"

272

"Long flights over water were lonely, even if I had a gunner. I felt like I was on the moon. The sheer vastness of the Pacific really scared the hell out of me. My best friend disappeared while on patrol. It was the first time I could put a face on death. It was troubling, confusing and a very real message that one could get killed here!"

"Combat experiences shaped us and bonded us together. These experiences are vey personal and intimate and something you just learn to hide away. Why explain them to anyone who hasn't experienced it? It's kind of like a woman trying to explain having a baby to man. He just doesn't get it. But when she explains it to another woman, boy there is an unwritten degree of understanding. So it is with veterans. If you are not a veteran (or a mother), you'll never understand. Never!"[4]

"....the defining moment of my life was my time in the service, and to me, the most important part of my life was my time in the USMC. Getting your Navy wings of gold is, I don't know how to express it, except you are walking on air."[5]

Coleman and I went down similar paths on the way to careers during WWII and in life. We both started in the V-5 aviation program of the US Navy. The path to our USMC commissions was similar, pre-flight school at a college campus and flight training in similar types of planes. Both of us shared the thrill of receiving the Gold Wings and eventually flying combat in the mighty Corsair! We were flying Corsairs at the same time in the Solomon Islands and were both recalled to active duty after WWII. We each spent time in minor league baseball. My adult 25-year career was coaching college baseball. Of course I did not play or coach in the World Series...but did take a University of Wyoming team to the College World Series in 1956! Coleman and I retired as Lieutenant Colonels from the military. I served twenty-nine years in the *USMCR and ARMY Corps of Engineers National Guard.* And, we both knew that the best accomplishment in our careers was when we received the GOLD WINGS and our time in the Marine Corps.

Epilogue   Final Thoughts On Men And War

War never ends! There are surrenders, peace treaties, armistices, diplomatic agreements, territorial walls constructed and the process of dividing up the spoils of conflict ... but ...

War continues in the hearts and minds of those who served their country, and remains in the memories of those lost, the frustrations and feelings of despair, the thoughts of senseless tragic events and the mystery of facing death with courage are never far from the surface.

Sharing those experiences, the men and women who served write their memoirs and historians, through their research, bring back to life the enormity of the decisions to wage war; wars that inevitably break people on all sides and wreak havoc.

Why then does war *NEVER* end? Despite the reflections of the evils of war, government leaders and the generals who make the command decisions are the old men who send young men to war. Some wars are just, some must be fought to defend life and freedom but these are rare indeed. My War, World War II, was a "just" war. But even "just" warriors in "just" wars make terrible mistakes that young men pay for.

WW-II has been described in a multitude of ways. My personal experience verifies these descriptions in books and videos of one of the bloodiest battles of the Pacific.

The *Battle of Peleliu*
"Bloodiest Battle of the Pacific War"
"The Forgotten Corner of Hell"
"Horror in the Pacific"
"The Forgotten War"

Proud Marines who serve our country stand tall and sing in memory of the fallen…

The Marine Corps Hymn

From the Halls of Montezuma
To the Shores of Tripoli
We will fight our country's battles
In the air, on land, and sea;
First to fight for right and freedom
And to keep our honor clean
We are proud to claim the title of

THE UNITED STATES MARINES

Appendices

"Lest We Forget"

OPERATIONAL ACCIDENTS

2nd Lt. Robert O'Sullivan
'43 CA
2nd Lt. Robert P. Brown
' 43 CA
2nd Lt. Lyman Gage
'43 Eva, HI
1st Lt. Robert Y. Brown
'44 Green Is.
1st Lt. Stuart Wessman
'44 Turtle Bay
1st Lt. Bob Meyes
'44 Eva, HI
1st Lt. Robert Smith
'44 Eva, HI
Maj. "Blackie" Bastian
MCAS New Orleans
1st Lt. Parker Reilly
MCAS El Toro

OFFICERS KILLED IN ACTION

1st Lt. William Hobbs
'44 New Ireland
1st Lt. Jim Parmalee
'44 New Ireland
1st Lt. Jiggs Smith
'44 New Ireland
1st Lt. Walt Telep
'44 New Ireland
1st Lt. Robert Spain
'45 Yap

1st Lt. Ken Wallace
'45 Koror
Maj. Robert "Cowboy Stout
'45 Koror

ENLISTED KILLED IN ACTION

CPL T. Mummaw
'43 Peleliu
Tech Sgt. R. Olsen
'44 Peleliu
Sgt R. Simpson
'44 Peleliu

POST WW-II

'Rump' Heinley
Mel Freeman
Ray Durham
Dave Johnson
"Blackie" David
"Wink" Balzer   '80
Nick Virgets   '87
Duke Gilchrist   '87
Dick Rash   '88
Sven Svare   '88
Larry Marshall   '89
Larry Herzog   '90
Sam Porter   '91
John Bernhart   '94
Lewis Kilbourne   '94
Dave Neiswanger   '95
Don Fisher   '95
Bill Sonnenberg   '97
Frank Pippen   '98

Bob Tucker	'98
Bob D'Arcy	'99
"Timo" Sullivan	'00
Zip Zabel	'00
Bill Elzey	'01
Frank Sullivan	'02
Pete Drury	'03
Bernie Boress	'04
Herb Mosca	'04
Boyd McElhaney	'05
Roy Reed	'05
Les Strandman	'05
Jack Conger	'06
Joe Wallace	'06
Wally Weber	'09
Bill Cantrell	'13
Gay Greenfield	'14

Mighty Corsair

VOUGHT F4U CORSAIR

My love affair with the mighty Corsair,
Started out with a bit of doubt!
Could I fly this big bad awesome thing,
Did I have the guts to find out?

Some called it "hose nose" (a loving term),
Because of its extra long snout.
To others it was "bent wing bird",
Or "bird cage" (can't see out.)

To most it was the "F4U",
with a mind all of it's own!
The first few hops the plane flew you,
A bit of a twilight zone!

Although its over 60 years
Since my initial flight,
I won't forget that feeling,
Great excitement … mixed with fright!

"Cleared for take off" said the tower,
Am I finally ready to go?
I locked the tail-wheel-added power,
I really didn't know!

Be still my heart, go back to your place,
Why are you up here, so close to my face.
Stop all that damn pounding, I can't hear at all,
If the engine should quit, the angels might call!

At 90 some knots, the tail comes up,
By George there's a runway I see,
Now I'm off the ground, the wheels come up
What's wet? … did I take a pee?

COWBOY DOWN

The field is dropping away quite fast,
I just pulled up the flaps,
The gauge reads over 2000 feet,
I've got it made ... perhaps!

2000 horses working hard,
That purring sound is sweet,
Was on the ground five minutes back,
And now ... lO,OOO feet!

So smooth the turns, light the controls,
A thoroughbred for sure,
It's better than expected,
A pleasure to endure!

Down wheels and flaps, ease back the stick,
Let's try a landing stall,
How come I'm flat on my back?
And brother, that ain't all!

I'm headed for the deck it seems,
And very fast at that,
Rollout and gain some speed you dummy,
Before the spin goes flat!

Hot-damn, the bottom sure dropped out,
Don't do that low and slow,
Or you'll go home in a big pine box,
To watch the daisies grow!

Now back to base, all soaked in sweat,
The hardest part's ahead,
I've got to get this sucker down,
Or I'm as good as dead!

500 feet, down wheels and flaps,
Read landing check off list (GUMP),
A nice one-eighty turn to port
Down-wind ... I've got the gist!

100 knots, while on base,
Rollout at 85 ...
A three-point landing? Bounced but oh,
By God! I did survive!

And now I've got your number,
Ole' "bent-wing bird" Corsair,
The next time I will be in charge,
When we are in the air!

And if I don't abuse you,
My best friend you will be,
And always bring me safely home,
When we go out to sea!

REMEMBER VMF-114!!! SEMPER FI!

Aircraft Flown 1942-1984

AIRCRAFT FLOWN: US MARINE CORPS-ARMY NATIONAL GUARD-CIVILIAN

150 HP Luscombe "all-metal" low level trainer	Breese Field, Laramie, WY
N2S Stearman Bi- Wing Trainer "open cockpit" Yellow Peril	NAS Pasco, WA
N3N Navy Factory Bi-Wing Trainer Yellow Peril	NAS Pasco, WA
BT 18 Vultee "Vibrator" Low-Wing "enclosed tandem cockpit Trainer"	NAS Beeville, TX
SNJ "Texan" Advanced Fighter Trainer	NAS Kingsville, TX
FM-1 Grumman "Wildcat" Combat Fighter	NAS Green Cove Springs, FL
FM-2, FM-3, FM-4, FM-FJA Grumman "Wildcat" Combat Fighter	NAS Green Cove Springs, FL
F4U-1 Corsair "Bird Cage Cockpit" 2200 HP Combat Fighter	MCAS El Toro, & South Pacific
FG-2 Corsair Goodyear "Bubble Cockpit" 2200 HP Fighter	MCAS El Toro & South-Pacific
F6F-5-9 Grumman "Hellcat" Navy Fighter 2000 HP Fighter	MCAS El Toro and South Pacific
C-46 Curtis Commando Twin Engine Transport	Peleliu- Hollandia, New Guinea
TBM Grumman Torpedo Bomber "Turkey"	VRF-3 NAS Terminal Island, CA
JRB Beechcraft "twin engine low wing" multi-purpose aircraft	VRF-3 NAS Terminal Island. CA
PV-2 Ventura "Lodestar" twin engine bomber	VRF-3 NAS Terminal Island, CA
JRF-2 Grumman "Goose" twin engine multi-purpose	VRF-3 NAS Terminal Island, CA
PBY-5A Consolidated Catalina (respectfully called "Dumbo")	VRF-3 NAS Terminal Island, CA
TD2C-1 Culver PQ-14 (Target Drone)	VRF-3 NAS Terminal Island, CA
Cessna 182 & De Havilland DH2 "Beaver"	Wyoming National Guard HQ, Cheyenne, WY

Private Aircraft/Civilian Flying

Pitts Special (aerobatic)	VMF 114 Reunion, Springfield, MO
Piper Lance	Cozumel, Mexico
Cessna 310	Cabo San Lucas, Mexico
Beechcraft (night flight refresher training)	Tucson, AZ

Marine Birthday Ball Speech

USMC 232nd Birthday Ball November 10, 2007
LTC GLENN R "Bud" DANIEL, Guest of Honor
Spoke to the Marines from his heart:

We are the Marines-the few and the proud!

The history of the Corps is long and honorable made possible only by you – the men and women who choose to serve our country.

Today we celebrate the 232nd birthday of our beloved Corps. HAPPY BIRTHDAY MARINES, AND MAY GOD CONTINUE TO BLESS YOU and OUR CORPS!

We are the Marines…and damn proud of it!

I thank your for inviting me to be your speaker. 64 years ago, I was a 21 year old, flying combat missions, in a Marine Corsair. Never did I imagine that I would be with you tonight.

I suspect some of you are wondering why you have an old baseball coach from Wyoming up here speaking on this special occasion. Perhaps I am here because there are not many like me still around – the combat Veterans of WWII who flew the Corsair. Our numbers are becoming smaller each day. We are truly "the FEW and the PROUD".

I might be here tonight because I am a volunteer in Hanger 4 at the Pima Air Museum, and have acquired a reputation for telling thrilling tales of "blood and thunder" during aerial combat in '44 and '45.

Or it might be because I have the distinction of being, perhaps the only Marine pilot, who wound up as a commanding office of an Army Combat Engineer Battalion. It was quite a journey from Marine Aviation to building bridges and airfields, then blowing them up.

283

Why, after spending 14 years in the Marine Reserves did I switch to the Army Corps of Engineers? It was a hard, civilian job related decision…but I always considered myself just to be on loan to the Army. However, I continued to war my pilot gold wings on that Army uniform-the wings that represented the badge of my family, the Marines!

Since I have had the opportunity to serve in the Marines—spent time on a Navy Carrier—was attached to the Air Force—and served in the Army—I can concur with Colonel David Hackworth _(despite having been warned not to quote an Army officer at a Marine function!)_ when he wrote:

The AIR FORCE is like a French Poodle – it looks pretty-is pampered and always travels first class. It is the country club of the services. BUT the poodle was bred as a hunting dog, and in a fight is very dangerous.

The ARMY is like a St. Bernard-it's big and heavy-sloppy and a bit clumsy. BUT it is powerful, has a lot of stamina and is built for the long haul.

The NAVY is like a Golden Retriever-good natured-great around the house- their hair is a bit long. They go off wandering around for a long time and they love the water.

Now MARINES come in two breeds: Rottweiler and Dobermans----
Some are BIG AND MEAN----SOME ARE SKINNY AND MEAN
They are aggressive on the attack and tenacious on defense. They have really short hair and
ALWAYS GO FOR THE THROAT!

For years the Devil Dogs have been known as the first to fight. It has been our way of life since November 10th 1775, when in the Tun Tavern in Philadelphia, a group formed the Continental Marines. Since then, from the Halls of Montezuma –to the deserts of Afghanistan and Iraq, Marines have distinguished themselves with HONOR, BRAVEY AND SELF SACRIFICE for their brother Marines and for their country.

When you get to be my age, the word family assumes a grater importance, and tonight my theme is family – the Marine family. All Marines are family—*Brothers in Arms*—ready to go into harm's way at a moments notice. We wear a small badge of recognition that sets us apart- the *Eagle, Globe and Anchor*. We serve in the air on the land and on the sea.

I come from a proud family of Marine fighter pilots –The Marines of VMF 114. I was accepted into this family on August 11th 1943 when I pinned on the Globe and Anchor, 2nd Lt's Bars and proudly those Wings of Gold.

As a young Lt stationed at MCAS El Toro, we were issued our '45 caliber pistols and immediately, as per the OLD CORPS tradition, we flame grained the holsters with cordovan shoe polish. We were supposed to meet four young ladies at the O Club at 4 PM, but were anxious to fire the new pistols, so we headed for the hills – and returned really late. Our dates made sure we regretted that decision!

I soon fund myself in the cockpit of the mighty F4U Corsair— known to the Japanese as *"Whistling Death"*. VMF 114 –the Death Dealers Squadron was formed at El Toro in Oct 1943. I became a member of the 114 family in June '44, and selected as Major "Cowboy" Stout's wingman. How proud this 2nd Lt. was to be flying the wing of an ACE from Guadalcanal- a hero awarded the Navy Cross. The saddest day of my life was when he was killed in action on a low level Napalm mission at Koror.

Twenty four Corsairs of 114 departed Espiritu Santos in September '44 for a 2600 mile flight, island hopping to Guadalcanal-Bouganville-Emirau –and finally Peleliu. There we joined the 1st Marine Division in their fierce battle.

It was there I developed my admiration and complete appreciation for Marine Infantry. These men were courageous warriors dedicated to winning – no matter the price to be paid. I will carry my respect and reverence for them forever.

Our flying *"Band of Brothers"* lived in tents through typhoons---dropped thousand pound bombs and, from an altitude of a few hundred feet, delivered 265 gallon Napalm Tanks on the Japanese cave entrances on Bloody Nose Ridge.

For eight month we flew long, over water missions, survived Aussie Mutton, and 120 degree heat on the coral sands of Peleliu. After the battle was over and the war won, we came home to many different lives.

Only seven pilots from my squadron remain to tell the tale of a group of men who did their job – and did it well. Our "Lucky Seven" continues the tradition of keeping our Marine Family together. We have met annually for the last twenty-eight years and in September, in Tucson, we marked the *64th Anniversary* of our squadron's formation. We were honored to have your Color Guard lead us in a salute to our country and to the Marines.

In any place, and in any task, for a United States Marine, there is only one standard: *Do Your Duty and Do It Right*. For 232 years we have defended this nation, representing the best that is in it.

WE MARINES BELIEVE IN OUR COUNTRY, AND OUR COUNTRY BELIEVES IN US.

We proudly gather on this, our 232nd birthday to honor the spirit of the Corps, and the men and women it continues to inspire.

HAPPY BIRTHDAY MARINES --- GOD BLESS YOU ALL

SEMPER FI

Heaven for Naval Aviators

I hope there's a place, way up in the sky,
Where Naval Aviators can go, when they have to die.

A place where a guy could buy a cold beer
For a friend and comrade whose memory is dear.

A place where no blackshoe or porkchop could tread,
Nor a Pentagon type would e're be caught dead!

Just a quaint little O'club; kind of dark, full of smoke,
Where they like to sing loud, and love a good joke.

The kind of place, where a lady could go
And feel safe and protected by the men she would know.

There must be a place where old Navy pilots go
When their wings get too weary, and their airspeed gets low.

Where the whiskey is old and the women are young,
And songs about flying and dying are sung,

Where you'd see all the shipmates you'd served with before,
And they'd call out your name, as you came thru the door,

Who would buy you a drink, if your thirst should be bad
And relate to the others, "He was quite a good lad!"

And then thru the mist you'd spot an old guy
You had not seen in years, though he'd taught you to fly.

He'd nod his old head and grin ear to ear,
And say, "Welcome shipmate, I'm pleased that you're here!"

For this is the place where Naval Aviators come
When the battles are over, and the wars have been won.

They've come here at last to be safe and afar
From the government clerk and the management czar,

Politicians and lawyers, the feds and the noise,
Where all hours are happy, and these good old boys

287

Can relax with a cool one, and a well-deserved rest!
This is Heaven, my son, you've passed your last test!"

CAPT E. Royce Williams, USN (Ret.)
(Navy + Marines = Naval Aviators + GOLD WINGS)

A Christmas Poem

A VISIT FROM GOOD OLD "YOU KNOW WHO"
Commander George Matais, USN

T'was the night before Christmas
And all through the carrier
Not a sound could be heard
Not the "clang" of a barrier

The Ensigns in the bunkroom
Were snug in their bunks
While visions of "Jo-sans"
Danced in their heads

I was down in the wardroom
Having my last cup of "Joe"
We were far out at sea
There was no where to go

When up on the roof
There arose such a clatter
I raced to the flight deck
To see what was the matter

When out at the "90"
I saw: "What the heck?"
A big old snow sled
Making a run at the deck

The pilot was flawless- not a nugget
And when he called "Roger-Ball"
We new in a tick
It was the old pro, good old St. Nick

The moon on the crests
Of the white caps below
Gave an eerie green luster
It was quite a show

They hit the deck softly
And pulled hardly some wire
They took number three
Without blowing a tire

His team that I spotted
Was strange to be sure
And my memory trembled
Never was there an Air Group ever assembled

There were a "Hornet" and "Tomcat"
Together up there
And a "Cougar" and "Skyhawk"
Then two "Corsairs"-a pair

Then following on
Like something to lean on
Were a gutless "Cutless"
And even a "Demon"

What I then saw
Made me want to stand tall
The mighty great "Spad"
Was leading them all

The pilot leap from the cockpit
And gave a slight bow
Then he looked all around
And asked, "What's for chow?"

His helmet was scratched
As were his visor and boots
His G-Suit was tarnished
With ashes and soot

A butt of a "gar" he clamped
Tight in his teeth
And the smoke it encircled
His head like a wreath

Then from PRY-FLY
There came a loud shout
"Down on the flight deck
The smoking lamps out"

He spoke to the fuel gang
"Fill them up full, son"
I've a long way to go
Before you see the sun

There are many young sailors
Out there on the sea
Looking for comfort
And that comfort is me

He went down below
Gave the crew all their wishes
Then sampled the "mid-rats"
Even helped with the dishes

Then he rang up the ladder
As we did long ago
Then sprang to the cockpit
And to the "sling shot" said "no"

He fastened his harness
His helmet and radio
Then started his engines
To make sure they'd go

He saluted the colors
Went to "Burner Zone Five"
And away they all roared
Like a Polaris C-5

I went down to Combat and saw
The message he had left on the PPI scope
"Happy Christmas to all
And a New Year of hope"

Bibliography

The following are resources that inform, present historical documentation and relate personal perspectives of Marine Corps Aviation and World War II battles in the Pacific.

Anton, Todd, "No Greater Love, Life Stories From The Men That Saved Baseball" Rounder Books, Burlington, MA 2007

Anton, Todd & Nowlin, Bill (Editors)"When Baseball Went To War" Triumph Books, Chicago, IL 2008

Astor, Gerald, "Semper Fi In The Sky"
Ballentine Books, New York 2005

Boardman, Robert, "C-Rations For the Warrior's Heart",
ACW Press, Oregon 2003

Boardman, Robert, "Unforgettable Men In Unforgettable Times"
Selah Publishing Group, Surprise, Arizona 1998

Brand, Max, "Fighter Squadron at Guadalcanal"
Naval Institute Press, Maryland 1996

Camp, Dick, "Last Man Standing -1st Marine Regiment on Peleliu"
Zenith Press, Quayside Publishing Group 2011

Cantrell, Bill, "Friends, Dear Friends & Heroes"
Freebooter Publishing Company, Springfield, Missouri 1987

Guyton, Boon T. "Pilot's Handbook F4U Corsair"
(Prepared with Paul S. Baker & L. A. Bullard Jr.)
Vought - Sikorsky Aircraft, Division of United Aircraft Corp.
Stratford, Connecticut July 24, 1942

Guyton, Boon T. "Whistling Death, The Test Pilot's Story of the F4U Corsair"
Orion Books, New York 1990

Marine Aircraft Group 11, Report on Palaus Operation

Mersky, Peter B. "U.S. Marine Corps Aviation"
The Nautical & Aviation Co of America, Annapolis, Maryland
1983

Moran, Jim & Rottman, Gordon, "Peleliu 1944, the Forgotten
Corner of Hell"
Osprey Publishing Ltd, UK   2002

Newman, Rick & Shepperd, Don, "Bury Us Upside Down, The
Misty Pilots And The Secret Battle For The Ho Chi Minh Trail
Ballantine Books, New York   2006

Pearn, Victor, "Devil Dogs and Jarheads"
Busca, Inc. New York   2003

Shaw, Antony, "World War II Day by Day"
Chartwell Books, Inc.   New York   2010

Sherrod, Robert, "History of Marine Corps Aviation in World War
II", Combat Forces Press, Washington, 1952

Sierra Middle School Students, "They Opened Their Hearts,
Tucson Elders Tell WW-II Stories to Tucson Youth"
Voices, Inc. Tucson, Arizona   2005

Sledge, E.B. "With the Old Breed at Peleliu & Okinawa"
Novato Presidio, CA   1990

Sloan, Bill, "Brotherhood of Heroes, The Marines at Peleliu, 1944-
The Bloodiest Battle of the Pacific War"
Simon & Schuster, New York   2005

Sullivan, Jim, "F4U Corsair in Action"
Squadron / Signal Publications, Texas   2010

Thoreson, Richard, "Someone to Remember"
West- Press, Tucson, Arizona   1998

Tillman, Barret "Corsair, the F4U in WW II & Korea"
Naval Institute Press, Maryland   1979

Weiland, Charles P. "Above & Beyond"
ibooks Inc. Simon & Shuster, New York 1997

VIDEOS

"Cowboy's War" VMF114 Squadron Commander's Personal Story
Told through Letters & Photo's Sent Home
Narrated By His Grandniece, Cassady Alaya, Cheyenne, WY
2006

"Last Flight Home, Searching For & Finding MIA'S"
Bent Star Project, Davis, CA   2007

"Marine Corps/ PALAUA '44, The Palua Operation"
ARP Video's Inc. Hollywood, CA   1989

"PELEIU, The Forgotten War"
Dateline, NBC News Video, New York   August 4, 1995

"PELEIU, 1944, Horror In The Pacific"
American Hero Film, Minneapolis, MN

"The Lost Evidence, Peleliu"
The History Channel, A & E Television Network   2006

"Vought F4U Corsair"
Roaring Glory War Birds, Teleteam   2006

"Wings Of The Navy...100 Years of Naval Aviation"
Sponsored by USS Midway Museum, Rositzke & Associates
2011

VMF(AW)-114 - Wikipedia, the free encyclopedia. (n.d.).
Retrieved from http://en.wikipedia.org/wiki/VMF-114

Photos

If not cited, the author owns the photo. Listed photos are in the public domain and, period pictures were taken by US Government photographers during WWII.

Pages 27 and 166, SNV BT-13 Vultee " Vibrator"
Source: http://en.wikipedia.org/wiki/File:Vultee_BC-3_prototype_in_flight_c1940.jpg

Page 28, SNJ Advanced Fighter Trainer
Source: http://en.wikipedia.org/wiki/File:SNJ_washed.jpg

Page 34 and 167, F4F Grumman Wildcat
Source: http://www.history.navy.mil/photos/ac-usn22/f-types/f4f.htm

Page 162, PBY-5A
Source:
http://www.pby.com/WebPages.nsf/1ea472b5d881a626882565c90
0643ab9/9fa2c15aeceea1b988256b320022f237!OpenDocument

Page 166, 150 HP Luscombe "all-metal" low level trainer
Source: http://en.wikipedia.org/wiki/File:Luscombe.8a.g-ccrk.arp.jpg

Page 167, SNJ Advanced Fighter Trainers
Source: http://en.wikipedia.org/wiki/File:North_American_AT-6A_(NΛ-78)_in_flight_(00910460_099).jpg

Page 168, C-46 Curtis Commando
Source: http://en.wikipedia.org/wiki/File:Curtiss_C-46_Commando.JPG

Page 168, TBM Torpedo Bombers
Source: http://en.wikipedia.org/wiki/File:TBM_VT-90_CV-6_Jan1945.jpg

Page 169, JRF Grumman "Goose"
Source: http://en.wikipedia.org/wiki/File:JRF-5_NAS_Jax_1942.jpg

Page 169, PV-2 Lodestar Multi-Purpose
Source: http://en.wikipedia.org/wiki/File:PV-2_NAN9-2-45.jpg

Page 169, JRB Beechcraft Multi-Purpose
Source: http://en.wikipedia.org/wiki/File:Beechcraft_UC-45F_00910460_118.jpg

Page 170, TD2C-1 Culver PQ-14 Target Drone
Source: http://en.wikipedia.org/wiki/File:Culver_TD2C-1_drone_in_flight_c1945.jpg

Page 170, PBY Consolidated Catalina "Dumbo"
Source: http://en.wikipedia.org/wiki/File:PBY-5A_VPB-6(CG)_over_Narssarsuak_Greenland_1945.jpeg

Page 171, Cessna 182 Source: Source:
http://en.wikipedia.org/wiki/File: Cessna182A.jpg

Page 171, DeHavilland "Beaver"
Source:
http://en.wikipedia.org/wiki/File:De_Havilland_Canada_DHC-2_Beaver_(N130WA).jpg © Raimond Spekking / CC-BY-SA-3.0 (via Wikimedia Commons)

Page 171, Piper Lance
Source: http://en.wikipedia.org/wiki/File:PiperPA-32R-300LanceC-GTSC01.JPG

Page 172, Cessna 310Q
Source: http://en.wikipedia.org/wiki/File:Cessna310Q.jpg

Page 172, Beechcraft B19 Musketeer
Source:
http://en.wikipedia.org/wiki/File:BeechcraftB19MusketeerC-
GDYW.jpg

Page 172, Pitts Special Acrobatic
Source: http://en.wikipedia.org/wiki/File:Pitts_Special_S-1T_C-
GZRO_02.JPG

End Notes

[1] Sledge, E.B. "With the Old Breed at Peleliu & Okinawa" Novato Presidio, CA   1990

[2] Hyperwar: USMC Monograph – The Assault on Peleliu, Major Frank O. Hough, USMC, Appendix E, Aviation at Peleliu http://www.ibiblio.org/hyperwar/USMC/USMC-M-Peleliu/USMC-M-Peleliu-E.html

[3] Sloan, Bill, "Brotherhood of Heroes, The Marines at Peleliu, 1944-The Bloodiest Battle of the Pacific War" Simon & Schuster, New York   2005

[4] Anton, Todd & Nowlin, Bill (Editors)"When Baseball Went To War" Triumph Books. Chicago, IL 2008

[5] Anton, Todd, "No Greater Love, Life Stories From The Men That Saved Baseball" Rounder Books, Burlington, MA 2007

41824294R00166

Made in the USA
Lexington, KY
30 May 2015